070 4905

WORLD PRESS PHOTO
07

 Thames & Hudson

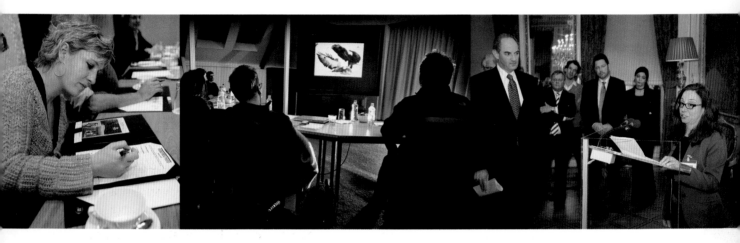

It took the jury of the 50th World
Press Photo Contest two weeks of
intensive deliberation to arrive at
the results published in this book.
They had to judge 78,083 entries
submitted by 4,460 photographers
from 124 countries.

World Press Photo

World Press Photo is an independent non-profit organization, founded in the Netherlands in 1955. Its main aim is to support and promote internationally the work of professional press photographers. Over the years, World Press Photo has evolved into an independent platform for photojournalism and the free exchange of information.

In order to realize its objectives, World Press Photo organizes the world's largest and most prestigious annual press photography contest. The prizewinning photographs are assembled into a traveling exhibition, which is visited by over two million people in more than 45 countries every year. This yearbook presenting all prizewinning entries is published annually in six languages. Reflecting the best in the photojournalism of a particular year, the book is both a catalogue for the exhibition and an interesting document in its own right.

Besides managing the extensive exhibition program, the organization closely monitors developments in photojournalism. Educational projects play an important role in World Press Photo's activities. Seminars and workshops open to individual photographers, photo agencies and picture editors are organized in developing countries. The annual Joop Swart Masterclass, held in the Netherlands, is aimed at talented photographers at the start of their careers. They receive practical instruction and professional advice from leaders in the profession.

World Press Photo receives support from the Dutch Postcode Lottery and is sponsored worldwide by Canon and TNT.

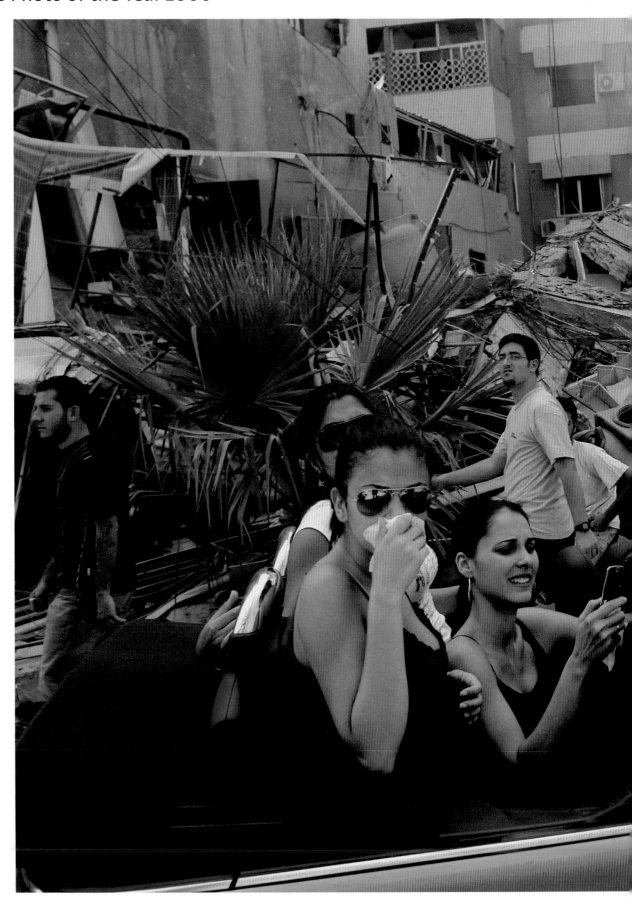

Spencer Platt
USA, Getty Images
1st prize Daily Life Singles

Young Lebanese drive down a street in Haret Hreik, a bombed neighborhood in southern Beirut, Lebanon, on August 15. For nearly five weeks Israel had been targeting that part of the city and towns across southern Lebanon in a campaign against Hezbollah militants, whom it accused of sheltering in residential areas and launching cross-border attacks. As a ceasefire brokered by the United Nations gradually came into force from August 14, thousands of Lebanese began to return to their homes and villages. According to the Lebanese government, 15,000 homes together with 900 factories and

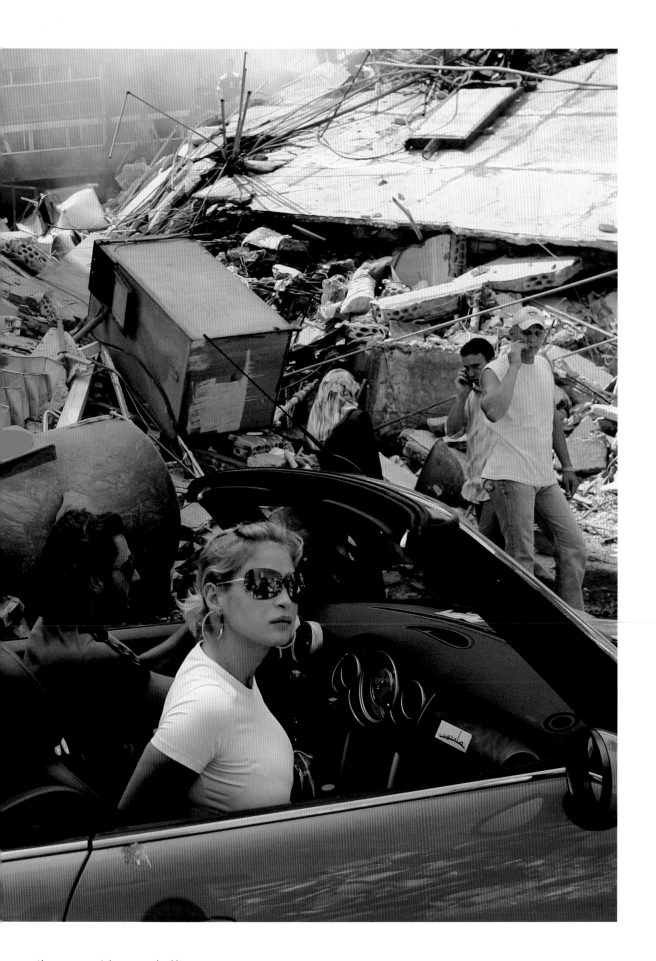

other commercial concerns had been
damaged, and 630 kilometers of
roads and 78 bridges were destroyed.
It estimated the bill for repairs to the
country's buildings and infrastructure
alone would reach US$4 billion.

Spencer Platt is from Westport, Connecticut. After graduating from Clark University in 1994 with a degree in English, he worked at numerous newspapers as a photographer. Platt joined Getty Images in 2000 as a staff photographer. Besides domestic stories, Platt covers international assignments in Iraq, Liberia, Congo, Indonesia and Lebanon, among others. Platt has received awards in both the Pictures of the Year International and the NPPA Best of Photojournalism contests, for work in Liberia and Albania. He recently won first place in the Atlanta Photojournalism Seminar contest for his coverage of the war in Lebanon.

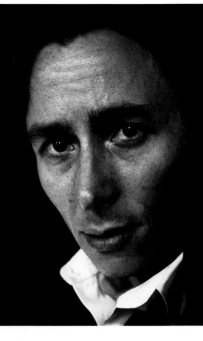

Spencer Platt

Spencer Platt, winner of the World Press Photo of the Year 2006, responded to questions about his work.

How did you become involved in photojournalism?
I had wanted to be a writer, but had the good sense early on to realize my limitations in that profession. My friend Tyler Hicks got me into photojournalism. We grew up together in a small town in Connecticut, and both got newspaper internships that led to staff jobs. I eventually found a place at Getty Images. They have given me the time and space to find my voice as a photographer.

What is it that motivates you as a photographer?
I am very much a wire shooter. I will be one for the rest of my career. Wire services, which send news and images immediately to a wide range of outlets, serve the public in a way that few media outlets can. I want my images to be viewed and understood by as many people as possible. I have always admired the great wire photographers. They are often the first media on the ground and have to be slaves to the satellite phone and deadline...file, file, file. This is good; it keeps you on your toes and saps your anxiety. It is also very much a team effort at a wire service. You must always be prepared to drop everything and edit a disk for a colleague. This is good, it keeps you humble.

Can you describe the circumstances that led up to your taking the winning photo?
I took the image of the young people driving in a red Mini through the devastation of Beirut after a long morning walking through rubble and documenting people returning to what was left of their homes. It had been a difficult day due to the tension between members of Hezbollah, who controlled this area of town, and the media who wanted to document an important story. I was lucky to have a terrific fixer by the name of Wafa who, by being a Shiite, was able to get me into various parts of the city. Only the previous day I had been running through those same streets, which were totally deserted because of continual Israeli bombing. The contrast between the two days was both astonishing and indicative of the resilience of the Lebanese people. On approaching a street packed with families in battered cars surveying the wreckage, I saw out of the corner of my eye the people in the convertible. There was only a second to capture that moment; no time to meter, focus or compose the subject. The moment had vanished in seconds. Once I had a moment to analyze the image I realized just how unusual this tableau was. We often think we know what war looks like, but it is not until we get to war that we realize it looks like us.

What impact do you think the photo may have?
The image is certainly not a critique of these people in any sense. I do not know the people in the car. For all I know they have lost their homes in the war like thousands of other Lebanese had. Like everyone in Lebanon, their lives are complicated and resist simple definition. There is a temptation to classify these individuals as Sunni or Shia, Christian or Druze, rich or poor. For me they transcend all of that, they are simply the great Lebanese. No one was immune to the bombs that fell.

I think some in Lebanon are a bit uncomfortable with the image as it acts as a mirror on them. It is OK when we, the media, are covering the bloody aftermath of an Israeli bombing, but not when we turn the camera on the contradictions of the war. If anything, the picture starts a conversation. It asks you to reconsider stereotypes of victims of war.

Did the assignment carry any emotional impact for you?
It was distressing at times to work in Lebanon, as we were never sure what was simply done for the media's benefit and what was authentic. The Middle East has become incredibly media savvy. They are more aware of the power of imagery than just about anyone in the world. There were many situations where I and other journalists were suspicious of what was actually going on. What I feel most proud of about my winning image is that it is a valid depiction of a moment in Beirut in the turbulent summer of 2006.

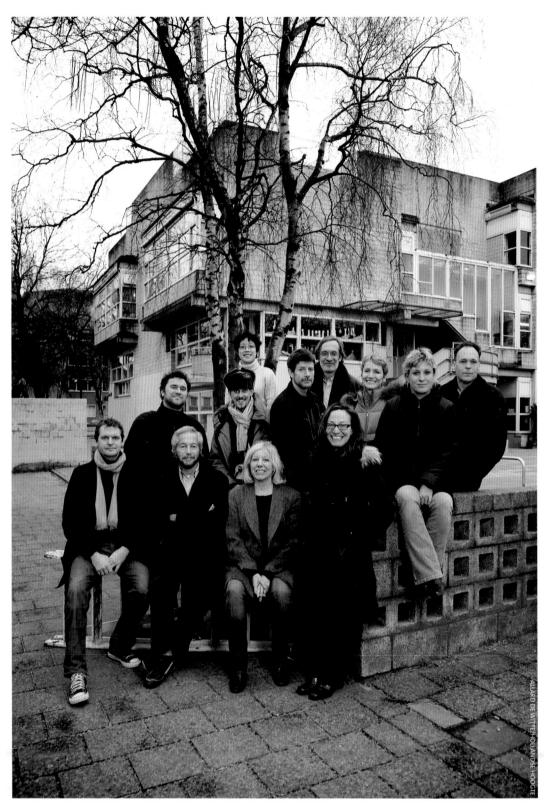

THIS YEAR'S JURY.
FRONT ROW, FROM LEFT TO RIGHT:
Adrian Evans, UK
Diego Goldberg, Argentina
Ruth Eichhorn, Germany
Michele McNally, USA (chair)

MIDDLE ROW, FROM LEFT TO RIGHT:
Jerry Lampen, The Netherlands
Philip Blenkinsop, Australia
Stephen Mayes, UK (secretary)
Maria Mann, USA
Maya Goded, Mexico
Peter Bialobrzeski, Germany

BACK ROW, FROM LEFT TO RIGHT:
Wen Huang, People's Republic of China
Jean-François Leroy, France
(Alexander Joe, Zimbabwe, not in picture)

ALLARD DE WITTE/HOLLANDSE HOOGTE

Foreword

Why is it that a newspaper can state in words that over 60,000 people were killed in a tsunami, even in a bold headline, but it is when a picture of the victims appears that the editor gets numerous letters of concern? Or that it is not the story of US soldiers being killed in Iraq, but a photograph of the event that comes under scrutiny from all sectors and attracts pleas not to publish. Or that a photographer working with the Mahdi Army is accused of being a traitor. All of these events may be reported in words, but it is always the pictures that incite public reaction. They just seem more real.

I think this speaks to the power of photojournalism, to its ability to make historical events tangible, to cause an instant visceral reaction. Still images have a way of fixing in your memory in a way that words can not.

When I tell someone I am a Director of Photography, they always ask what makes a good picture? They are looking for a definitive answer, even if they believe they already know it. Everyone thinks they know what a good photo is, because they have been looking at pictures since before they could read, so in a sense images are a more universal language than text.

So what does make a great press photograph? I believe it should be historical, defining a particular time, place, and event. It should be sociological, explaining what people do and what people do to each other. It should have a psychological and emotional tone, making the viewer feel something. It should also have an aesthetic component, drawing in the viewer, urging them to learn more about the story the picture is telling. Above all, it should be truthful. It is this quality of veracity which sets an important picture apart, and which highlights the crucial role of the photojournalist. This is evident in many of in the photos presented here, as photojournalists – often risking great danger – sought fairness in their visual reports while covering the ubiquitous tragedy in civilians' lives.

At first glance you wonder if the situation presented in the World Press Photo of the Year could possibly be true. Yet the people at the center of the photograph, in spite of their affluent appearance, are also refugees. Is reality simple? Like other winning photos in the contest, this is a complicated picture, truthfully reflecting the complex reality of the world we live in. And that complexity is what makes us linger even longer.

MICHELE MCNALLY,
Chair of the jury
New York, February 2007

9

Spot News

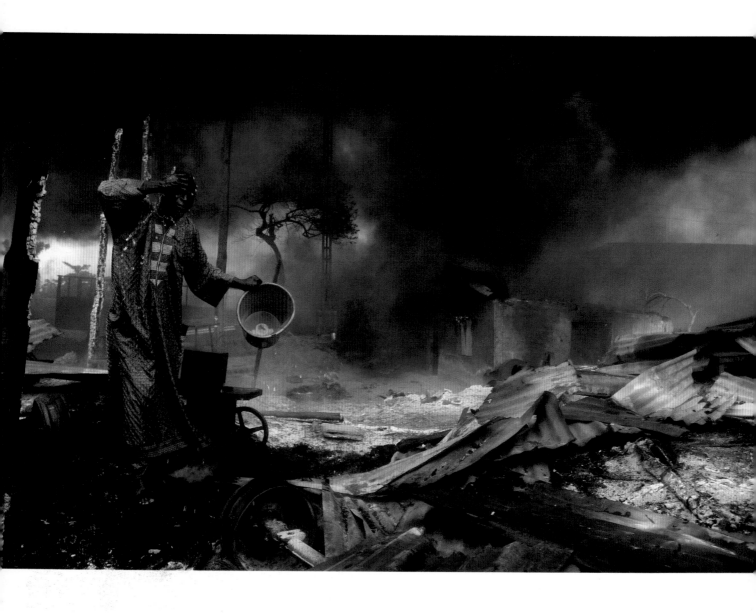

Akintunde Akinleye
Nigeria, Reuters
1st Prize Singles

A man rinses soot from his face at
the scene of a petrol pipeline
explosion in Lagos, Nigeria, on
December 26. At least 260 people
were killed after the punctured
pipeline caught fire. Thieves had
tapped it to fill tankers with petrol
for resale, and hundreds of residents
had gone to the scene to scoop up
leaking fuel in plastic containers.
Pipeline vandalism and fuel theft are
common in Nigeria, the world's
eighth largest exporter of oil, where
most people live in poverty.

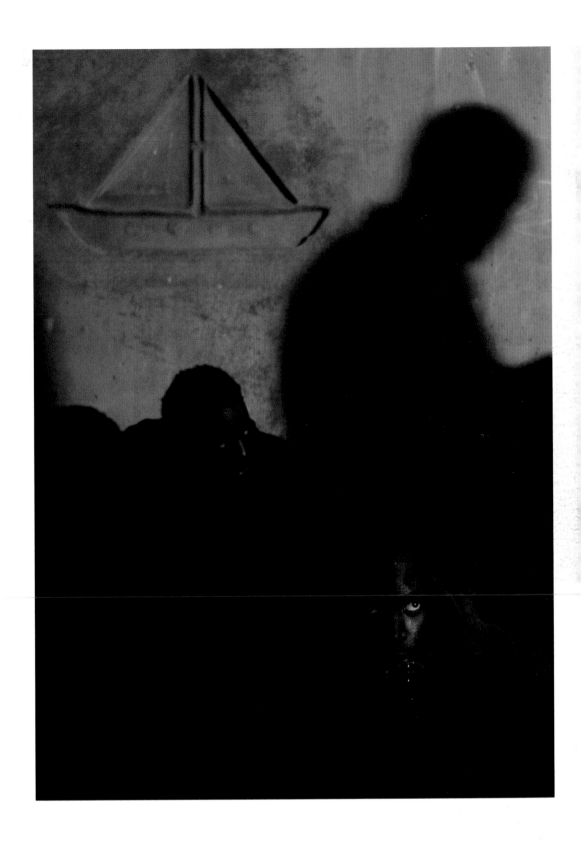

Arturo Rodríguez
Spain, The Associated Press
2nd Prize Singles

African immigrants wait on the quayside in the port of Los Abrigos on the Canary Island of Tenerife, Spain, on September 7. They will be transferred to a police station, and later to a holding center from where they will either be repatriated or sent on to the mainland. During 2006, the islands saw a fivefold increase in numbers attempting to enter the European Union illegally. Spanish officials estimated that more than 31,000 people reached the Atlantic islands during the year. In June, boats, planes and helicopters from the EU's border control agency, led by the Spanish Guardia Civil, began intercepting boats off the African coast and returning them to shore.

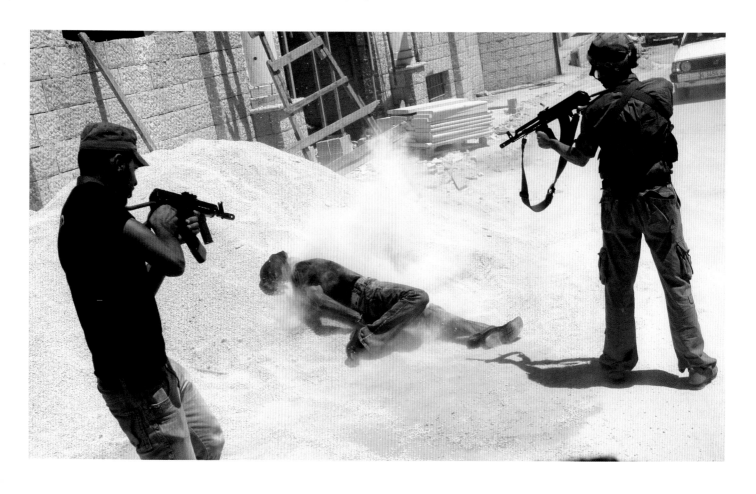

Mohammed Ballas
Palestinian Territories,
The Associated Press
3rd Prize Singles

Palestinian gunmen, who identified
themselves as members of the
militant Islamist group Islamic Jihad,
shoot a man in front of hundreds of
people in a public square in the West
Bank town of Jenin. The man was
identified as Bassem Malah (22),
who worked in the Israeli Arab town
of Umm al Fahm. He was accused of
collaborating with Israeli authorities,
imparting information that had led
to the death of two militants in a
targeted attack the week before.

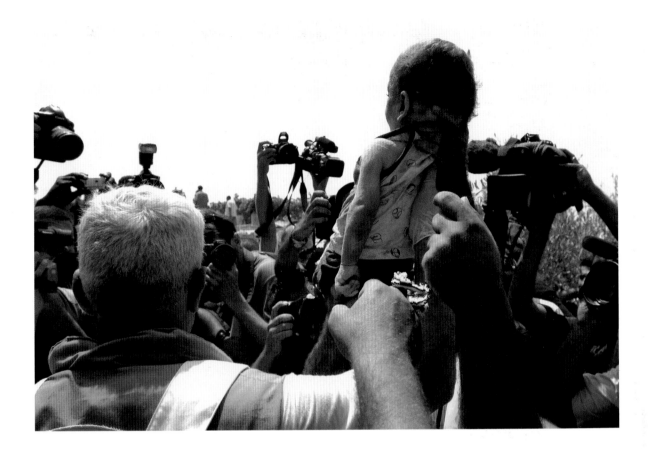

Jeroen Oerlemans
The Netherlands, Panos Pictures
Honorable Mention Singles

Paramedics hold up the dead body of a child before members of the press in the village of Qana, southern Lebanon on July 29. The boy's body had been recovered from the rubble of an apartment building, after an Israeli air attack in which at least 28 people, including 16 children, died. Hostilities erupted in Lebanon in July when the Israel Defense Forces carried out wide-ranging artillery and air attacks against Hezbollah. Both sides in the conflict in Lebanon were accused of manipulating the media to their own ends. Allegations were made – largely by bloggers over the Internet – that situations had been staged for the press for propaganda purposes.

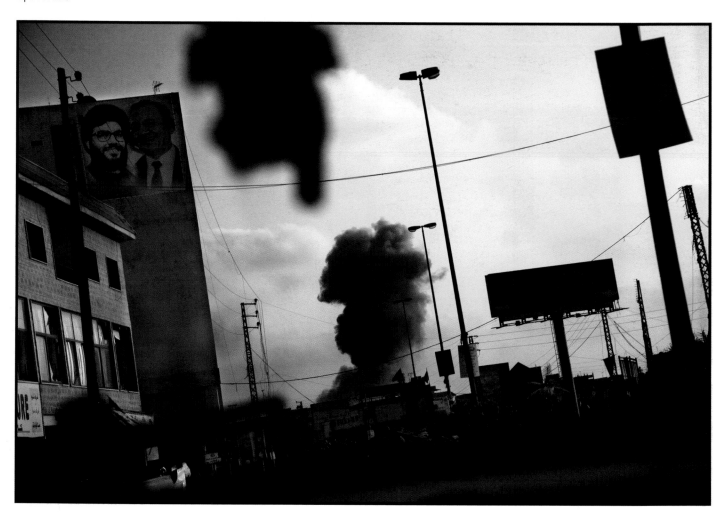

Davide Monteleone
Italy, Contrasto
1st Prize Stories

From July 12, the Israel Defense Forces (IDF) conducted a ground and air campaign against Hezbollah, the Islamist group with both a military and a civilian wing based in Lebanon. Israel claimed it was targeting pockets of Hezbollah fighters and missile-launching sites hidden in residential areas, but was accused of disproportionate reaction and indiscriminate bombing of civilians. This page: The center of Tyre, one of the worst-affected cities, after a bombing raid on July 26. Facing page, top: A man carries the body of a girl after the Israeli air attack on Qana, in which a three-storey building sheltering a large number of refugees collapsed. The air strike drew international condemnation and renewed calls for a ceasefire, and the IDF later issued a statement regretting the civilian deaths. Below: A bombed building in Tyre (story continues)

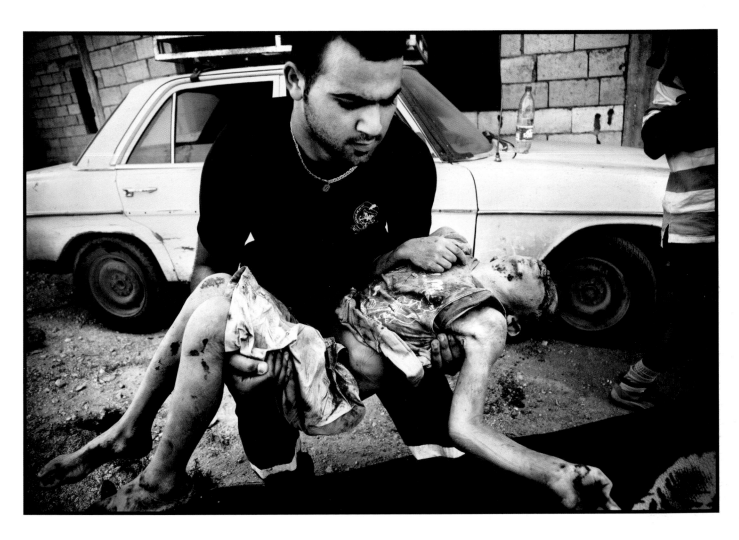

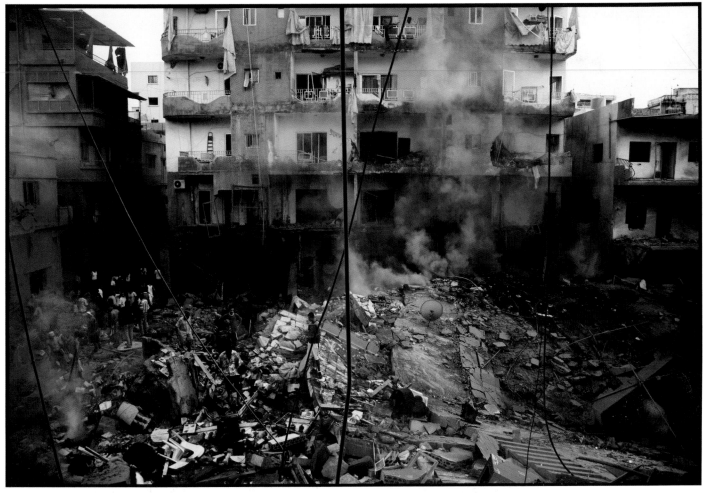

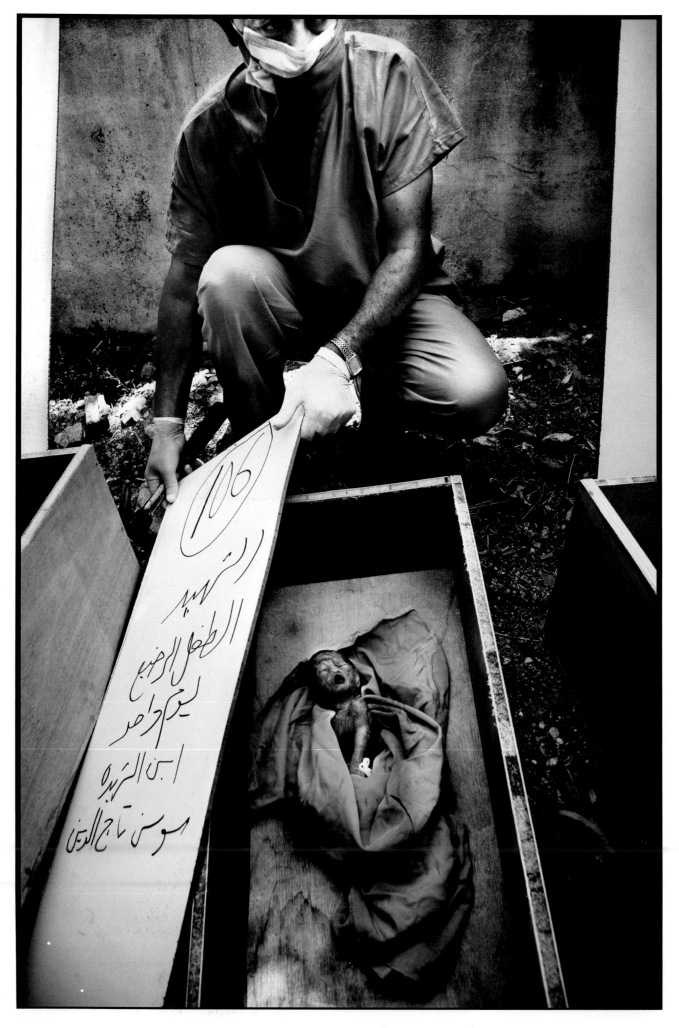

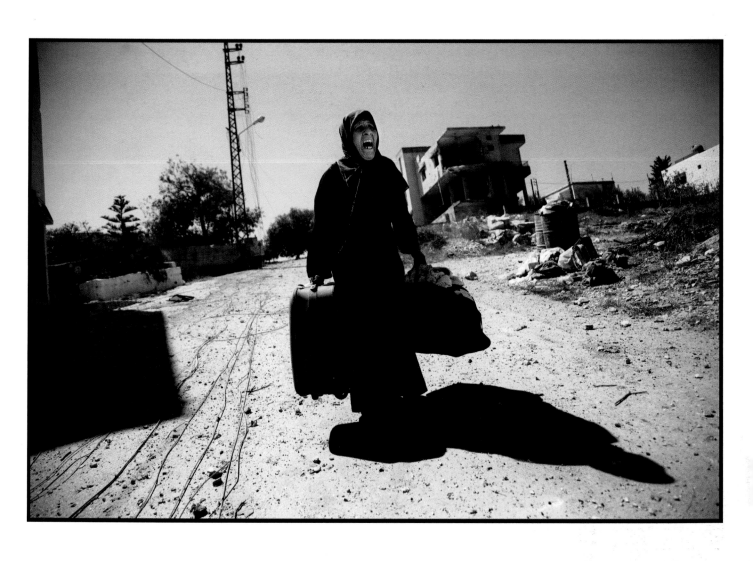

(continued) An internationally
brokered ceasefire put an end to the
conflict after five weeks. At least 116
IDF soldiers and 43 Israeli civilians
were said to have been killed in the
fighting. Official Lebanese figures
put their number of civilian dead at

1,109. Facing page: A baby of a few
weeks is buried during a mass
funeral in Tyre following an air
attack. This page: A woman flees the
town of Bent Jbail, which the Israelis
regarded as a Hezbollah stronghold,
following a heavy battle on July 31.

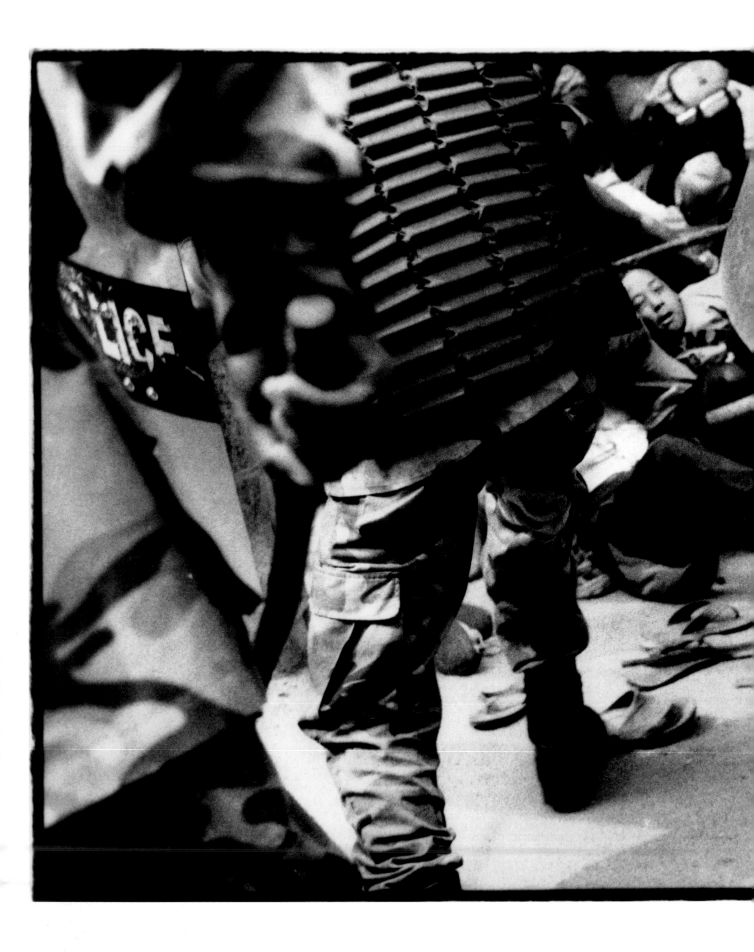

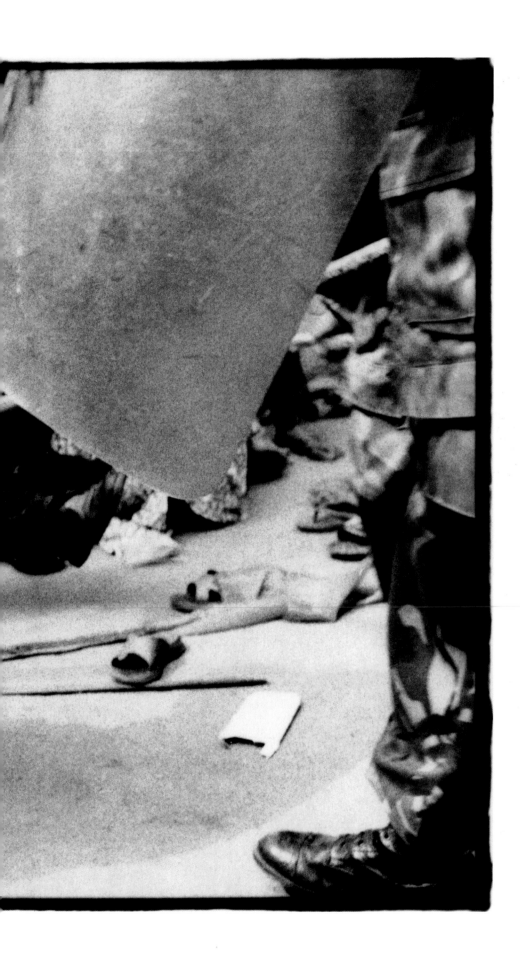

Agnes Dherbeys
France, Cosmos/Eve
2nd Prize Stories

Protesters march on the royal palace in Kathmandu, Nepal, in April, demonstrating against King Gyanendra. In February 2005, the monarch had dismissed the government of the country and assumed power, declaring a state of emergency and suspending civil rights. A general strike called by opposition parties in April 2006, was followed by an intensive campaign of anti-royal demonstrations and clashes with police around the country. These pages: A woman is buried under bodies as police beat protesters with bamboo sticks. (story continues)

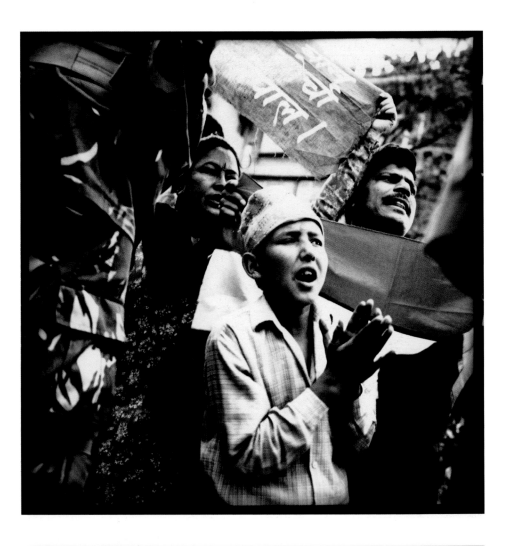

(continued) By the end of the month, the king had capitulated and agreed to the reinstitution of parliament. Opposition parties accepted, a new prime minister was appointed. This page, top: Protesters shout slogans against King Gyanendra in the early stages of the demonstration. Below: Shoes belonging to demonstrators who have fled from riot police lie beside blood from a boy wounded by bamboo batons. Facing page, top: Anti-monarchists burn tires on the ring road around Kathmandu's city center. Below: Protesters throw stones in the suburb of Kalanki, on the outskirts of Kathmandu.

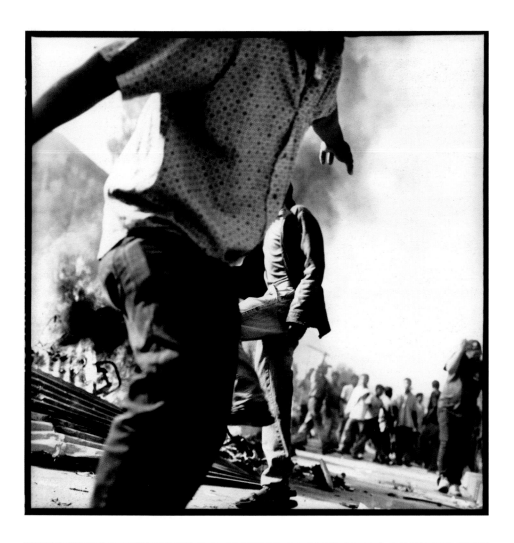

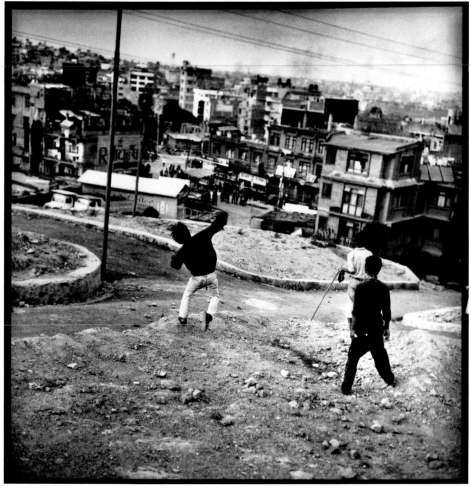

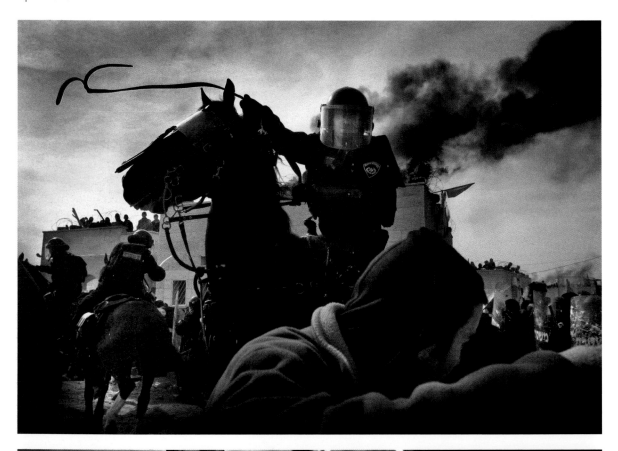

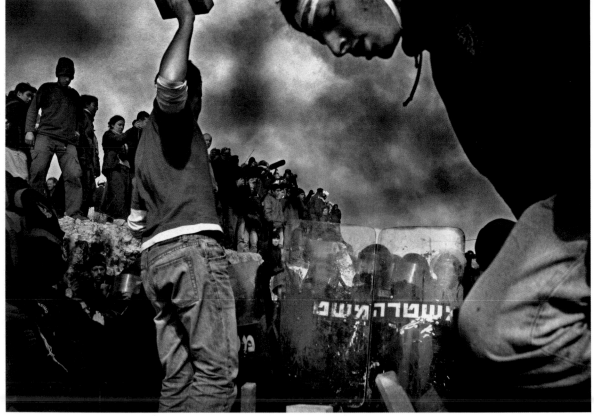

Yonathan Weitzman
Israel, Reuters
3rd Prize Stories

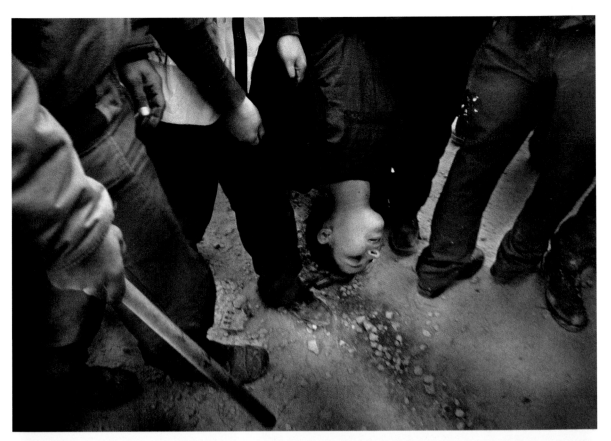

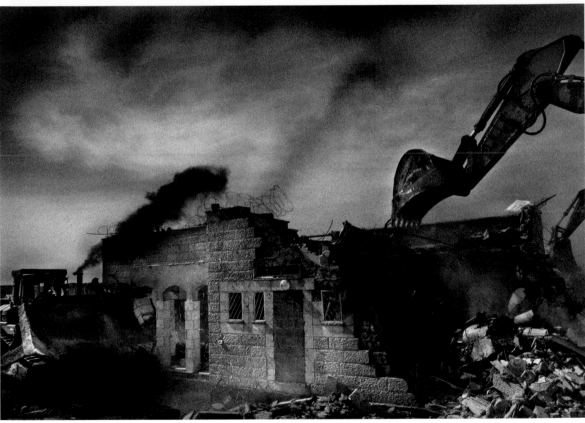

Jewish settlers clash with Israeli police in the evacuation of an outpost of the Amona settlement, West Bank, on February 1. The police had been ordered to tear down nine houses built without government permission on a hilltop near Ramallah. The order was part of a tougher stand on settler issues taken by Israeli acting prime minister, Ehud Olmert. About 5,000 protesters joined the settlers in their opposition. Facing page, top: An officer on horseback charges a settler. Below: Settlers throw stones and lumps of concrete at riot police, who responded with batons. This page, top: Israeli police drag a settler away. Below: After settlers have been removed, bulldozers move in to dismantle the homes.

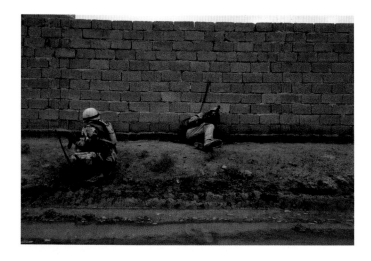 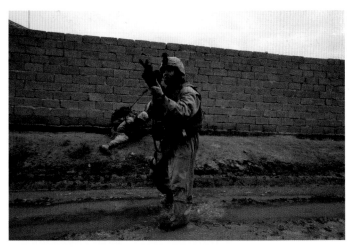

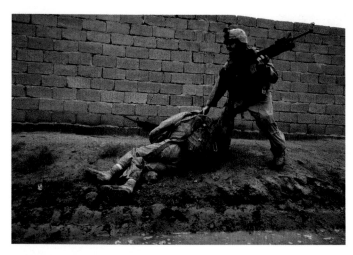 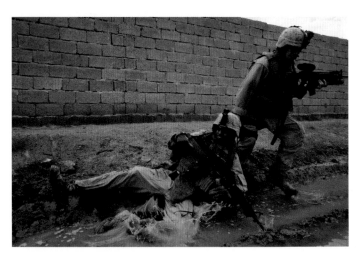

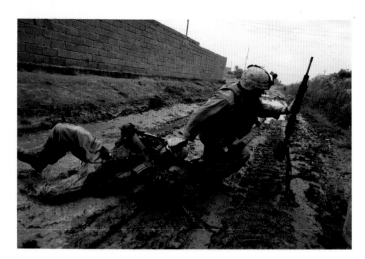 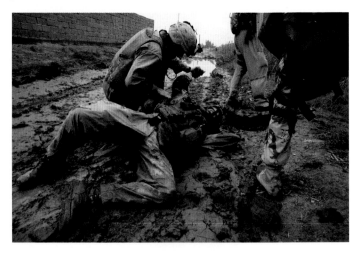

Joao Silva
South Africa, The New York Times
Honorable Mention Stories

Lance-corporal Juan Valdez-Castillo of the US Marines is shot by a sniper and dragged to safety by colleagues, during a joint patrol with the Iraqi Army in Karmah, northwest Iraq. The lance-corporal was a radio operator, a favored sniper target as radio provides links to other units. Valdez was shot through the right arm and torso, but survived the attack. By the end of the year, the US military death toll following the March 2003 invasion had passed 3,000. There was controversy about the number of Iraqi fatalities over the course of the conflict, with figures ranging from 55,000 to over 650,000.

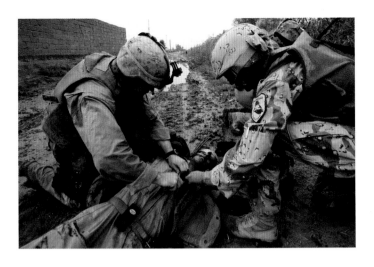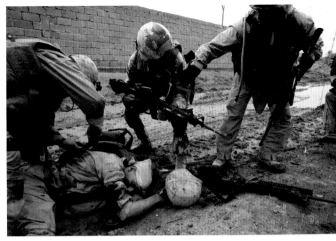

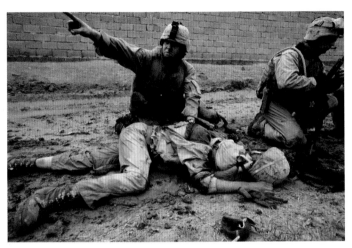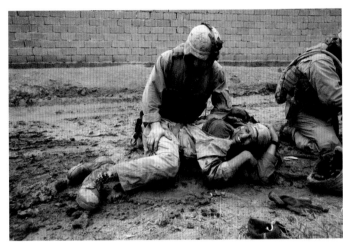

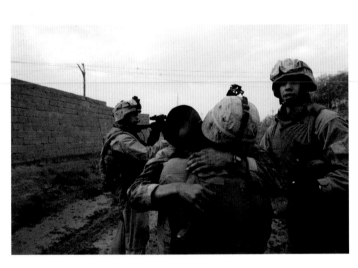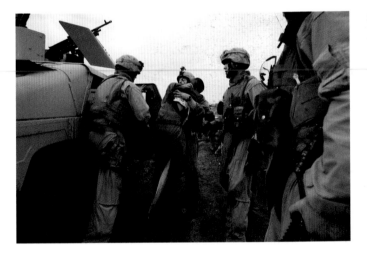

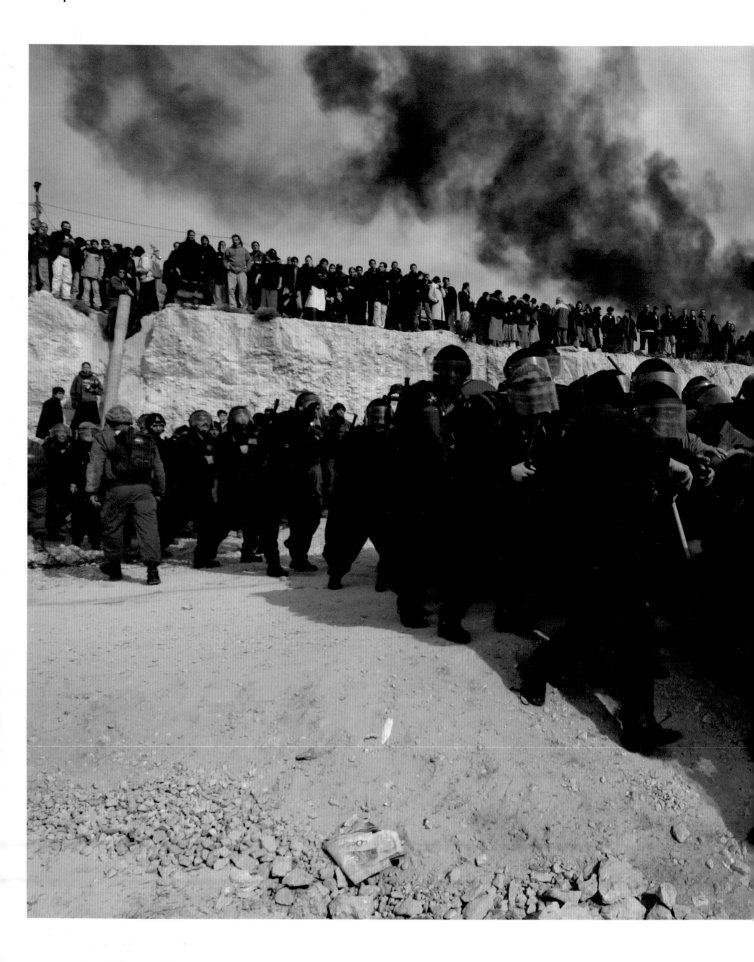

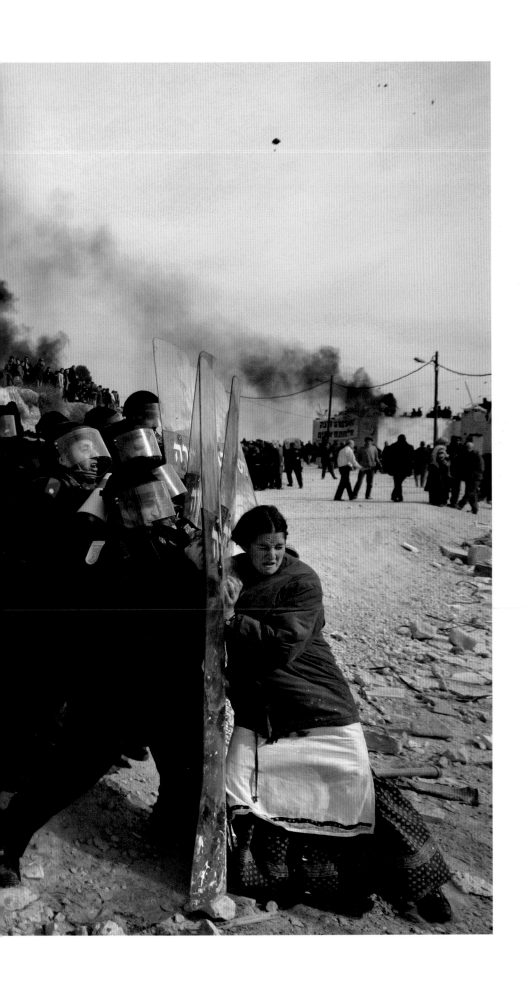

Oded Balilty
Israel, The Associated Press
1st Prize Singles

A Jewish settler resists Israeli riot
police enforcing a Supreme Court
order to evacuate and demolish nine
homes in an outpost of the Amona
settlement, West Bank, on February 1.
Residents of the settlement, joined
by thousands of other protesters,
raised barbed wire barriers to
protect the houses and clashed
violently with the police. More than
200 people were injured, including
80 policemen. Following hours of
confrontation, the settlers were
dragged away and bulldozers moved
in to begin the demolition.

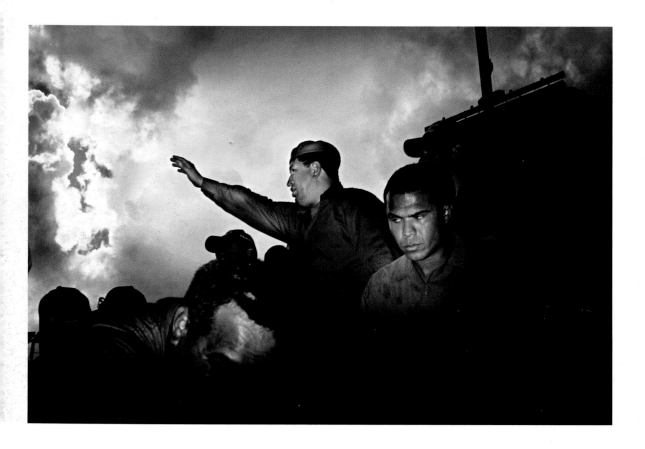

Christopher Anderson
Canada, Magnum Photos
for Newsweek
2nd Prize Singles

Venezuelan President Hugo Chávez greets supporters at a massive rally in downtown Caracas, just before his re-election in December. Chávez won by a landslide, saying that his third term in office would see a new phase in his plans for the country, which has the largest oil reserves in the Americas. The newly re-elected president immediately requested the National Assembly to grant him powers to rule by decree for 18 months, saying that the socialist revolution in Venezuela had begun in earnest. He won wide popular support by announcing a new luxury tax, and proposed plans to substitute the US with China as Venezuela's leading trade partner. Earlier, Chávez had referred to US president George Bush as "the devil" in a speech to the United Nations General Assembly.

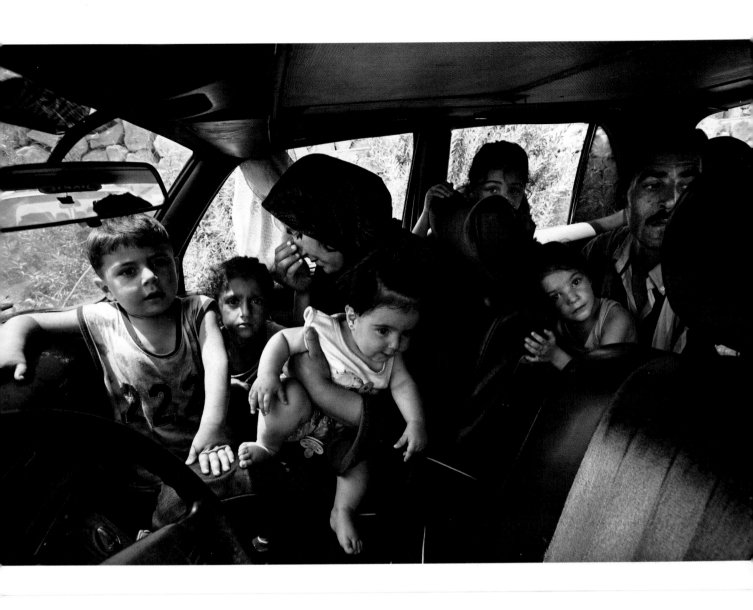

Stephanie Sinclair
USA, NPR
3rd Prize Singles

Families from a Lebanese border town flee along the dangerous coastal road between Tyre and Sidon, during the Israeli bombardment of the south of the country in July. The Lebanese government estimated that over 900,000 people, approximately 25 percent of the population, were displaced during the conflict. Travel became unsafe as Israeli bombs also hit roads in the offensive against Hezbollah bases in Lebanon.

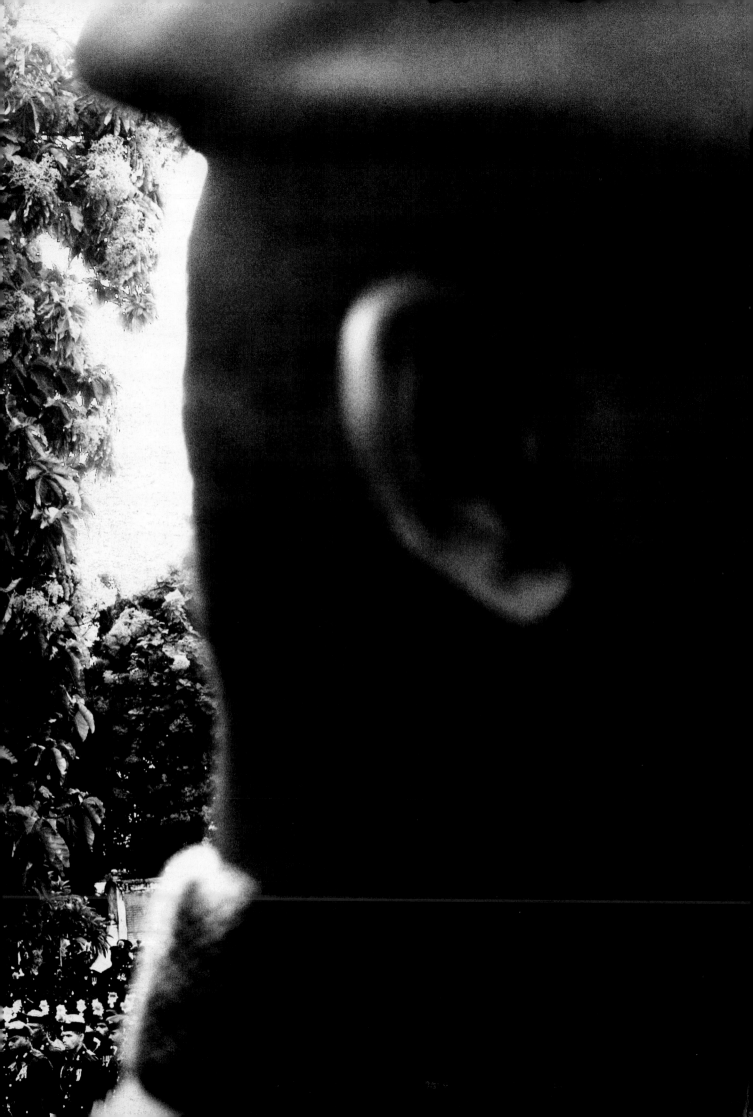

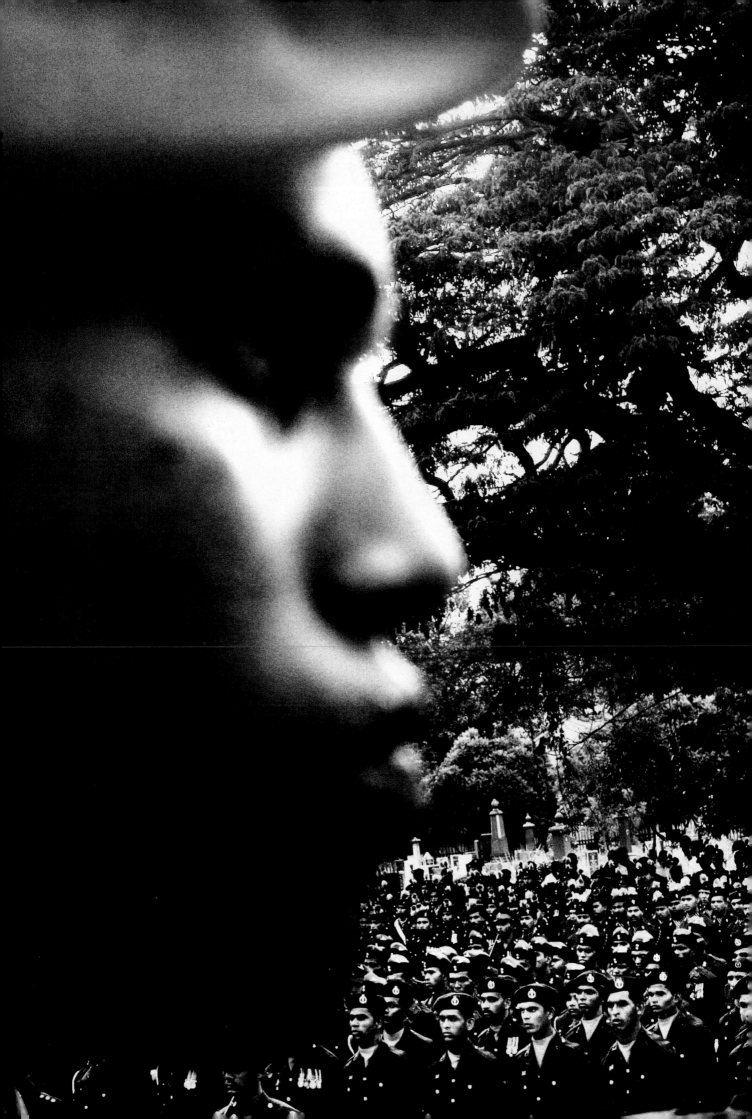

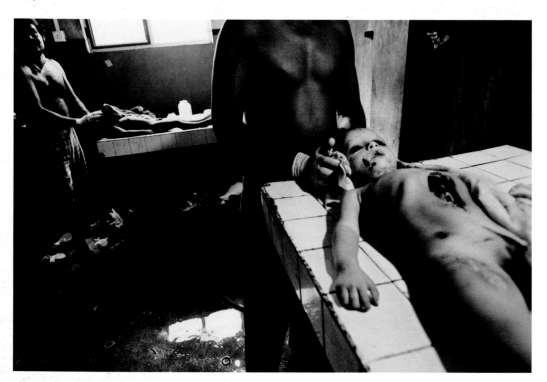

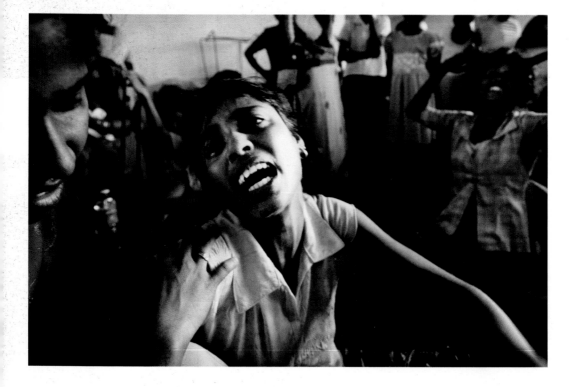

Q. Sakamaki
Japan, Redux Pictures
for Newsweek
1st Prize Stories

For decades Sri Lanka has suffered fighting between forces of the predominantly Sinhalese government and Tamil Tiger rebels, who want an independent homeland in the north and east of the island. Despite a four-year-old ceasefire agreement, conflict once again broke out in late 2005 and continued to escalate even though both sides initially reaffirmed their commitment to a viable peace. Previous pages: A soldier attends the funeral of Sri Lankan Army chief of staff Major General Parami Kulatunga, whose murder on June 26 led to an increase in violence. This page, top: Funeral workers prepare a child victim of the violence for mass burial. Below: Family members mourn victims of a June 15 bus attack, in which more than 60 people were killed. Facing page, top: Sri Lankan special forces patrol in a war-torn Tamil majority area in Jaffna. Below: Coffins lie ready for the mass burial of people killed in the June 15 bus attack. The government blamed rebels for the attack, but the Tamil Tigers denied the claim.

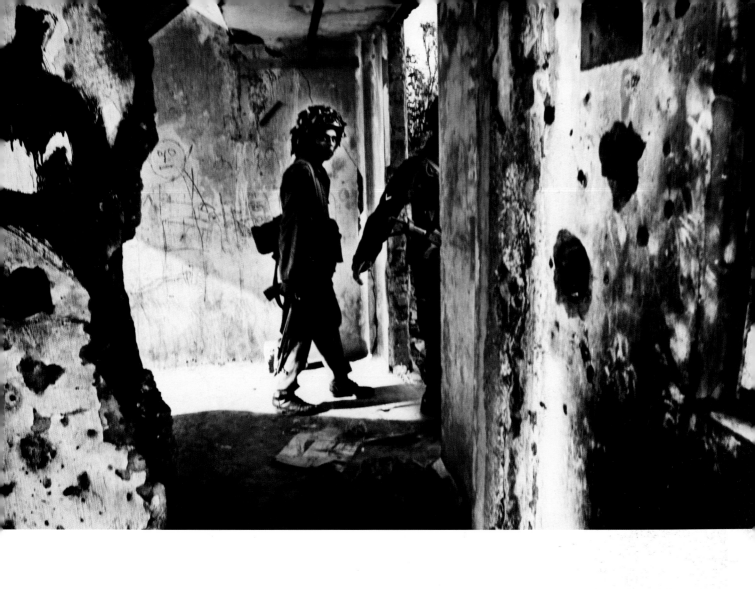
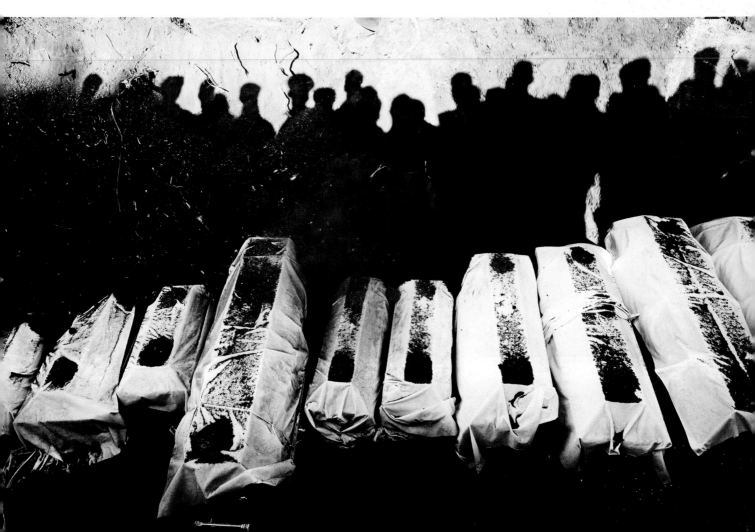

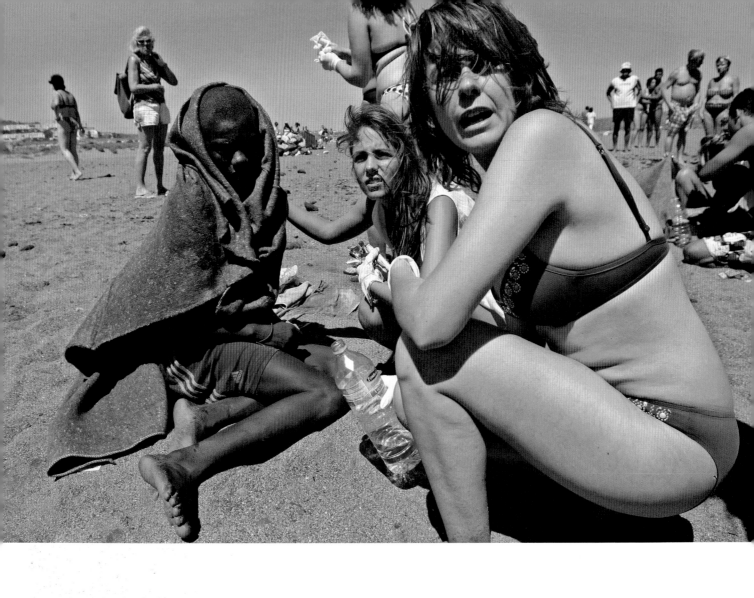
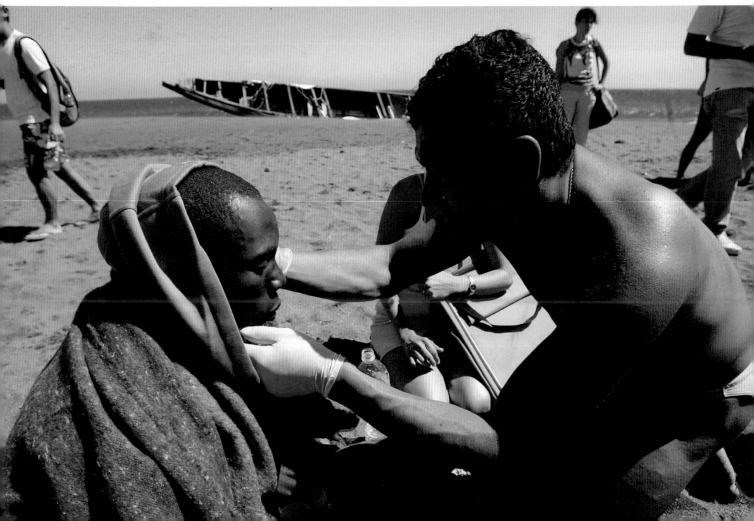

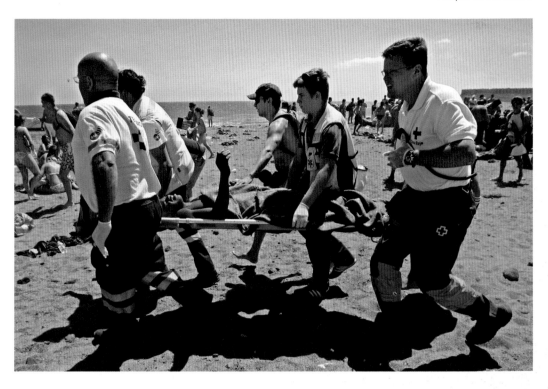

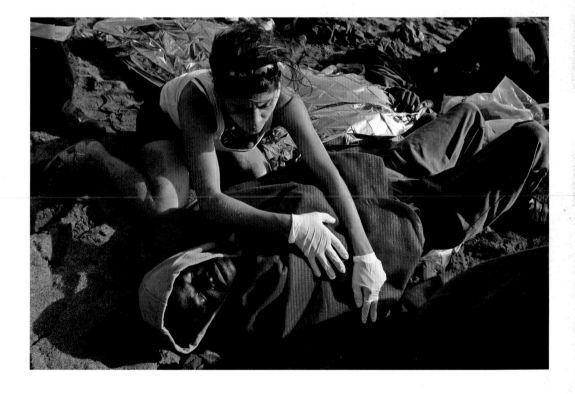

Arturo Rodríguez
Spain, The Associated Press
2nd Prize Stories

Summer tourists, members of the security forces, and Red Cross workers attend to African migrants who have landed on La Tejita, one of the most popular beaches on Tenerife, in the Canary Islands, Spain. Tens of thousands of similar migrants arrived in 2006, making the journey from the African coast in little wooden fishing boats with between 70 and 150 people crammed on board. An unknown number of boats sink during the perilous crossing. Migrants face a sea journey of up to 1,000 kilometers, and many arrive starving, dehydrated, or die on the way. According to the Canary Islands government, fewer than 10 percent of the immigrants are repatriated. Of the remainder sent on to mainland Spain, many end up in limbo, unable to gain work papers yet unwilling to go home.

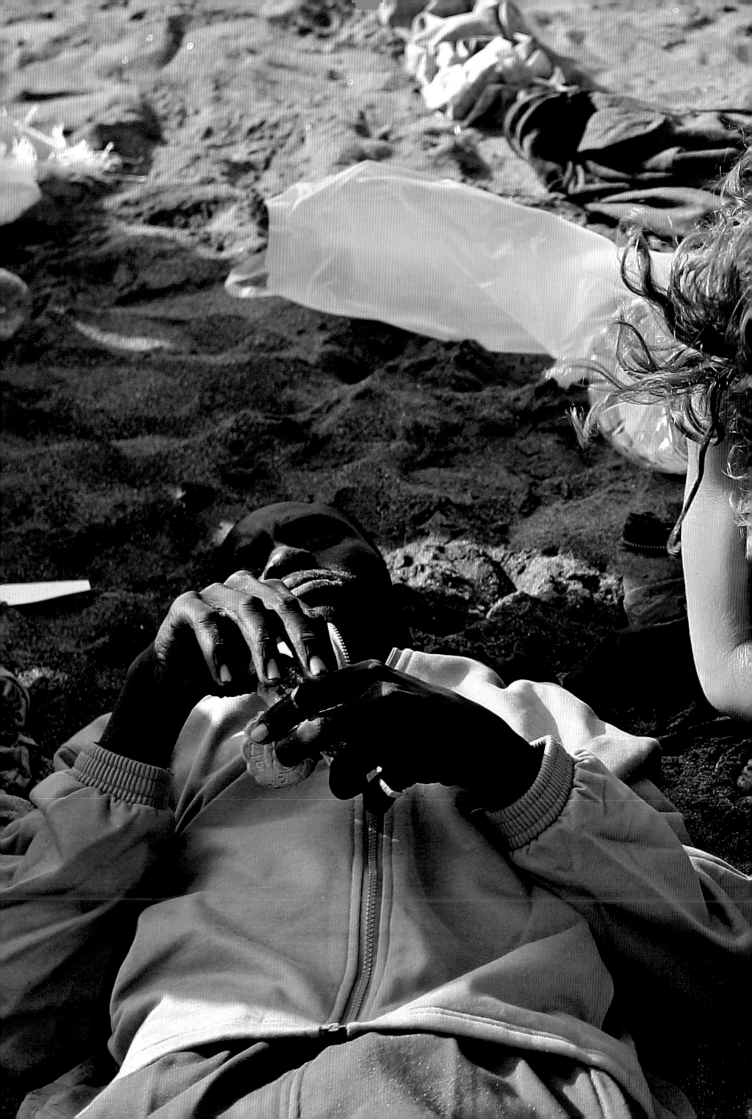

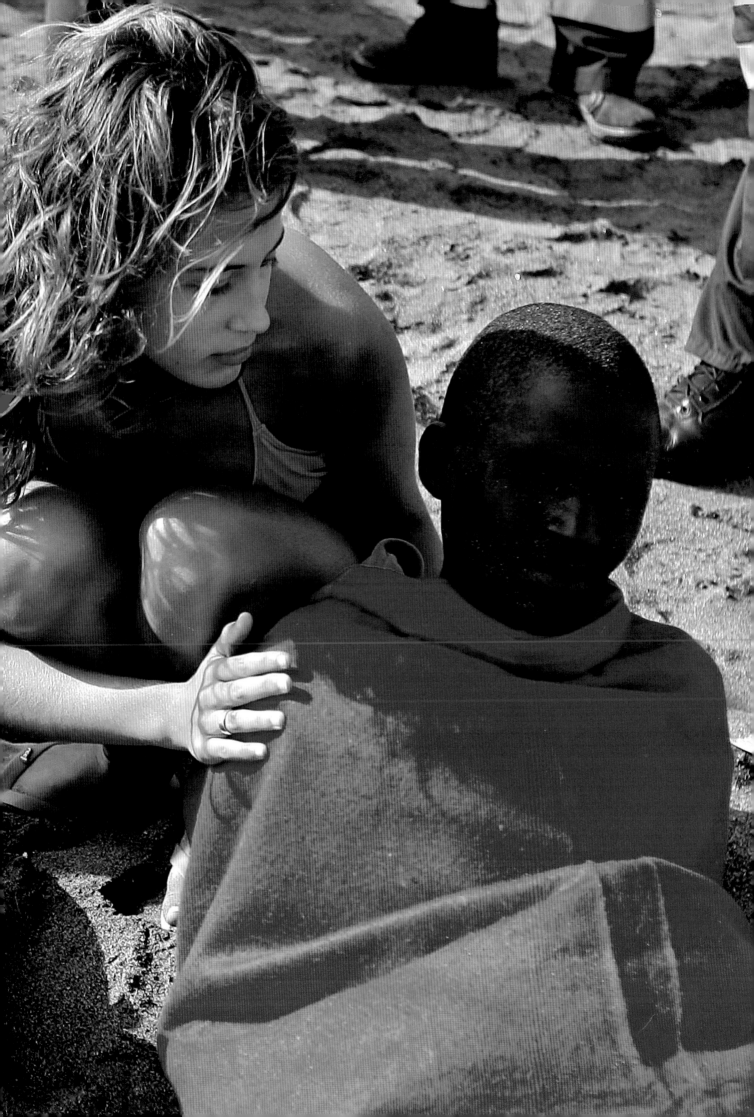

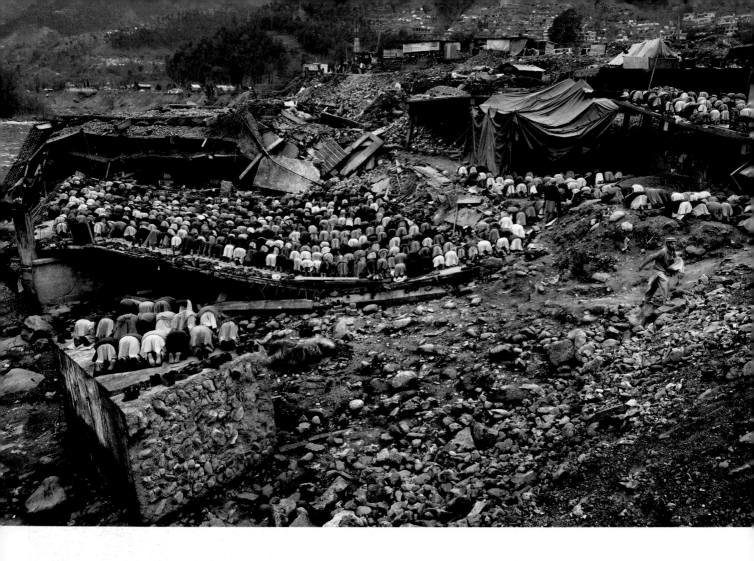

Espen Rasmussen
Norway, Verdens Gang
3rd Prize Stories

Three months after the October 2005
earthquake that devastated parts of
Kashmir, hundreds of thousands of
people were still homeless, many
living in tents and collapsed
buildings, facing icy winter conditions
in the mountains. This page: Over
3,000 people gather for Friday prayers
at the ruins of the main mosque in
Balakot, Pakistan, one of the worst-hit
towns. Facing page, top: People pray
in a collapsed mosque in the
mountain village of Jiggan, 2,350
meters above sea level. Middle:
Outside a tent in a refugee camp on
the road to Balakot, an old man who
broke his leg in the quake lies in the
bed he has occupied ever since.
Below: A boy starts singing to
entertain people waiting for an airlift
of food supplies in the mountain
village of Gujar Bandi, Pakistan.

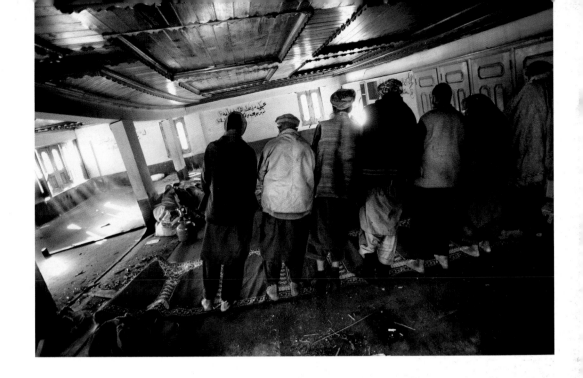

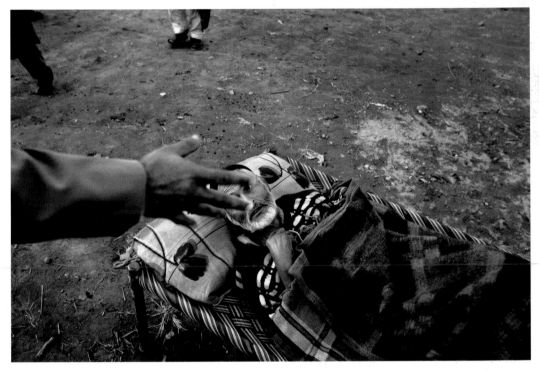

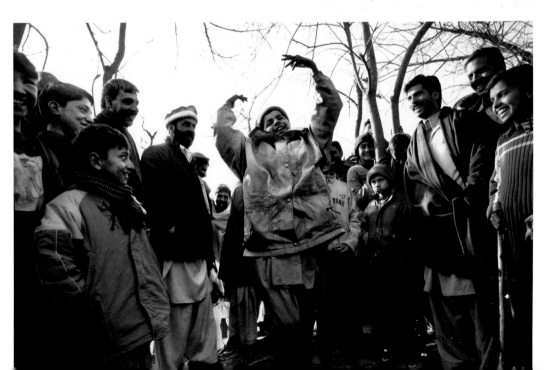

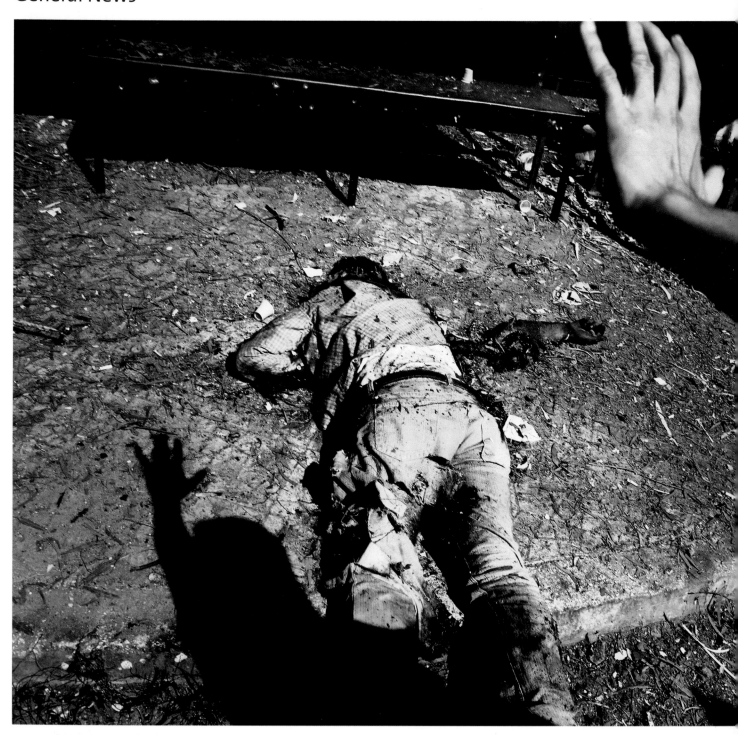

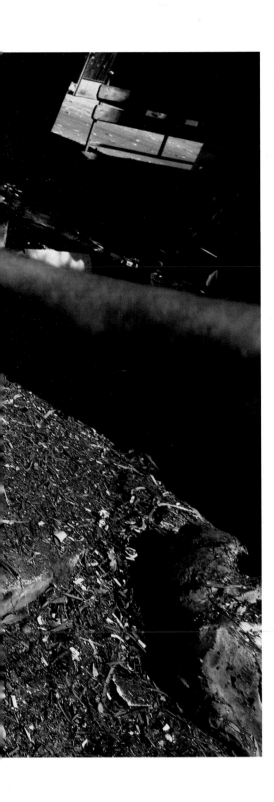

Paolo Pellegrin
Italy, Magnum Photos for Newsweek/
The New York Times Magazine
1st Prize Singles

A victim of an Israeli rocket attack lies
in the main road of the Lebanese city
of Tyre on August 6. Conflict had
been sparked by the capture of two
Israeli soldiers by the militant Islamist
organization Hezbollah, in a cross-
border raid three weeks earlier. Israel
responded by bombing areas across
southern Lebanon and in the
southern suburbs of Beirut, which it
said harbored Hezbollah militia and
missile launchers. On that day
Hezbollah launched its heaviest
rocket attack yet on northern Israel.

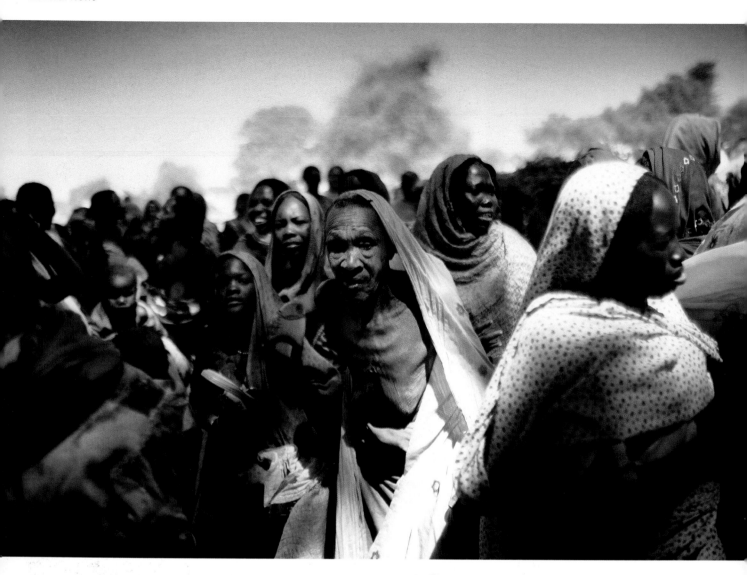

Jan Grarup
Denmark, Politiken/Newsweek
2nd Prize Singles

Displaced people wait for food distribution near the village of Habile, in Chad in November. Attacks by the Janjaweed, an Arab militia said to be backed by the Sudanese government, spread from the Darfur region of Sudan across the border to Chad. Janjaweed on horseback burnt the villages of black African farmers on both sides of the border, killing and raping inhabitants in a pattern of ethnic violence they had followed since 2003. The UN estimated that 400,000 people had been killed in the conflict over the years, and as many as 2.5 million were thought to have been displaced.

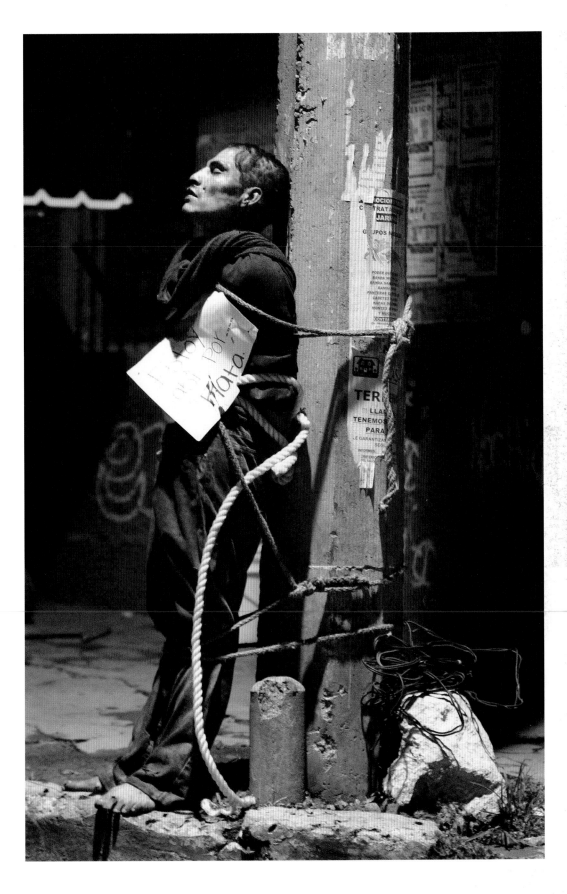

Daniel Aguilar
Mexico, Reuters
3rd Prize Singles

A man stands tied to a lamppost after being apprehended by members of the Popular Assembly of the People of Oaxaca (APPO) and accused of burglary, in Oaxaca City, Mexico, in October. The sign reads "Because I am a rat" (slang for burglar). A teachers' strike in June had developed into a widespread stand-off with authorities, involving other groups of activists under the banner of APPO, calling for the resignation of the state governor. Protesters took control of the city center, including government offices, for some months. At the time this man was caught only one public prosecutor's office was functioning. He remained tied up for several hours.

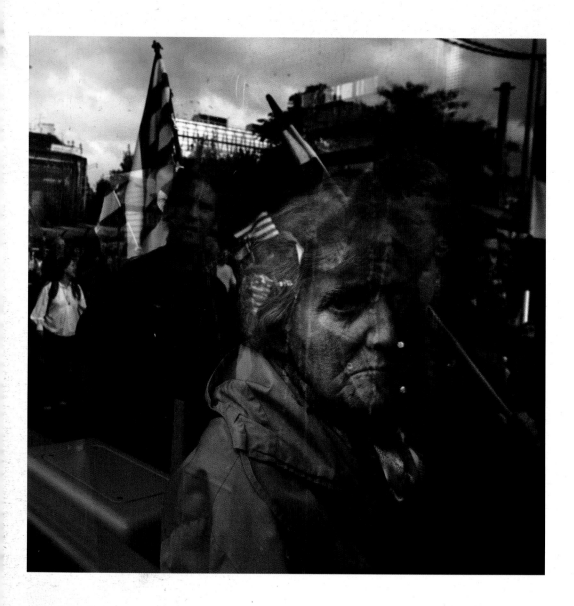

Zsolt Szigetváry
Hungary, for MTI
1st Prize Stories

Demonstrators and police clashed in the Hungarian capital Budapest in the run-up to the 50th anniversary of the country's revolt against Soviet rule. On September 17 Hungarian Radio leaked a tape on which Prime Minister Ferenc Gyurcsány could be heard admitting that the government had lied about the economy to secure re-election. The admission compounded growing anti-government feelings. Demonstrators converged on the Hungarian parliament, and a peaceful protest turned violent when a group stormed the building of the state television. This page: An elderly woman watches demonstrators from the window of a tram. Facing page: Riot police block the entrance to Hungarian Television. (story continues)

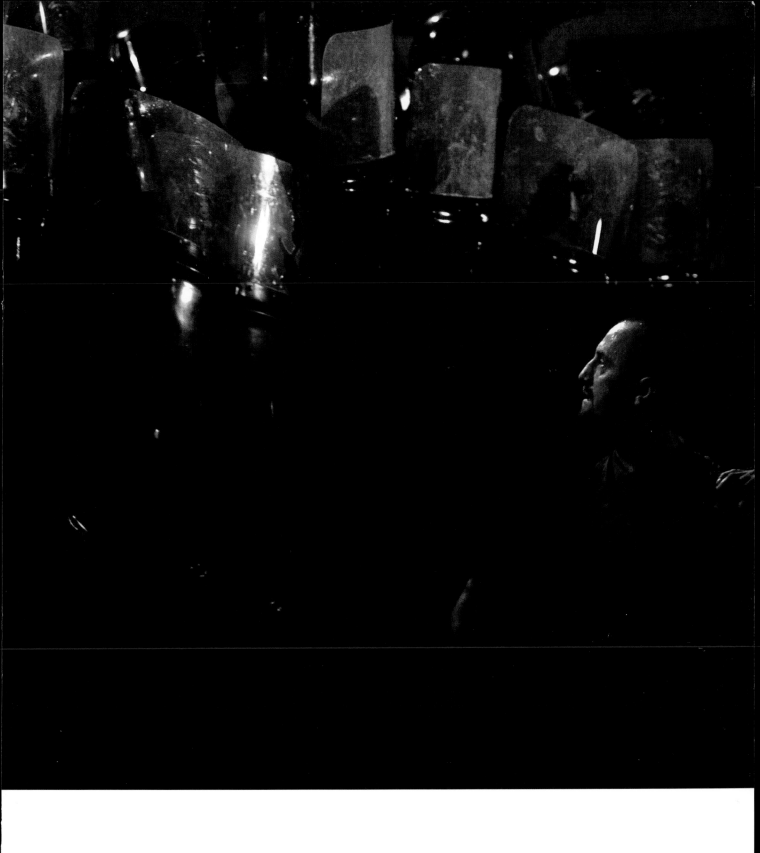

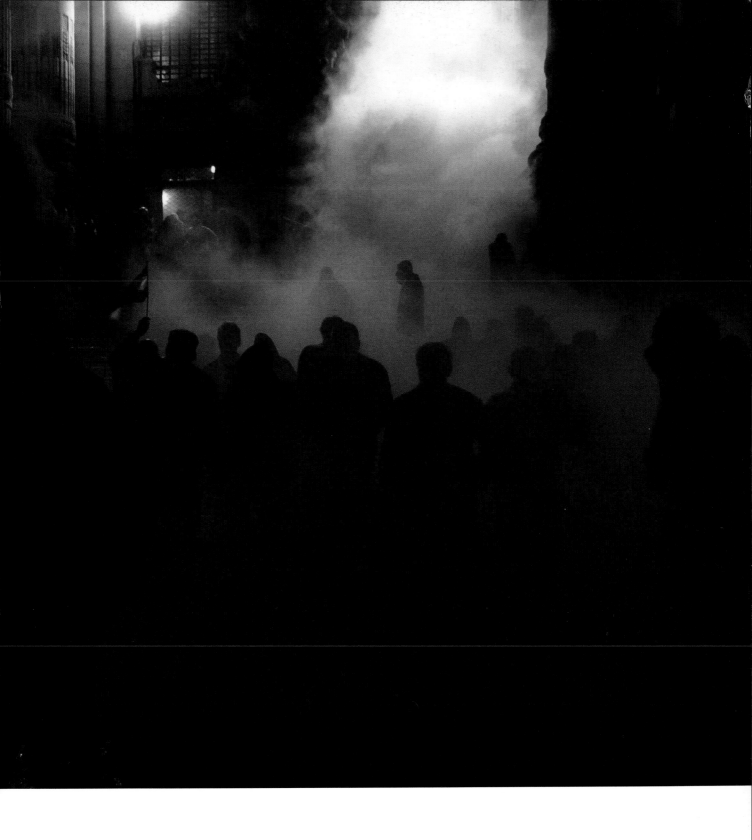

(continued) Violence escalated on October 23, the exact anniversary of the anti-Soviet uprising. Calm returned to Budapest only in November, even though Gyurcsány remained as prime minister. Facing page: Riot police defending the main gate of the television building spray demonstrators with a water cannon. This page: Tear gas is used to disperse crowds outside Hungarian Television.

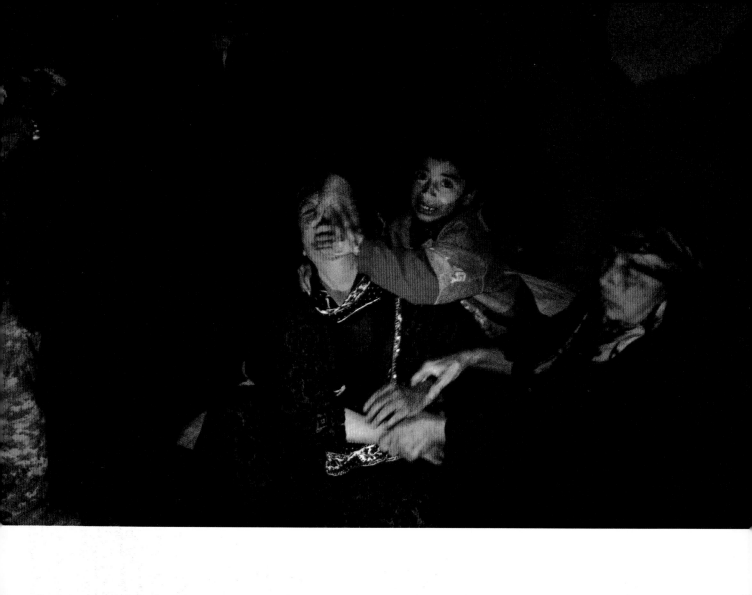

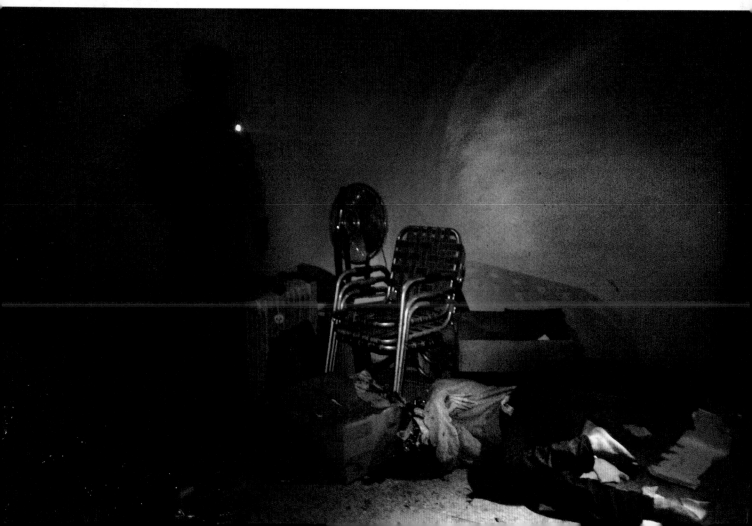

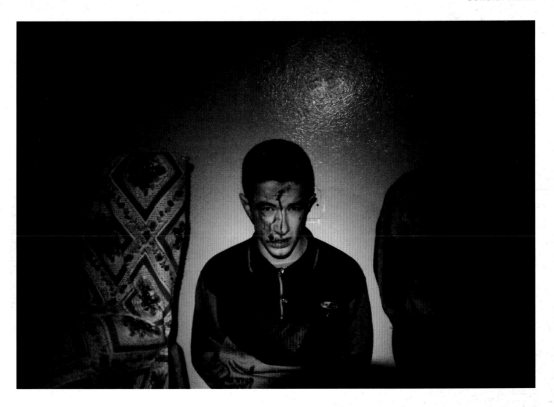

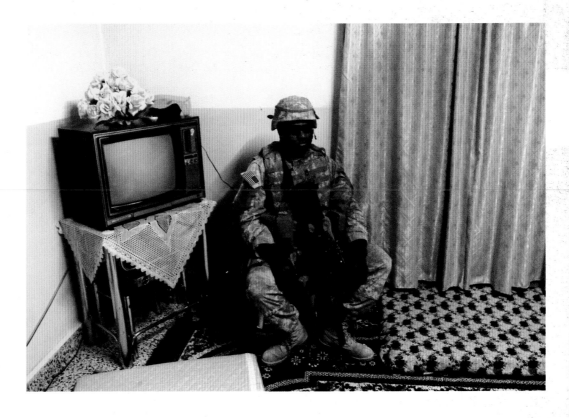

Peter van Agtmael
USA, Polaris Images
2nd Prize Stories

American soldiers conduct night raids on homes in Iraq, searching for suspected insurgents. The raids, sometimes carried out in conjunction with Iraqi security forces, were a common occurrence as insurgency increased. Facing page, top: A boy covers his grandmother's mouth during a raid. She had begun shouting and clawing at troops and had to be restrained by her family. Below: A US soldier stands over an Iraqi, whose limbs are locked in rigor mortis, after a late-night raid on a suspected bomb-maker's home in Mosul. This page, top: A young Iraqi stands handcuffed after he had attacked soldiers coming through the door to his home, and had been hit with a rifle butt. Bomb-making material was found during a search of the house, but the teenager was not arrested. Below: Sergeant Jackson of 172nd Stryker Brigade rests in the living room of a home after the detention of two suspected insurgents. Following pages: The younger brother of a suspect awaits interrogation while soldiers search the next room.

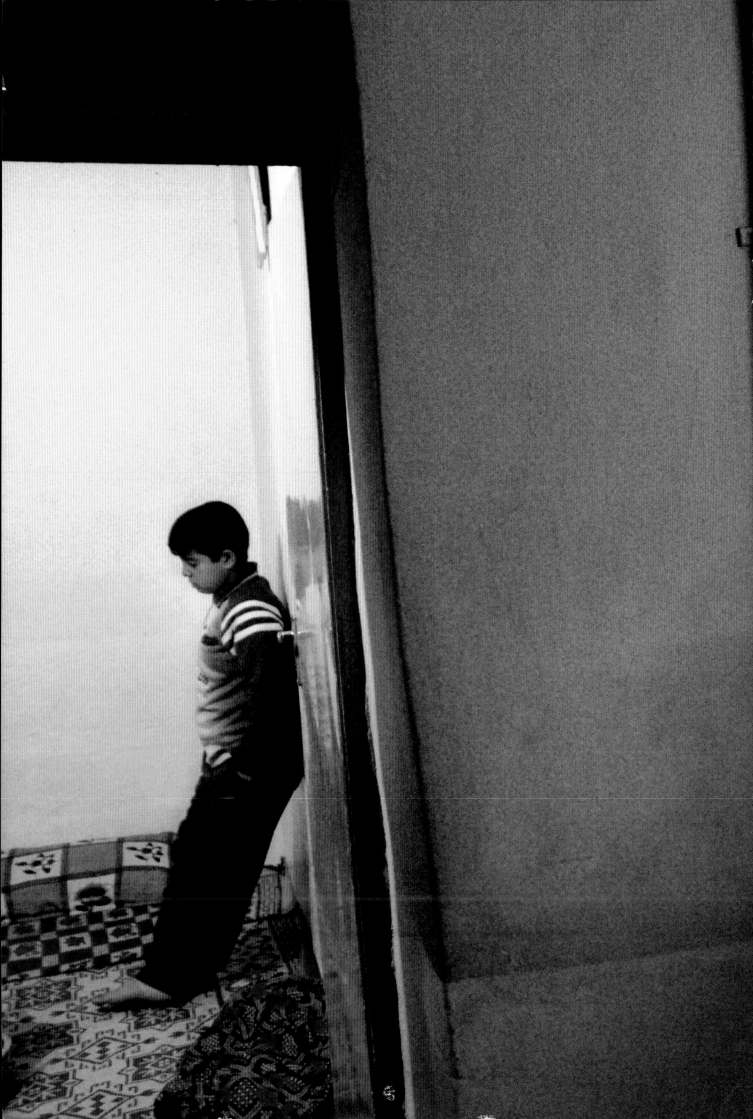

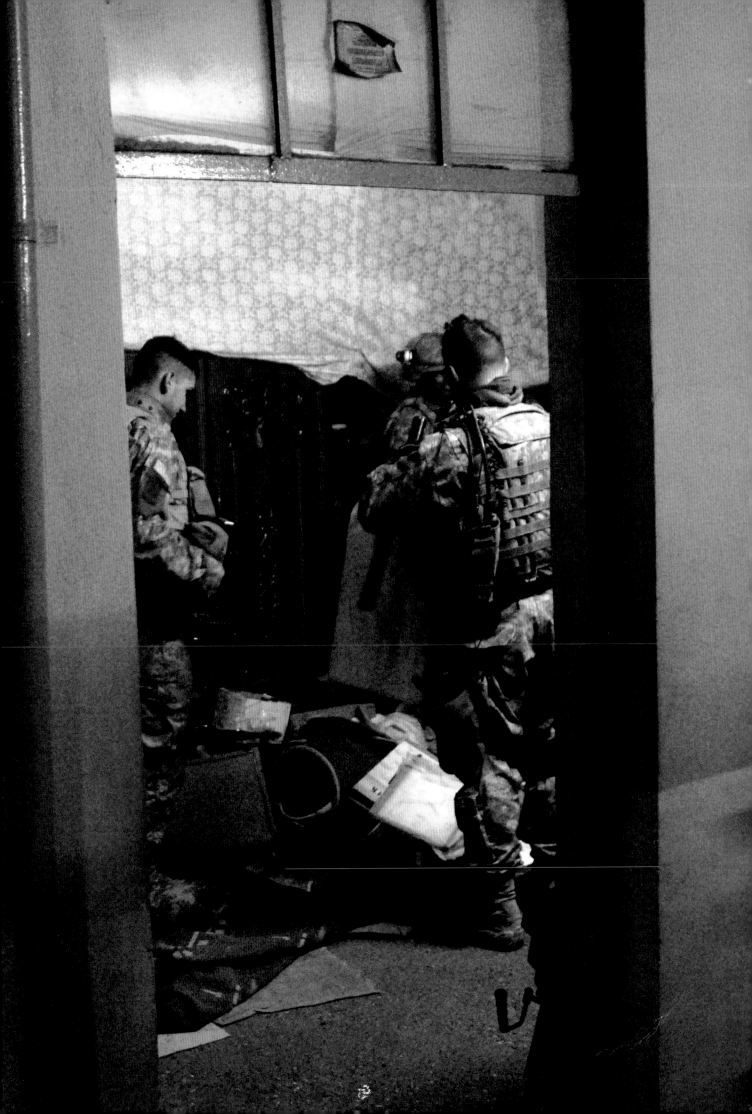

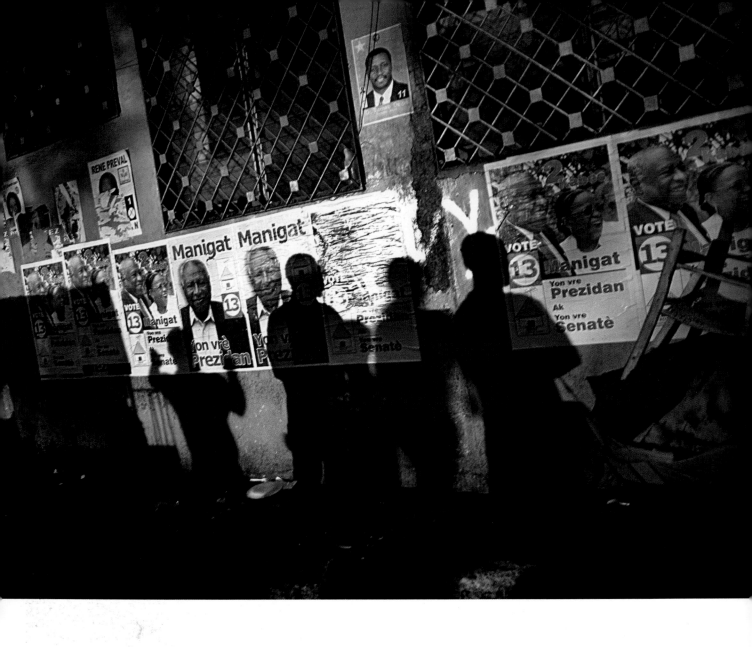

Moises Saman
Spain, Newsday
3rd Prize Stories

Haitians went to the polls in February, for the first elections since President Jean-Bertrand Aristide was ousted from power in 2004. The elections passed relatively calmly, though some violence erupted over a long delay in announcing results, and after early reports indicated that frontrunner René Préval had not reached the 50 percent of poll needed to prevent a March run-off. Later it was declared that Préval, a former ally of President Aristide, had indeed won with 51.15

percent of the votes. This page: Haitians wait for a bus beside a wall covered in posters for rival presidential candidate Leslie Manigat. Facing page, top: Voters line up at a poll station in Port-au-Prince early on election day. Middle: Préval supporters celebrate near the Presidential Palace as unofficial word of his victory spreads. Below: Supporters of Préval burn barricades and cars in Port-au-Prince in protest against delays in official election results.

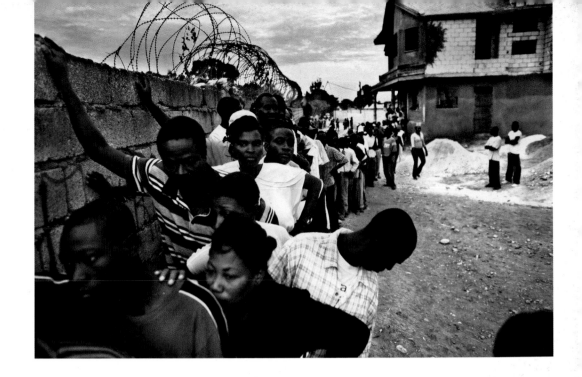

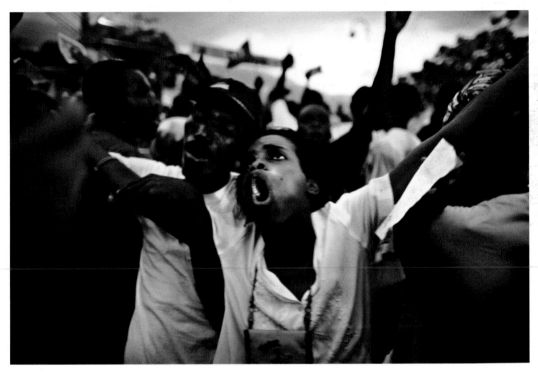

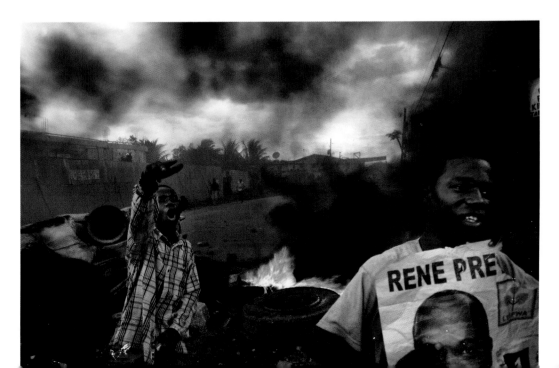

Contemporary Issues

Walter Astrada
Argentina, World Picture Network
1st Prize Singles

Public prosecutor's officials examine
the body of Maira Esperanza
Gutiérrez, 42, who has been killed by
16 shots fired by an unidentified man,
in Boca del Monte, Guatemala. Nearly
two women a day were murdered in
Guatemala in the first half of 2006
alone, part of a rising wave of assaults
against women that included rape,
torture and mutilation. Perpetrators
of what came to be called 'femicide'
appeared immune from punishment,
with only 14 out of nearly 2,000
murder cases being resolved since
separate records for women victims
began in 2001.

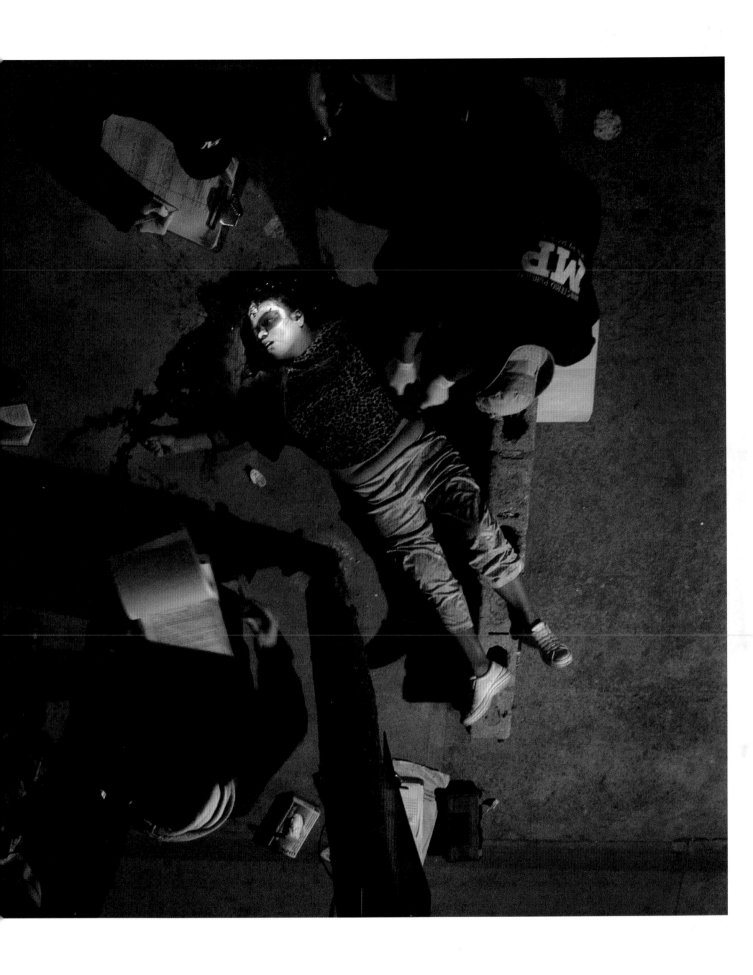

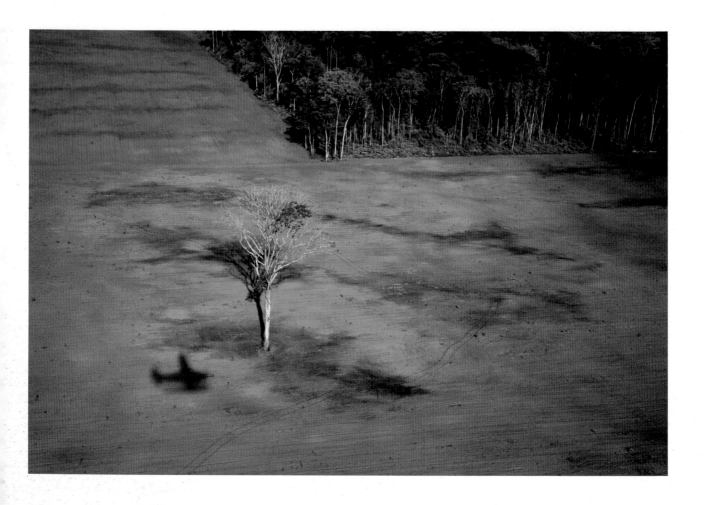

Daniel Beltrá
Spain, Zuma Press for Greenpeace
2nd Prize Singles

A tree stands isolated in a soybean
field on the edge of rainforest in
Belterra, near Santarém in the
Brazilian Amazon. Soy farming has
overtaken cattle ranching and
logging as a destroyer of rainforest.
Brazil's rainforest, one of the most
bio-diverse environments on earth,
is the size of Western Europe,
covering 60 percent of the country.
Experts believe that as much as one
fifth has been destroyed. Soy is used
widely in animal feed for high-
density farming, as well as for
human consumption and in other
products such as printing inks and
paint. Locally, soy farming provided
a source of income in what was an
economically depressed area.

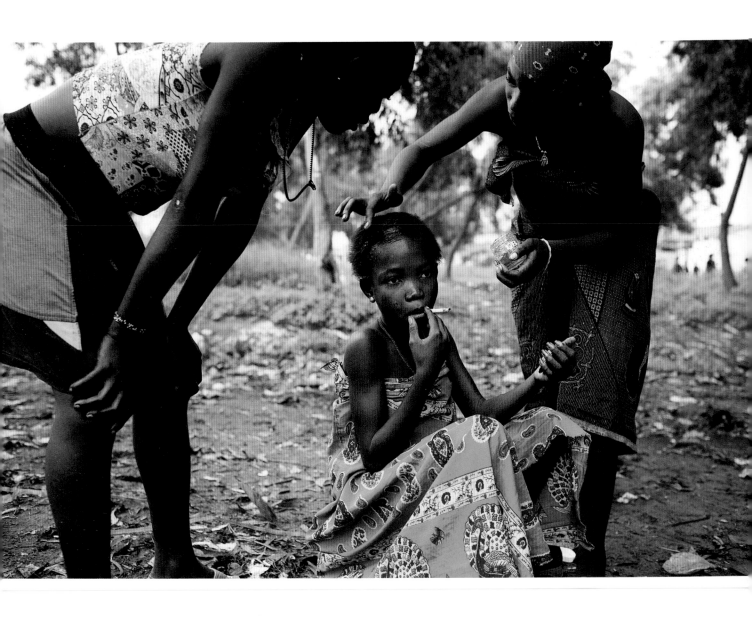

Per-Anders Pettersson
Sweden, Getty Images for Stern
3rd Prize Singles

Esther Yandakwa, 9, smokes a cigarette while her friends help her with her hair, in central Kinshasa, Democratic Republic of Congo. Esther is homeless and a sex worker, charging her clients as little as US$1. Conflict, internal displacement and HIV/Aids have long disrupted life in the DRC. Tens of thousands of child refugees, war orphans, and children abandoned by their families, live on the streets in Kinshasa and other urban areas around the country.

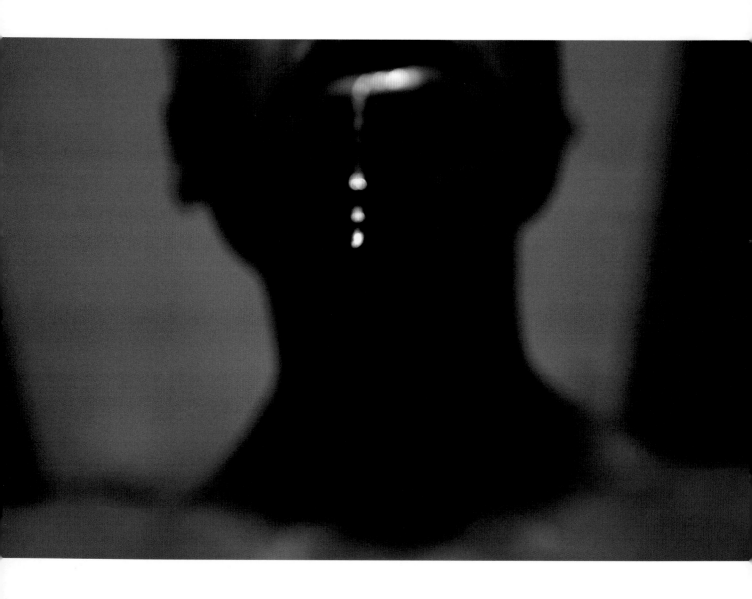

José Cendón
Spain
1st Prize Stories

In the conflict-torn Great Lakes region of Africa, where health care as a whole faces severe challenges, psychiatric resources are especially thin on the ground. People suffering post-war trauma live alongside those with a range of other mental disabilities in a handful of psychiatric hospitals. These pages: Inmates occupying isolation cells at the Kamenge psychiatric hospital in Bujumbura, Burundi, the only one in the country that treats people with war trauma. The center is run by a Belgian Roman Catholic order, the Frères de la Charité (Brothers of Charity). It is financed by the church, though patients contribute money for medicines and food. (story continues)

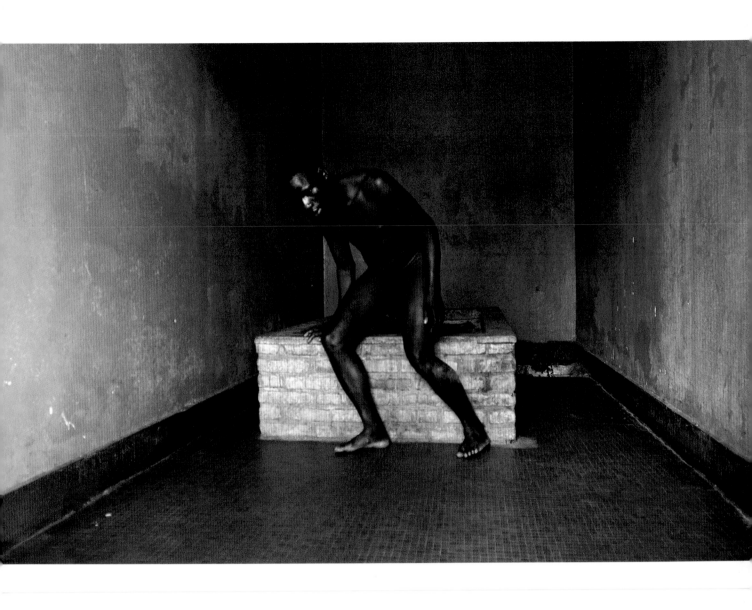

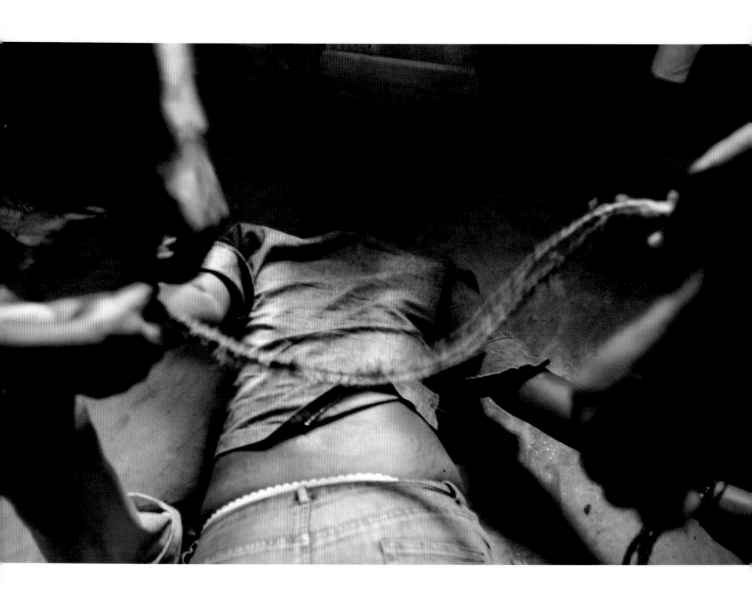

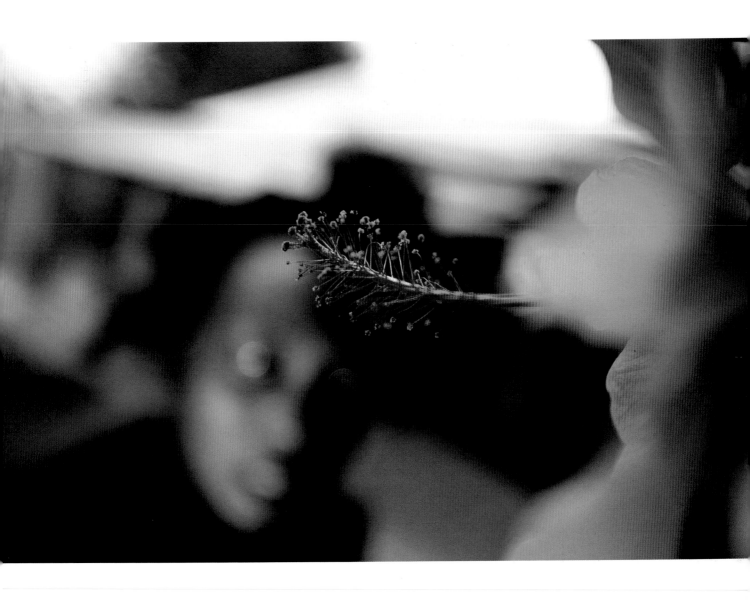

(continued) The Soins de Santé Mentale (SOSAME) psychiatric center is the only such facility in the Sud-Kivu province of the Democratic Republic of Congo, an area covering 69,000 square kilometers with a population of three million. The center has 60 beds for long-term cases, and treats some 50 outpatients a day. Family members are expected to help staff with patient care. Facing page: A patient is tied down by a member of her family and a nurse, after she tried to escape from the center. This page: A patient walks in the garden.

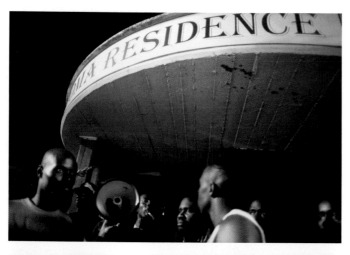
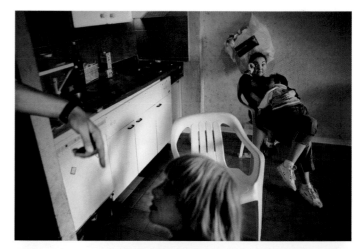
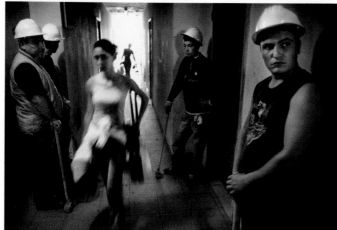
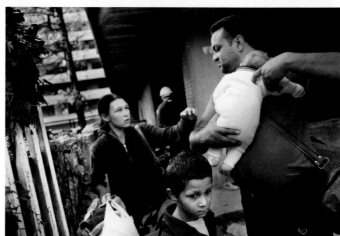
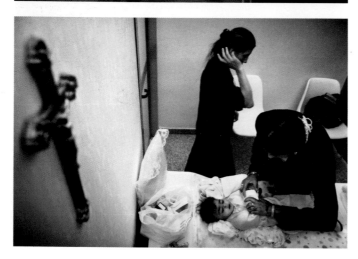
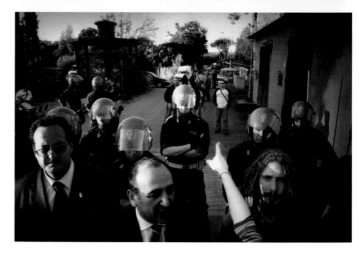

Massimo Berruti
Italy, Grazia Neri
2nd Prize Stories

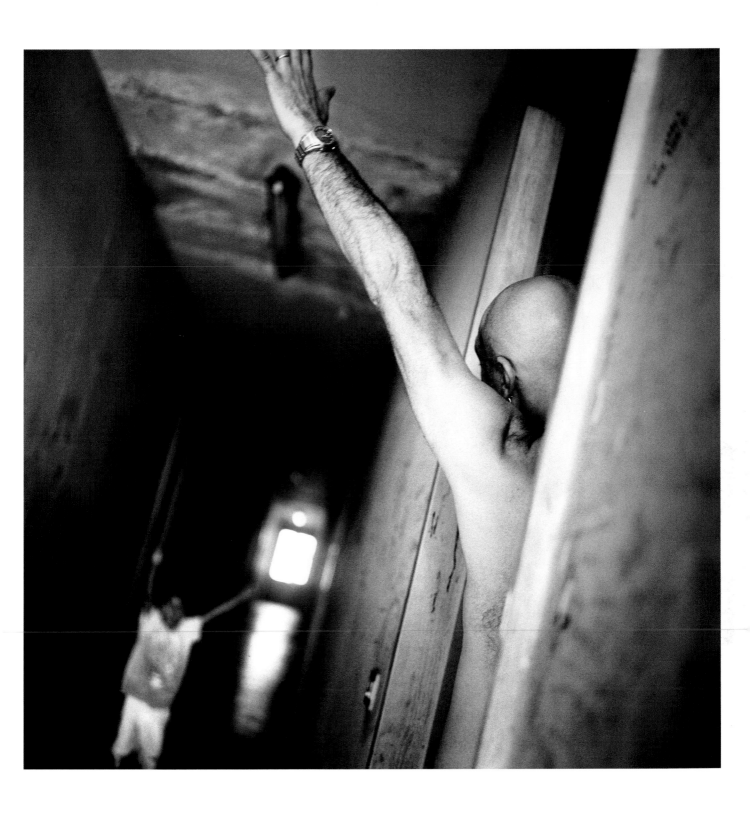

The Roma Residence is a group of apartment blocks just a kilometer from the Vatican in Rome. Built in the early 1980s when there was a housing crisis in the city, the complex has been through a succession of owners who let a proportion of its small apartments to local authorities for social housing. Over the years, maintenance was neglected and living conditions in the buildings declined. Given its choice location, the Roma Residence was scheduled for luxury redevelopment, but many of the mainly immigrant occupants who were evacuated had no rights to re-housing. Facing page, top left: Senegalese residents protest that the building's owners have cut off electric power to drive out tenants. Right: A family about to be evacuated. Middle, left: Women walk with their belongings past demolition workers on evacuation day. Right: A family is evicted from their apartment. Below, left: Women tend the body of a dead child. Right: Police barricade a protest by a housing and human-rights organization. This page: A man and child greet each other in one of the corridors.

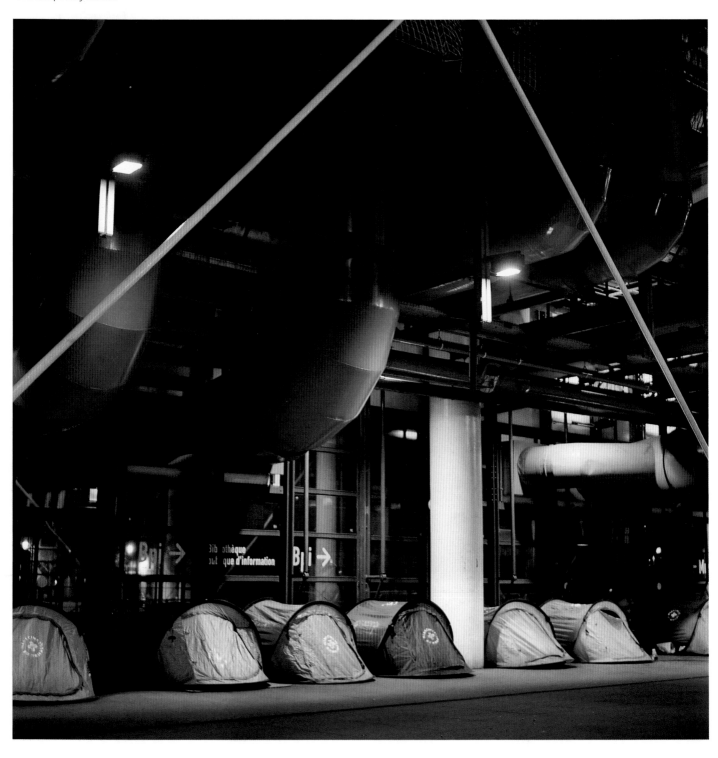

Bruno Fert
France, In Visu
3rd Prize Stories

In the winter of 2005 the charity Médecins du Monde began distributing tents to homeless people in Paris. The aim was not only to provide temporary shelter, but by the tents' high visibility to draw public and government attention to the situation of the homeless. Médecins du Monde handed out about 300 tents, but sympathizers gave away an estimated 200 more. Small tented communities began to spring up around the city, some in popular tourist spots. In August 2006, the French government pledged US$9.2 million for emergency housing in the capital, promising to create both extra hostel beds and longer-term accommodation. This page: Homeless people's tents erected in front of the Centre Pompidou. Facing page, from top left: Tents appear on the Quai d'Austerlitz, on Avenue de Wagram, on the stairs of Montmartre, and under the Pont Marie on the river Seine.

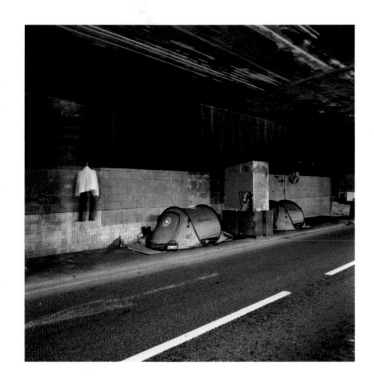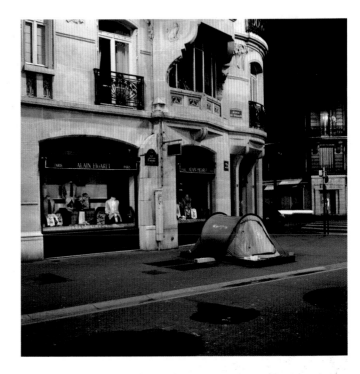
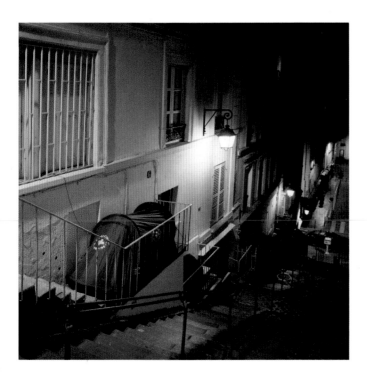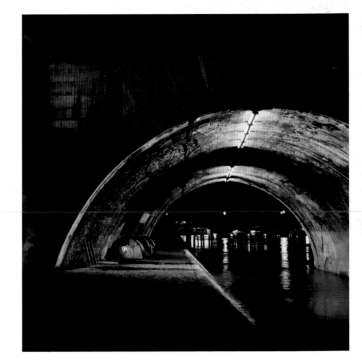

Daily Life

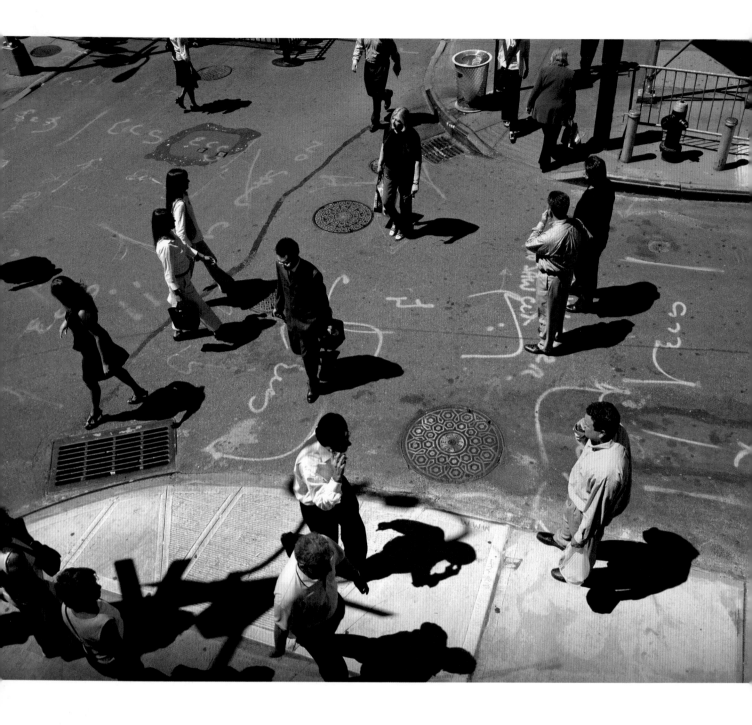

David Butow
USA, Redux Pictures for
US News & World Report
2nd Prize Singles

Pedestrians cross a section of Wall Street covered in painted construction markings, near the New York Stock Exchange, shortly before the fifth anniversary of the 9/11 attack on the city's World Trade Center. The former WTC site and parts of lower Manhattan were still in the rebuilding process following the attack.

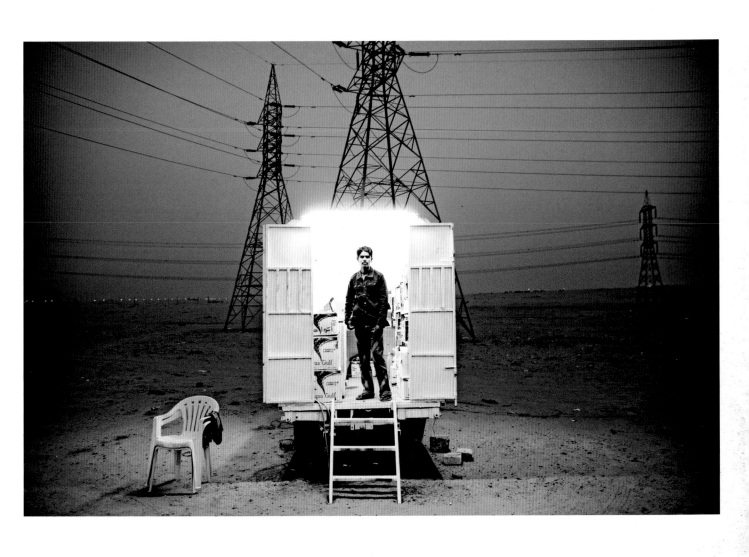

Steven Achiam
Denmark, Dagbladet Børsen
3rd Prize Singles

Hamal Munaf from Bangladesh works in temperatures of about 45° Celsius as sales person in an open-container kiosk in Kuwait. He is one of around 170,000 expatriate Bangladeshis working in Kuwait. They are often poorly paid and live in miserable conditions, but come in the hope of sending money home each month. Most workers arrive in the country legally on contracts to do cleaning and other menial tasks in a booming economy, but many claim that they end up receiving salaries drastically lower than those they were promised. Following Bangladeshi unrest in Kuwait in April, the Minister of Social and Labor Affairs promised a crackdown on unsound employment practices.

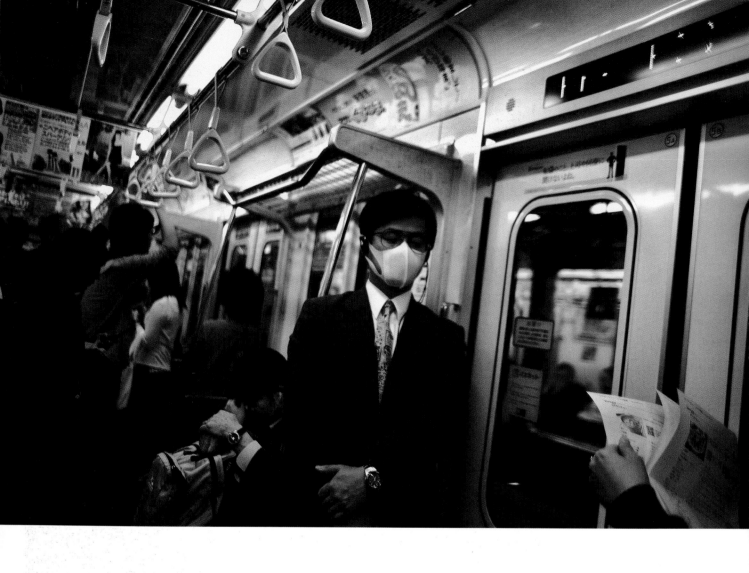

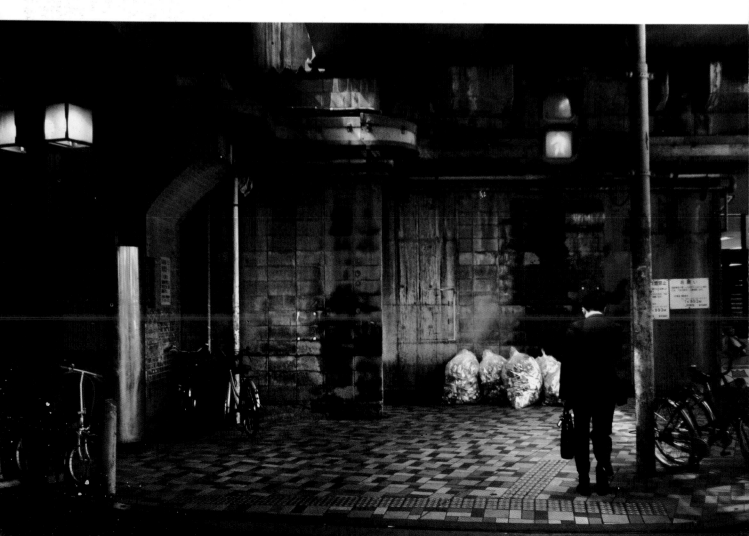

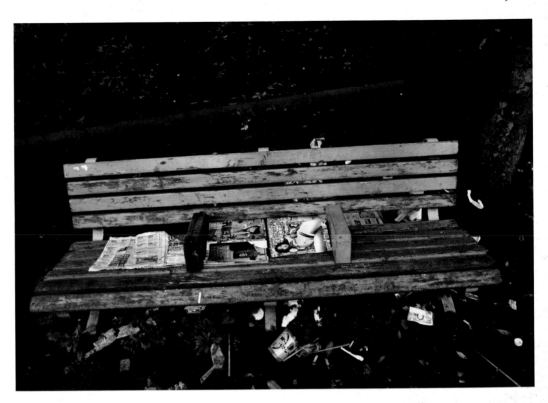

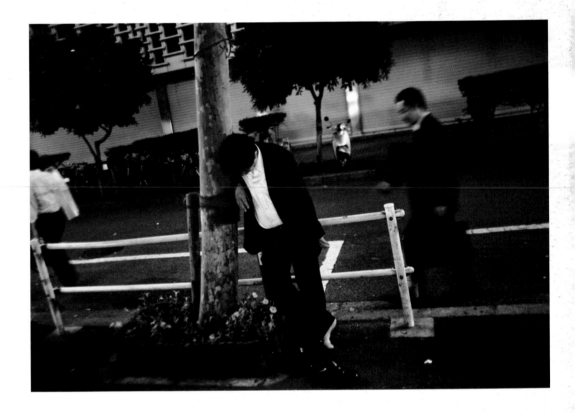

David Guttenfelder
USA, The Associated Press
1st Prize Stories

Traditionally, Japanese white-collar workers have been able to expect lifelong support and loyalty from their employers, in return for unremitting hard work. A 'salaryman' (a Japanese word that borrows from English) follows a punishing work regime that often affects social and family life. The term carries associations of long working hours, initial low prestige in the corporate hierarchy, and even *karoshi* – death caused by overwork. To relieve the tension of their working schedule many salarymen go out drinking at night. Facing page: Salarymen commute to their offices in Tokyo. This page, top: Men's magazines and newspapers abandoned on a Tokyo park bench. Below: A salaryman rests against a tree after drinking too much with fellow workers. Following pages: Central Tokyo.

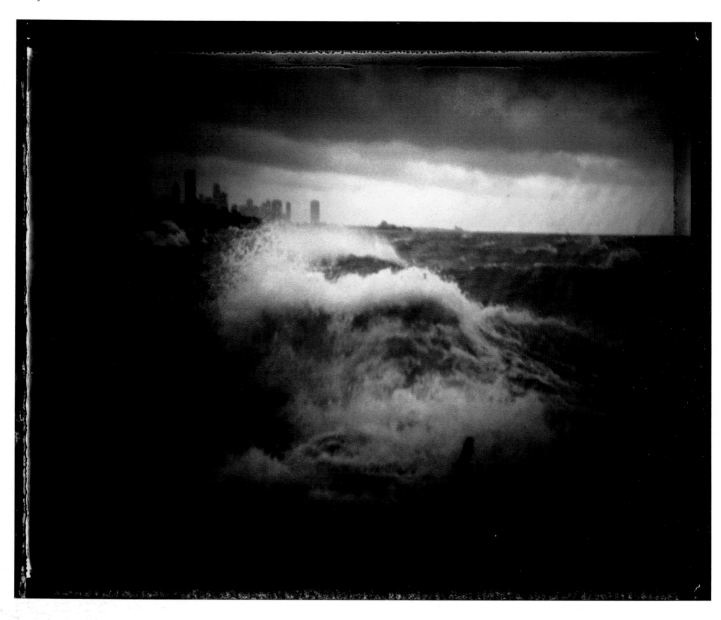

Jon Lowenstein
USA, Aurora Photos
2nd Prize Stories

Chicago South Side has long had a distinct identity, for much of the 20th century being associated with the city's African American population. In the 1970s and 1980s, the once thriving industrial communities of the South Side hit hard times, as Chicago's industrial base declined and city economy shifted from manufacturing to the service sectors. Unemployment, poverty, drugs and gang violence became major issues. This page: View from a South Side beach towards downtown Chicago during a summer storm. Facing page, top: Kokomo, a stripper, performs at a South Side bachelor party. Below: Reggie and his crew hang out on 72nd Street, in a neighborhood known as Pockettown and home to three rival gangs. (story continues)

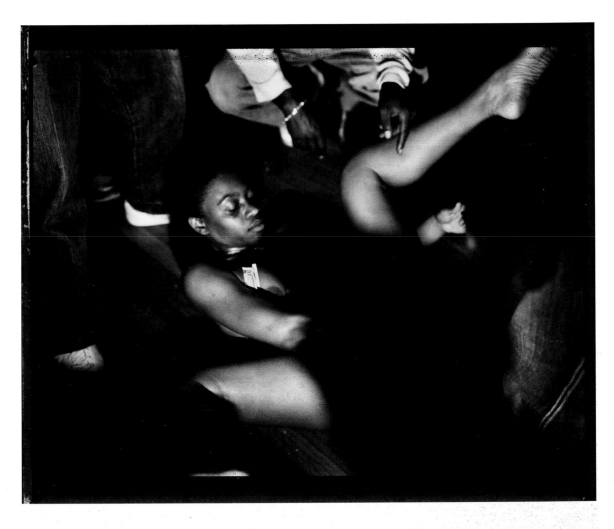

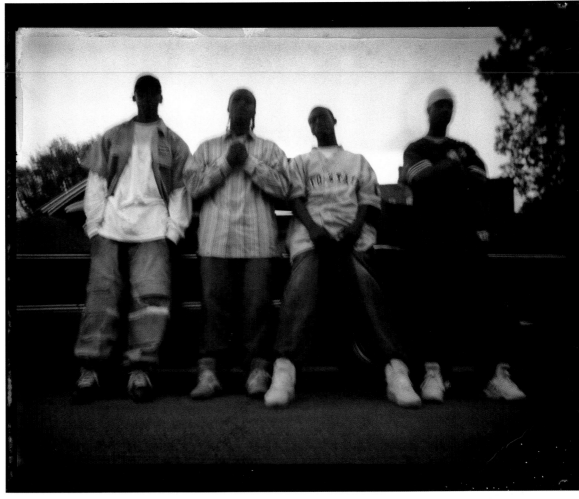

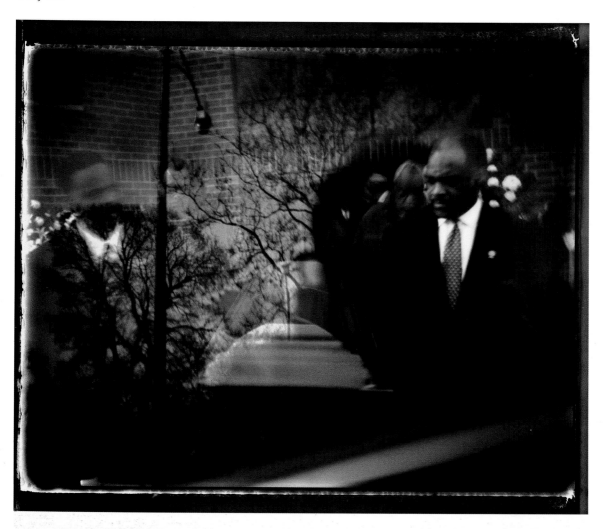

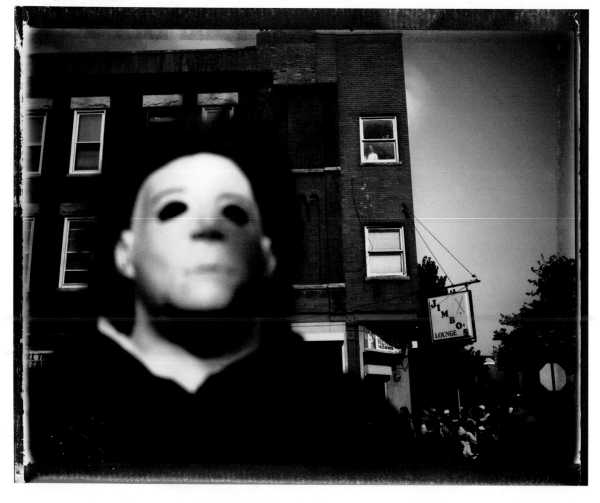

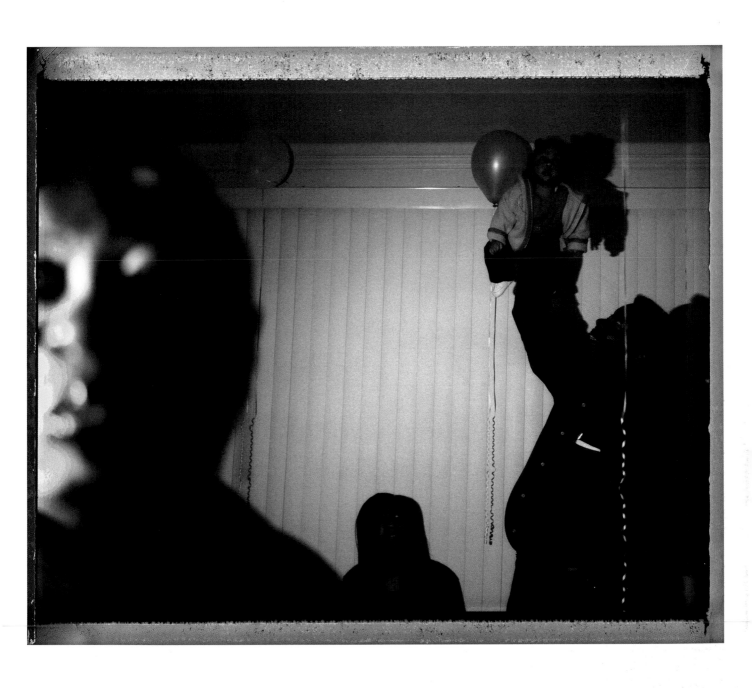

(continued) Despite their adversities, many South Side residents preserve a strong sense of community affection. But now many South Side residents are faced with displacement, as upscale redevelopment of some areas means that they can no longer afford to live there. Facing page, top: The funeral of Willie Jones Sr., a much-loved resident of Pockettown. Below: A man poses in a horror-movie mask in Bridgeport, an enclave known for its resistance to African American residents. This page: Uncle Al holds up his niece at Sam Binion's house on South Ellis Avenue.

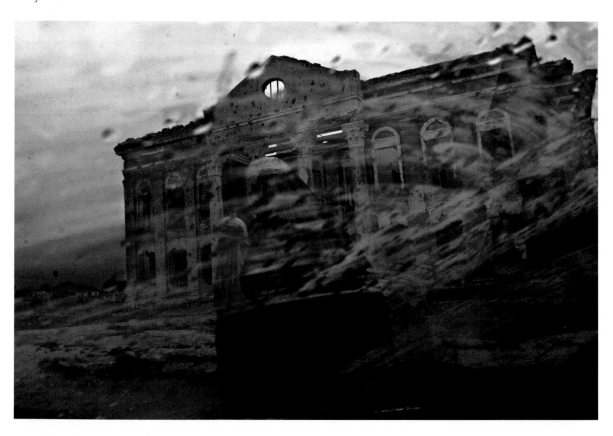

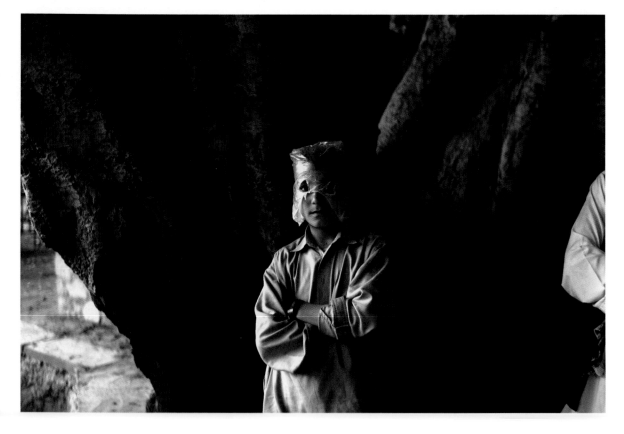

Moises Saman
Spain, Newsday
3rd Prize Stories

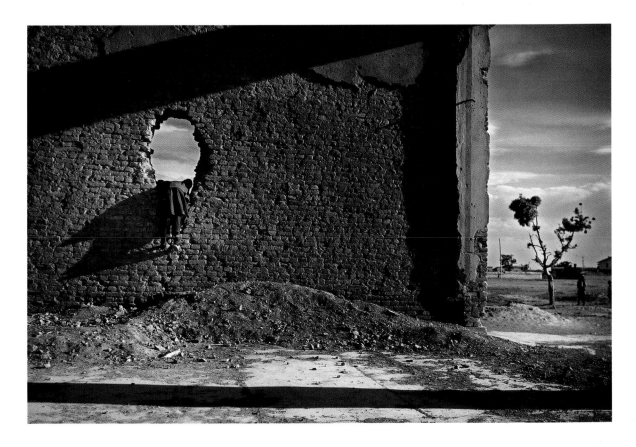

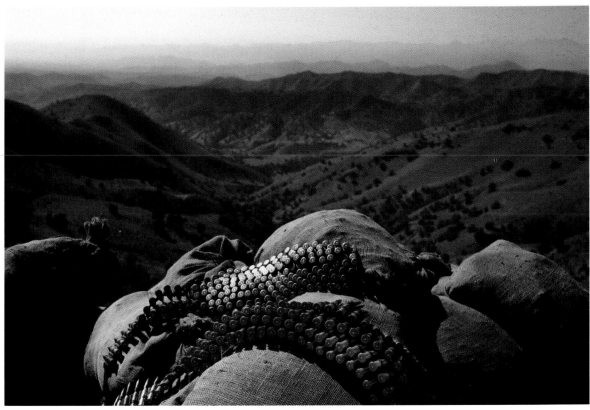

Five years after the American-led invasion to oust the Taliban from Afghanistan, efforts to reform the judiciary, towards religious freedom, and towards relaxing strictures on women were still underway. Daily life for most Afghans revolved around rebuilding the war-ravaged state. Facing page, top: Women wearing traditional burqas walk past a Kabul government building which was destroyed during the 1990s civil war. Below: Wearing a plastic bag for protection, an Afghan boy shelters from the rain. This page, top: A boy plays in a building damaged during the civil war, in the city of Gardez. Below: Machine-gun ammunition lies on top of a sandbag, in a position overlooking a mountain pass on the Pakistan border – a route used by Taliban insurgents.

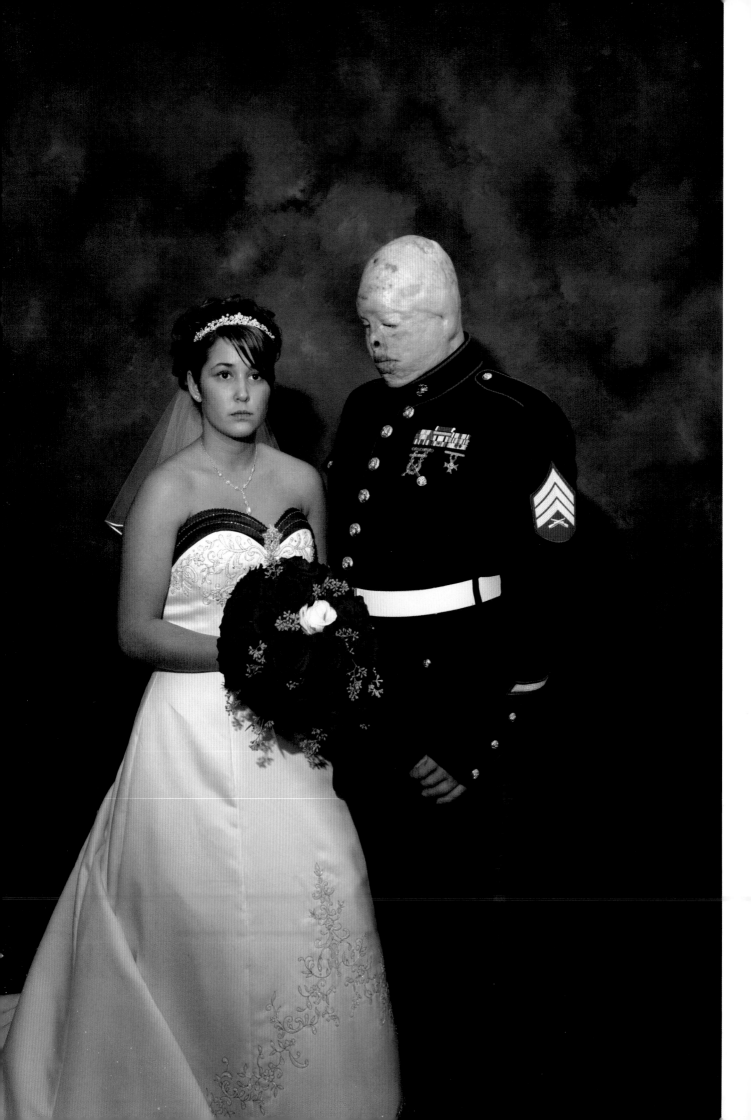

Nina Berman
USA, Redux Pictures for People
1st Prize Singles

US Marine Ty Ziegel poses with
Renee Kline before their wedding in
Washington, Illinois, in July. Ziegel
was severely wounded in a suicide
bomb attack during his second tour
of duty in Iraq. He was blinded in one
eye, had a shattered skull, and most
of his skin was burned off. The
couple were engaged following
Ziegel's first deployment in Iraq.
After Ziegel was injured, Kline lived
with him for over a year while he
recovered at a hospital in Texas.

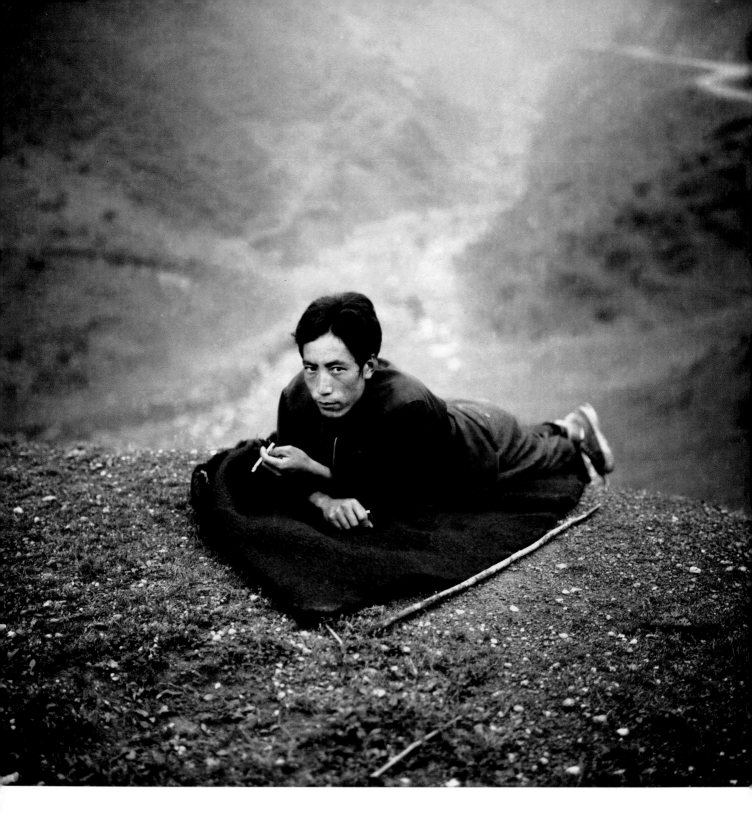

Wang Gang
People's Republic of China
2nd Prize Singles

A Yi shepherd takes a rest deep in the Daliang mountains of Sichuan, in China. There are around seven million Yis scattered mainly through the Sichuan, Yunnan, Guizhou and Guangxi provinces. The Yi ethnic group is said to stem from the ancient Qiang people of northwest China, and also to have Tibetan ancestry. They have their own language, and Yi characters – the earliest syllabic script in China – are still used today. Those Yi living in high mountain areas preserve a way of life that has changed little in centuries.

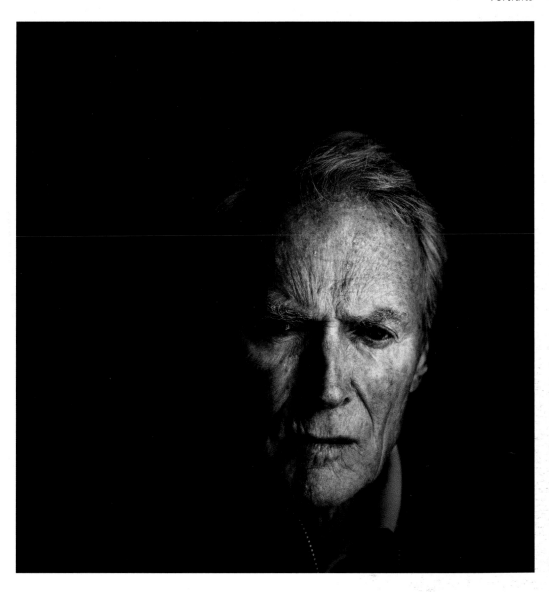

Damon Winter
USA, Los Angeles Times
3rd Prize Singles

Clint Eastwood, at the age of 76 in Burbank, California, on November 30. In 2006 Eastwood received the Légion d'Honneur from France's President Chirac, and the first ever humanitarian award from the Motion Pictures Association of America, which cited his decades of 'decency and goodness of spirit' in moviemaking. He also released two of the most acclaimed films of his career. *Flags of Our Fathers* and *Letters from Iwo Jima* tackled the infamous World War II battle of Iwo Jima from an American and Japanese perspective respectively.

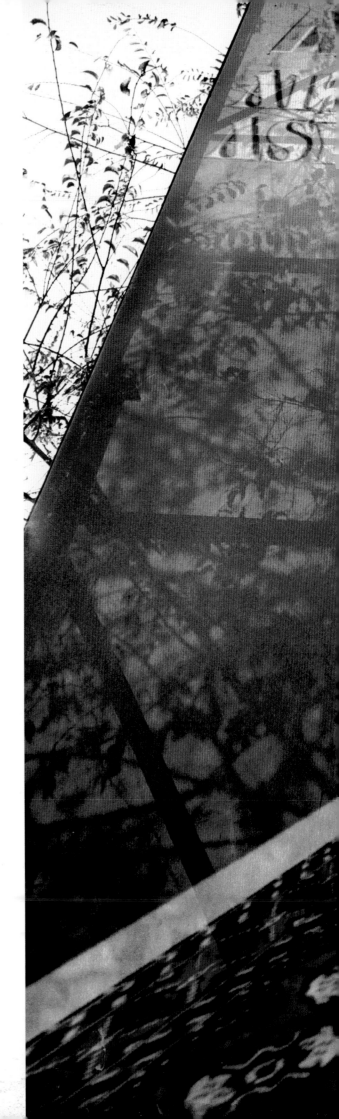

Nicolas Righetti
Switzerland, Rezo
1st Prize Stories

The authoritarian president of oil-
rich Turkmenistan, Saparmurat
Niyazov, died of a heart attack in
December, aged 66. Niyazov had
created a strong cult of personality
during his two decades in power,
styling himself Turkmenbashi, Father
of the Turkmen. Even months and
days of the week were renamed
after himself and his family. These
pages: A billboard depicting
President Niyazov. (story continues)

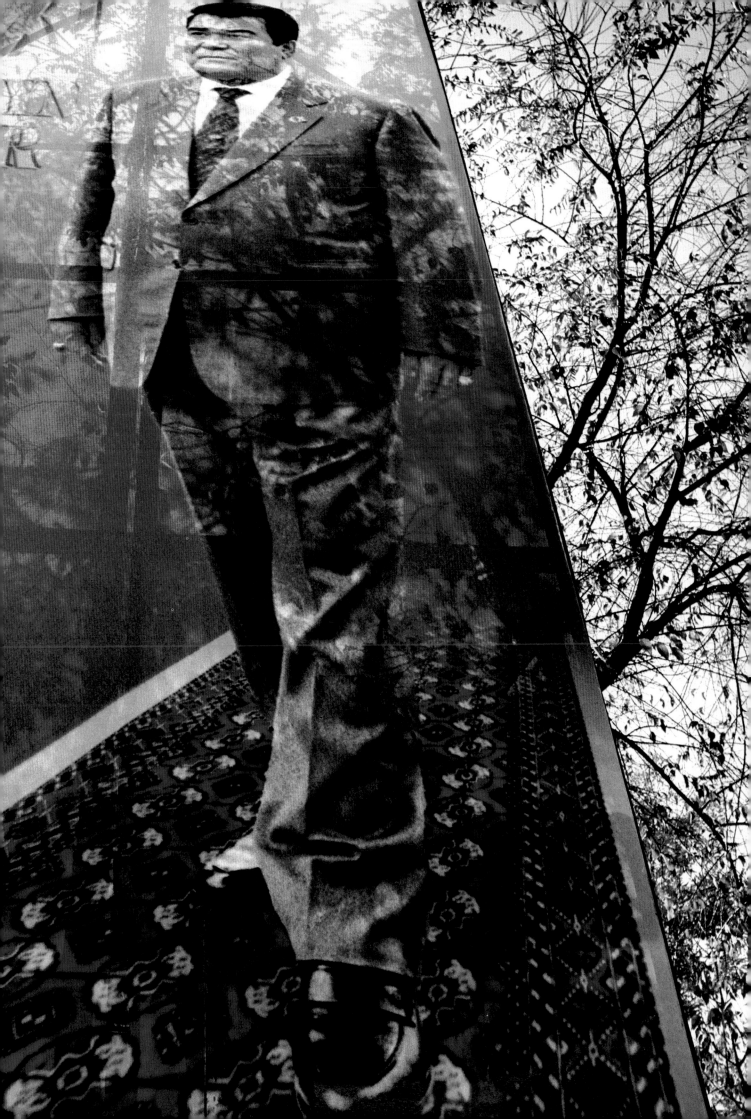

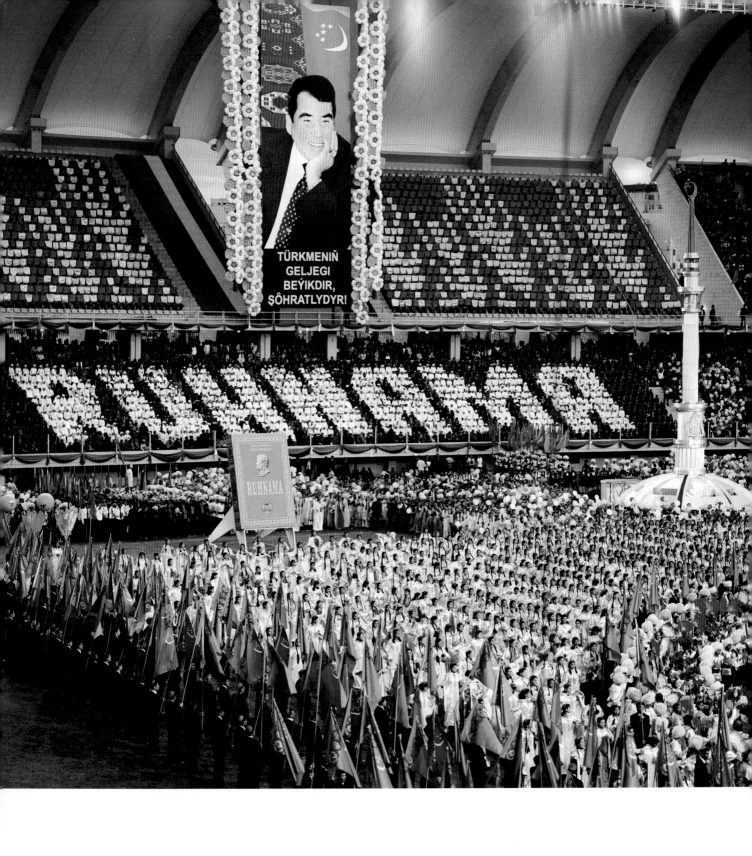

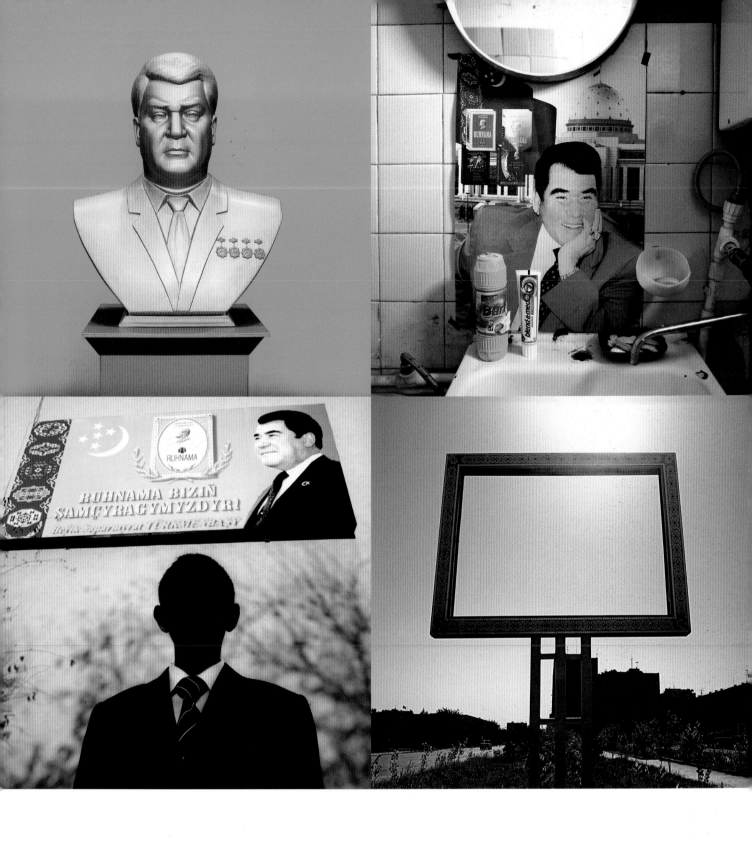

(continued) Niyazov wrote a spiritual guide *Ruhnama*, which became the nation's required reading. He tolerated no dissent, and there was no opposition or free media in Turkmenistan. Facing page: On independence day at the President Saparmurat Niyazov Stadium in the capital Ashgabat, citizens sing the praise of their leader and his book. This page, top left: A gilt bust of the president. Right: A presidential poster in a private bathroom. Below, left: A schoolboy beneath a representation of the president. Right: A hoarding frame devoid of its usual Niyazov image in Ashgabat.

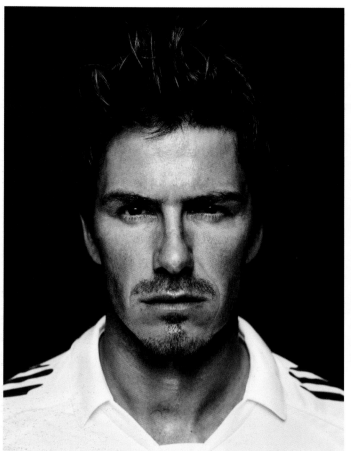 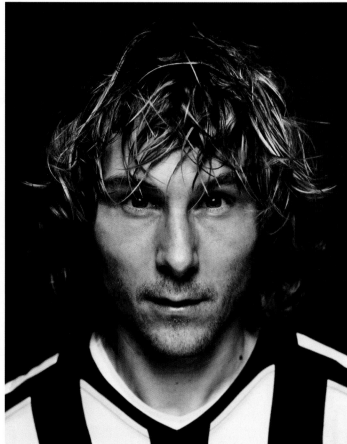

**Mathias Braschler &
Monika Fischer**
Switzerland, Grazia Neri for
L'Equipe/Guardian Weekend/
Sports Illustrated/Stern
2nd Prize Stories

Famous footballers, taken after the
final whistle of club matches. From
left to right: David Beckham, 31,
midfielder, after his club Real
Madrid's 4-0 win over Deportivo.
Pavel Nedved, 33, midfielder, after
Juventus lost 2-3 to AS Roma. Didier
Drogba, 28, forward, after Chelsea's
2-0 victory over Portsmouth. Carles
Puyol, 28, defender, after FC
Barcelona beat Real Sociedad 5-0.

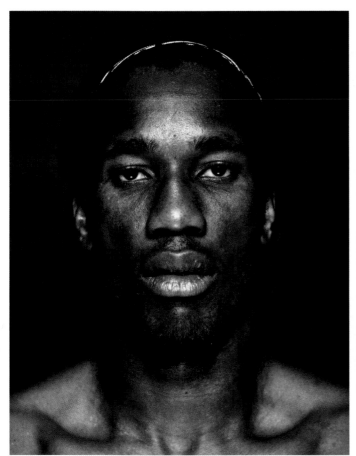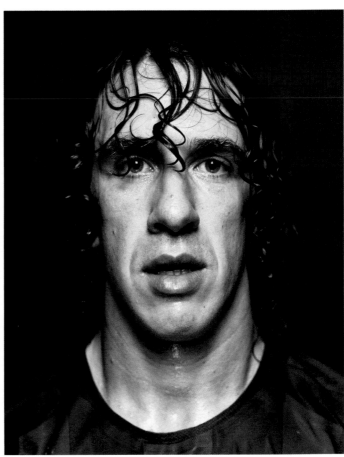

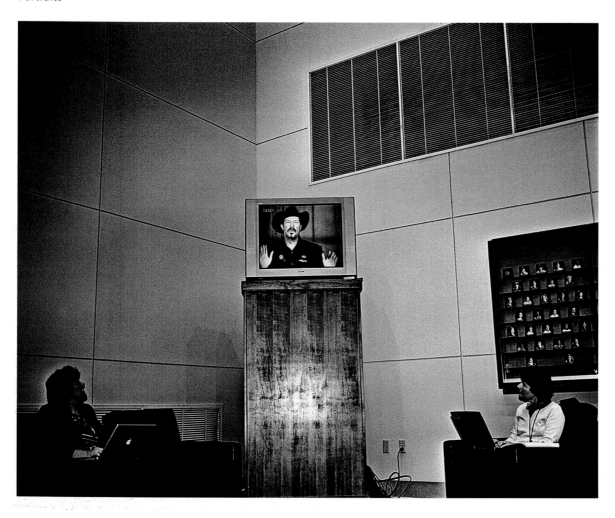

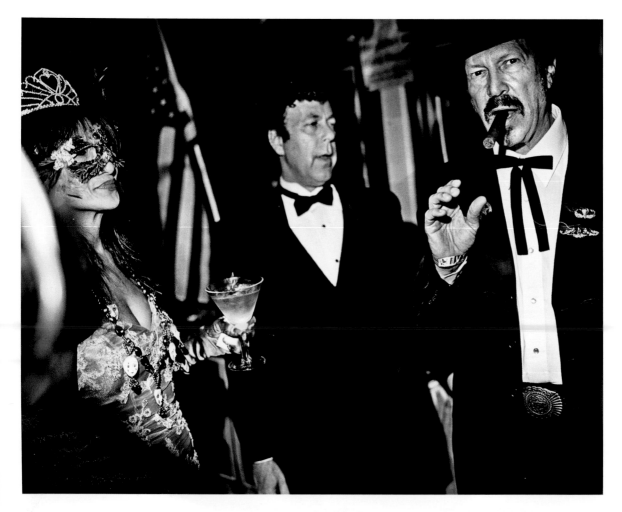

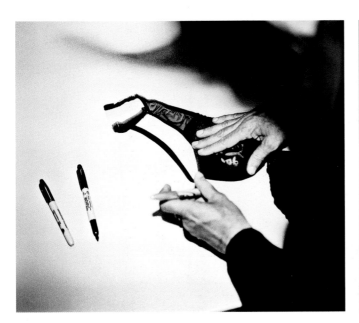 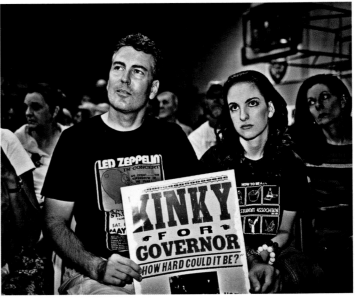

Erin Grace Trieb
USA
3rd Prize Stories

Flamboyant singer, songwriter, humorist and author Richard D. "Kinky" Friedman ran as an independent candidate for the governorship of Texas, receiving 12 percent of the vote. Known for his irreverent wit and enjoyment at causing outrage, Friedman announced policies ranging from support for gay marriage, to sending 10,000 troops to the Mexican border to deal with illegal immigration. Facing page, top: Friedman on the monitor debates with other gubernatorial candidates in October. Below: Friedman, with his characteristic cigar, attends the Houston Margarita Ball, in Houston. This page, left: Friedman autographs the brassiere of an admirer at Lamar University in Beaumont, Texas. Right: George and Maria C. Stavrou listen as Friedman gives a speech in Bastrop, Texas.

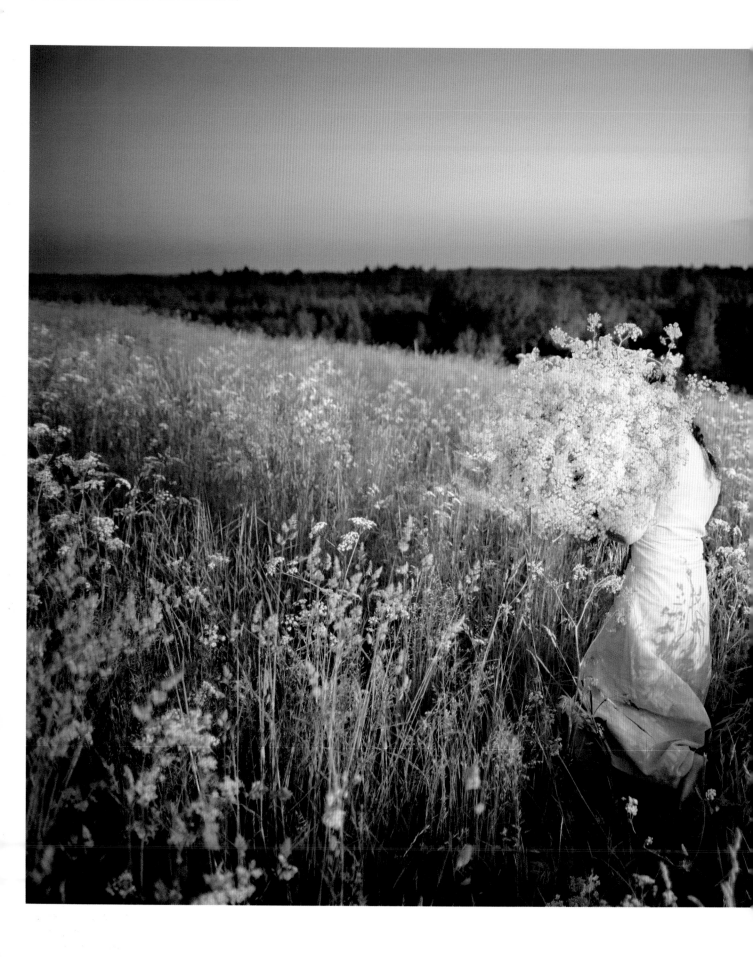

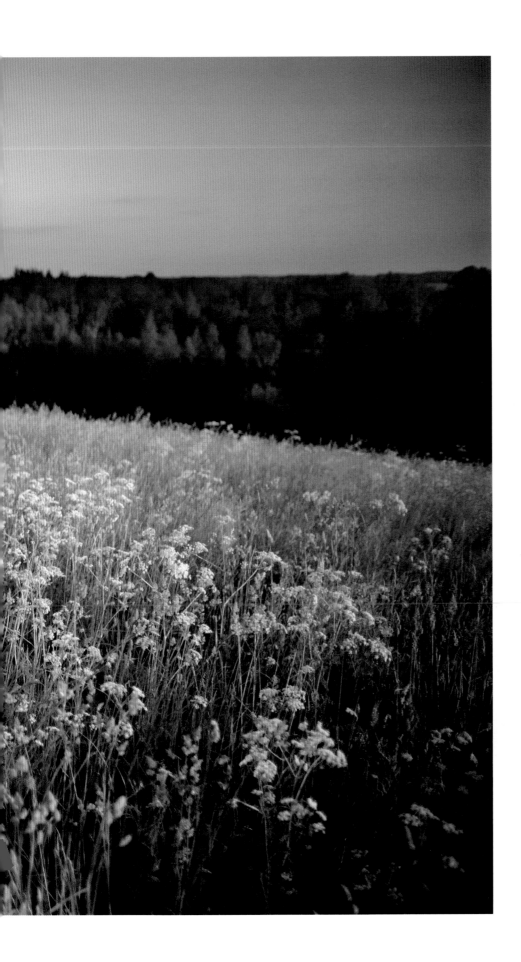

Espen Rasmussen
Norway, Verdens Gang
1st Prize Singles

A girl gathers flowers for midsummer
celebrations on a hill near the town of
Piltinkalns in Latvia. The rituals around
the summer solstice – the shortest
night of the year – have roots in pagan
belief, and are widely observed across
the Baltic region. Around 200 people
gather on the hilltop near Piltinkalns
on midsummer's night every year, to
sing, dance and make bonfires
through to dawn. On the day running
up to the festivities, women and girls
collect herbs and flowers to make into
wreaths to wear.

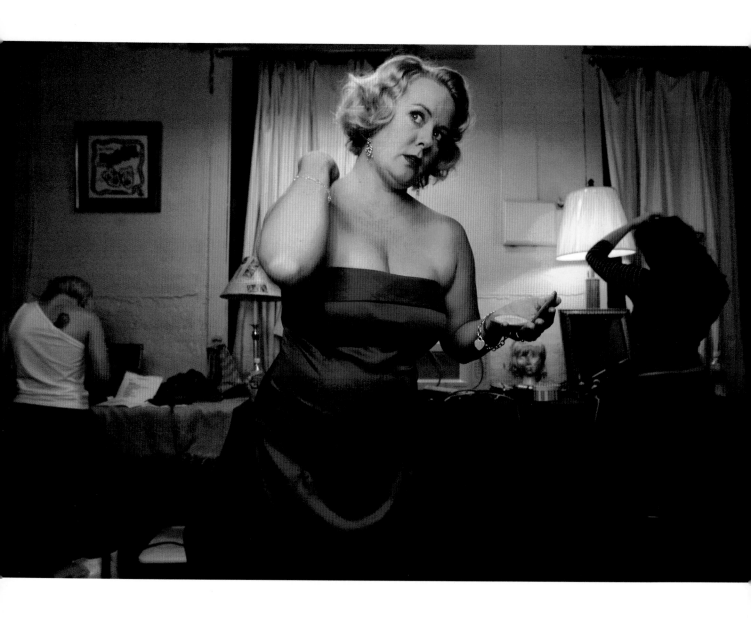

Carolyn Cole
USA, Los Angeles Times
2nd Prize Singles

Singer Debbie Davis puts on powder before the show at Tipitina's theater in the French Quarter of New Orleans, where the tradition of burlesque is making a comeback. Burlesque began as a raunchy working-class variety entertainment in 1880s New York, but by the latter part of the 20th century had declined into seedy striptease. The nationwide revival treats much of the erotic element of burlesque in a slightly tongue-in-cheek fashion, and includes a traditional touch of variety, with singers, comedians and jazz bands on the bill.

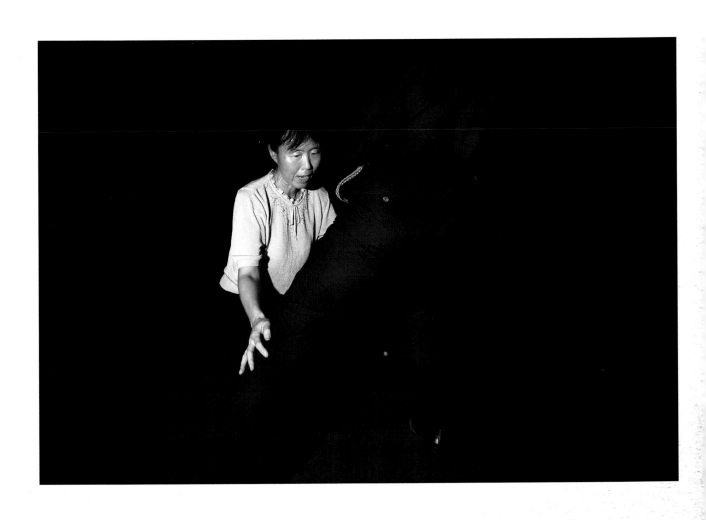

Paul Zhang
People's Republic of China,
The Beijing News
3rd Prize Singles

A blind woman touches her dancing
partner's legs in order to learn the
correct steps, at an activity center for
people with disabilities in Beijing.
Around 50 people with severe sight
difficulties gather for weekly Latin
dance sessions at the center. Each of
the pupils begins to pick up moves
with the sighted teacher, and is then
paired off with an experienced
partner. They learn everything from
rumba to tango by listening to
verbal descriptions, and by touch.

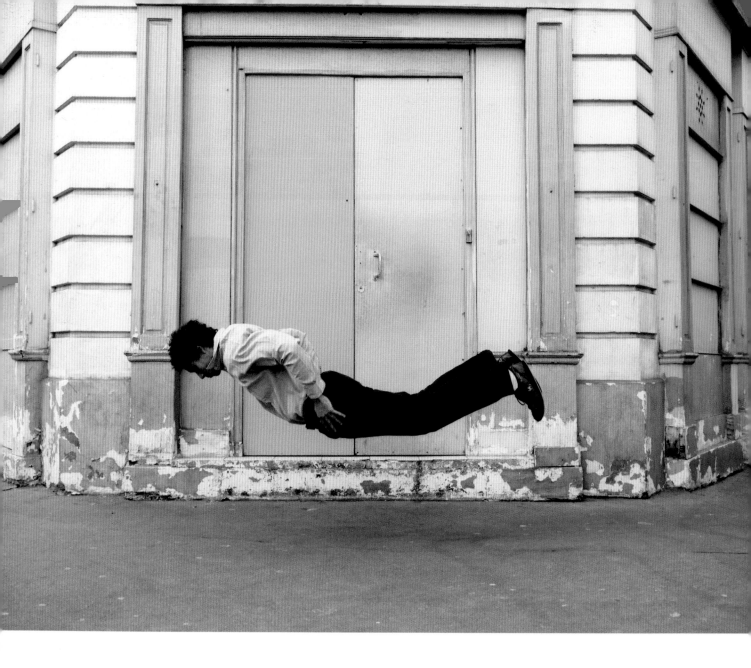

Denis Darzacq
France, Agence Vu
1st Prize Stories

Paris street dancers display their
skills at breakdancing, capoeira and
other personalized dance forms.
Breakdance evolved as part of the
hip hop movement among African
American youths in New York City in
the 1970s, and is arguably the best
known of hip hop dance styles.
Capoeira is derived from a Brazilian
martial art. (story continues)

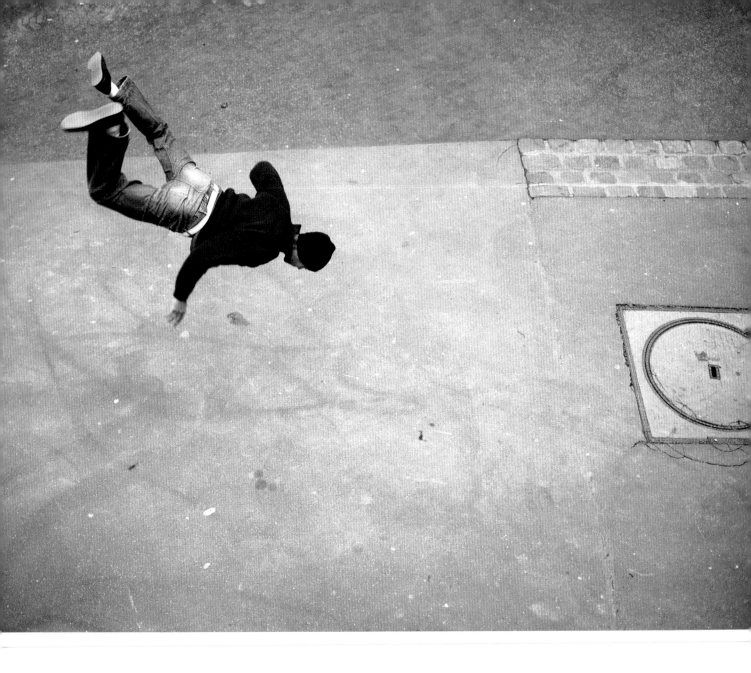

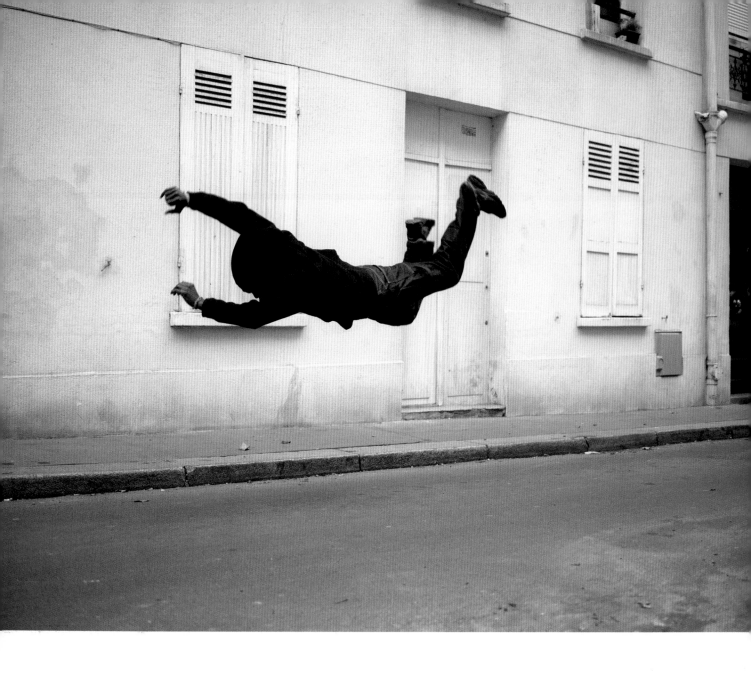

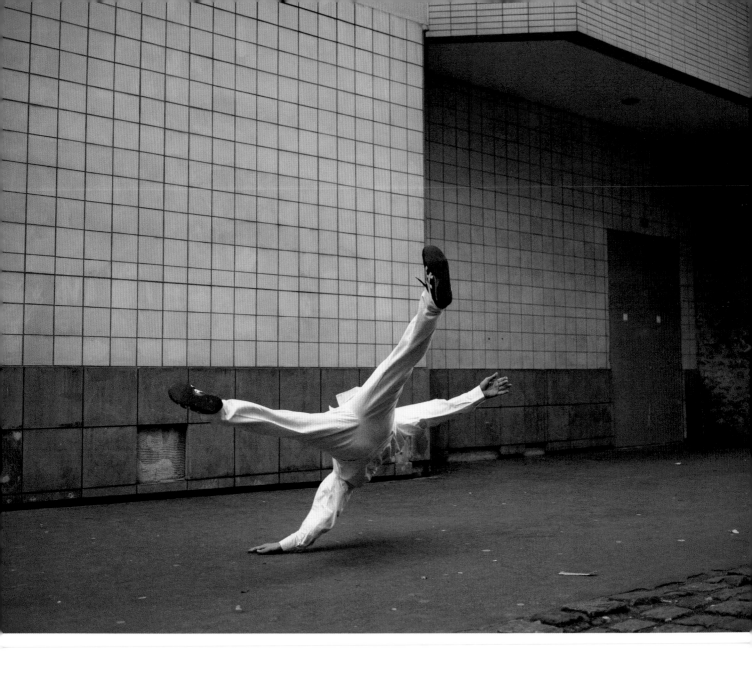

(continued) Although dances may
involve a known range of elements,
positions or steps, they are
unstructured, highly improvisational
expressions of individual technique.

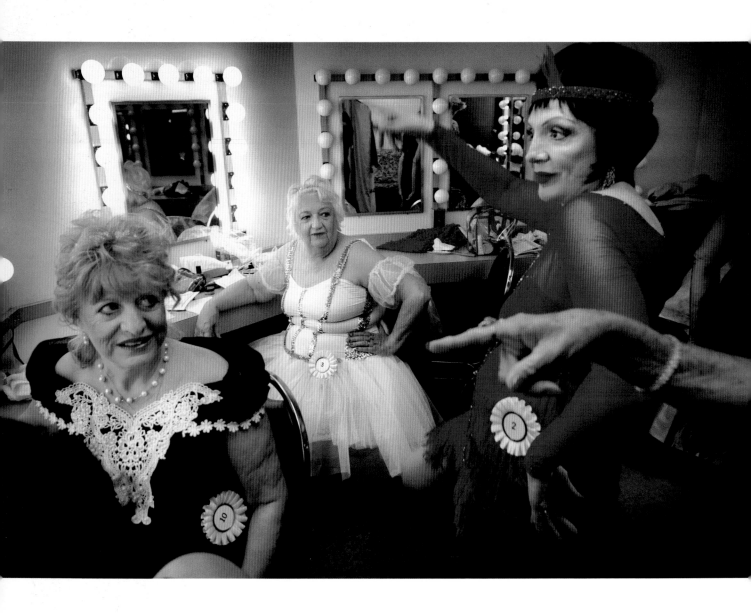

Magnus Wennman
Sweden, Aftonbladet
2nd Prize Stories

Women participate in the Ms Senior Sweetheart Pageant of America, in Fall River outside Boston. The pageant lasts for four days and involves a talent section, an evening-dress parade and an interview before a panel of judges. Contestants have to be at least 58 years old. This page: Doris Ulrich, Ruth Gibson and Francesca Piscottano ready themselves in the dressing rooms. Facing page, top: Previous pageant winners appear on stage during the finale. Middle: Janie Woods from Texas waits to go on stage during the talent section. Below: Winner of the 2006 contest Jacquelyn J. van Meter receives a congratulatory embrace.

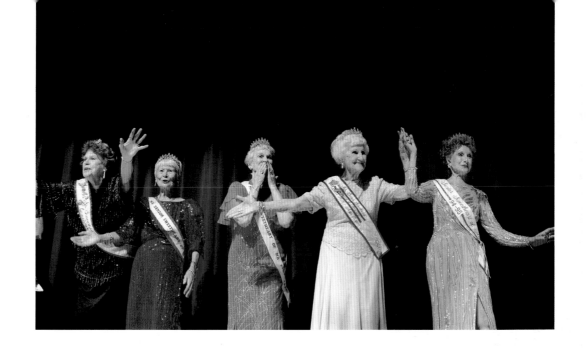

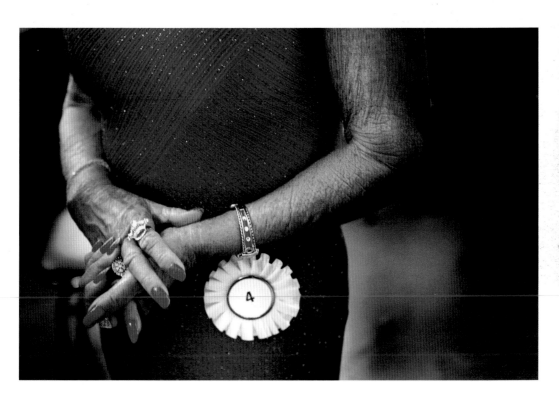

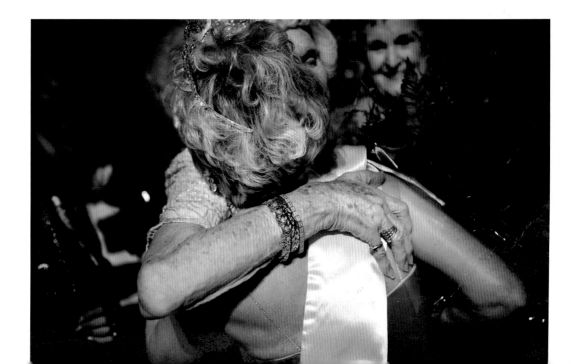

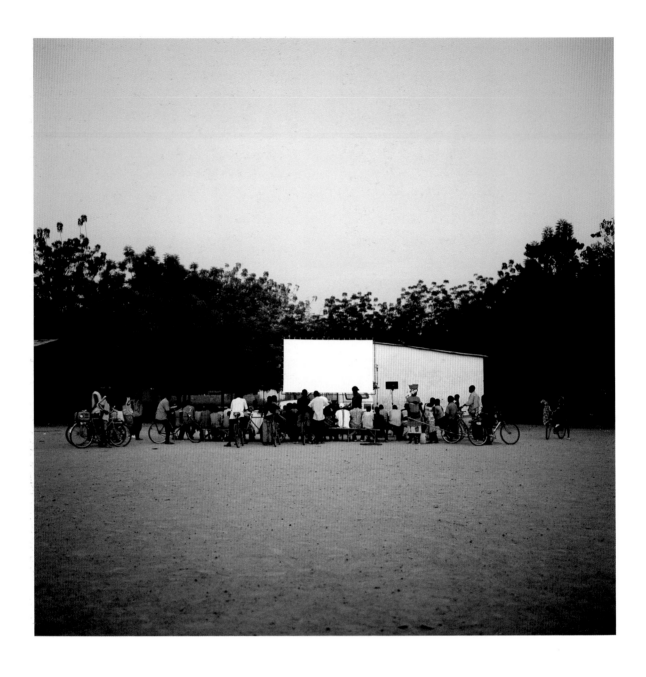

Meyer
France, Tendance Floue
for VSD/La Vie
3rd Prize Stories

Popular films and health messages reach remote communities in western Africa, brought by the Cinéma Numérique Ambulant (CNA, French for 'Mobile Digital Cinema'). With support from UNICEF and other NGOs, five mobile cinema projection vans travel to villages across Niger, Benin and Mali. Feature films are preceded by shorts on such topics as malaria prevention, HIV/Aids and water sanitation. Since its inception in 2001, the CNA has reached around 1.5 million people.

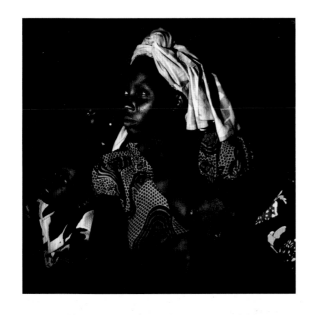

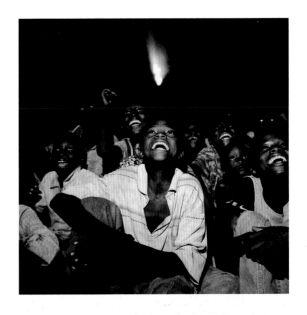

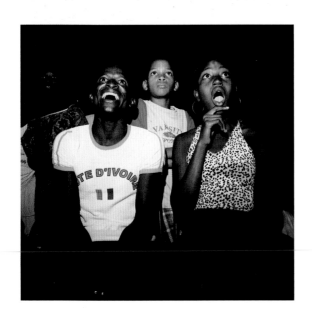

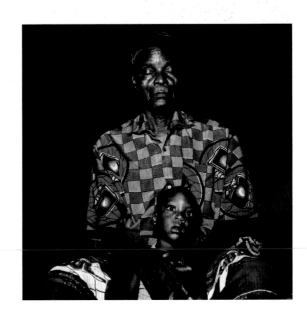

Nature

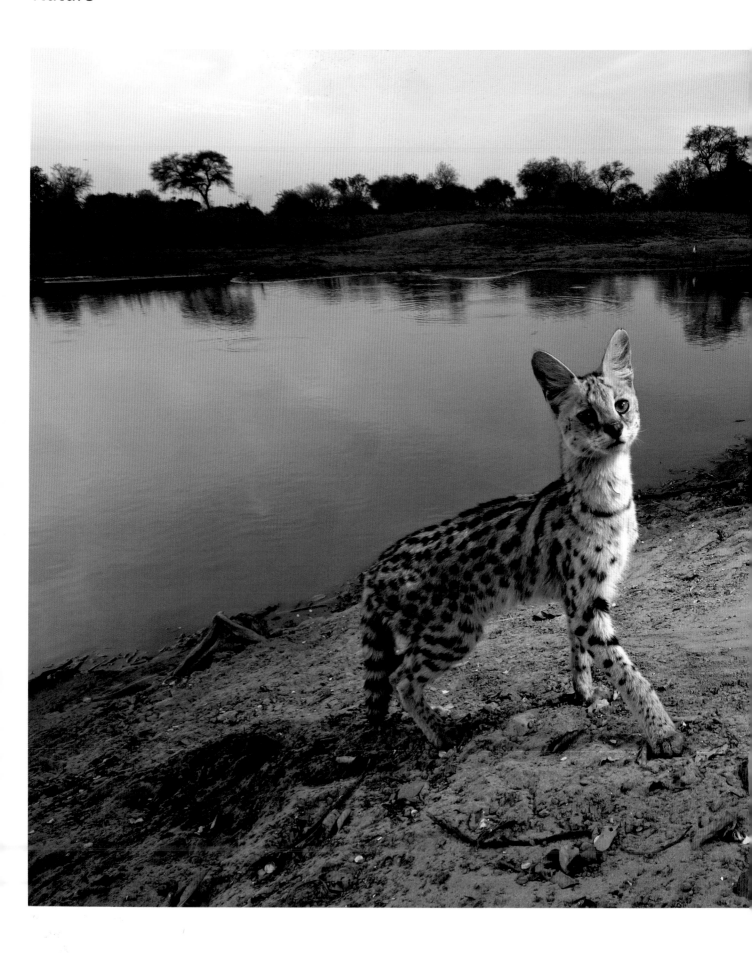

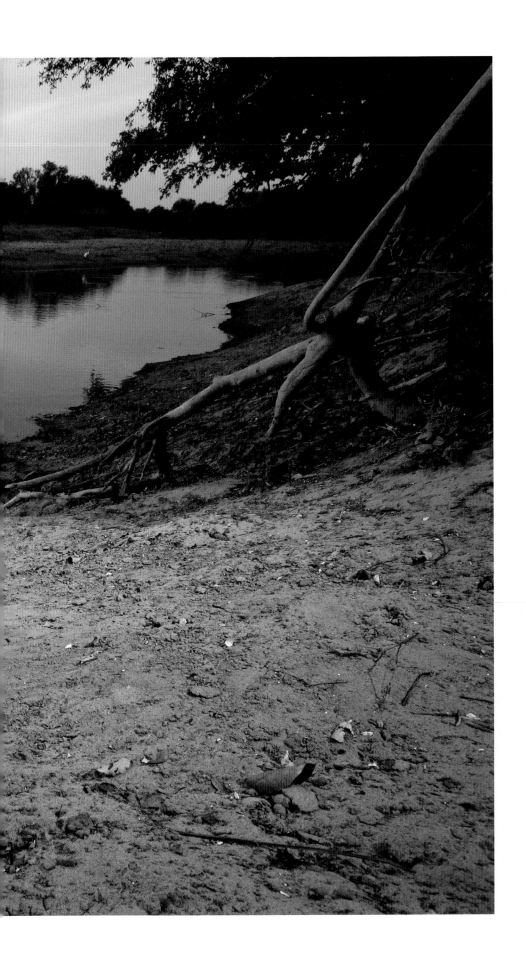

Michael Nichols
USA, National Geographic Magazine
1st Prize Singles

A serval cat hesitates momentarily on the banks of the Salamat river, Zakouma National Park, Chad. Servals are common though elusive predators living mainly on the African savannah. They feed chiefly on rodents, but also other small mammals, frogs, fish and insects. A long neck and legs together with acute hearing help the cat hunt in tall grass. Servals can even detect the sound of rodents burrowing underground, and will sometimes stand for up to fifteen minutes listening with their eyes shut while hunting.

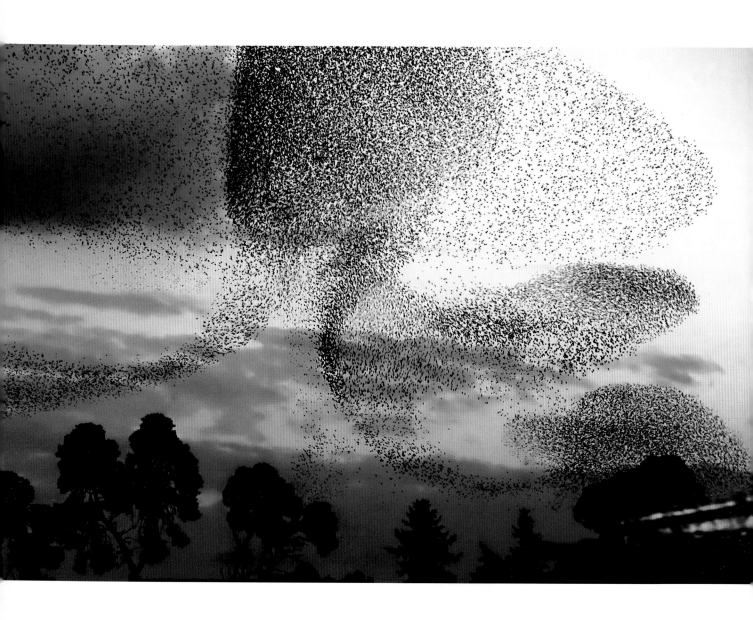

Fayez Nureldine
Palestinian Territories,
Agence France-Presse
2nd Prize Singles

A large flock of starlings flies over a park at sunset, looking for a place to roost for the night, in Algiers in January. Millions of the birds migrate annually to escape the northern European winter, seeking food sources further south along routes that appear to have evolved 10,000 years ago, after the last Ice Age. Some journeys span a third of the earth's circumference. It is not yet fully known how the birds navigate.

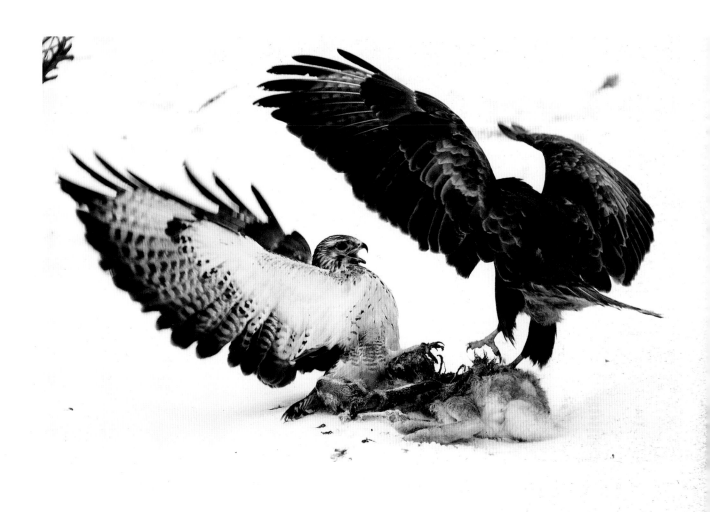

Jørgen Flemming
Denmark
3rd Prize Singles

Common buzzards fight over the
body of a hare, on the island of
Funen in Denmark in January. In
March, the country's first case of the
deadly bird-flu strain H5N1 was
confirmed in a wild common
buzzard, and the birds accounted for
a significant proportion of virus
carriers detected later. The first
outbreak of H5N1 avian influenza
occurred among a poultry holding in
Funen in June. The species of broad-
winged raptor is present across most
of Europe and parts of Asia.

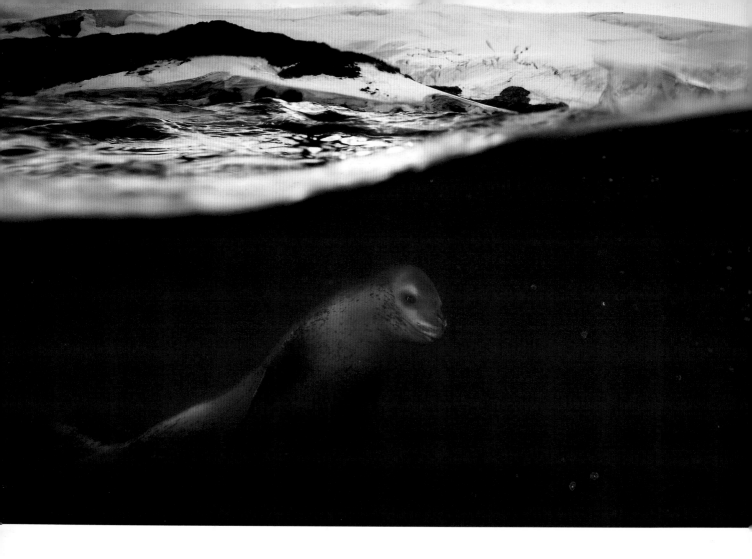

Paul Nicklen
Canada, National Geographic Magazine
1st Prize Stories

Leopard seals are the second largest species of seal in the Antarctic. Their reputation for ferocity grew in 2003, when a leopard seal attacked and killed a British scientist, Kirsty Brown. The seals are certainly the top predators of Antarctic waters, but may not always be as aggressive as believed. This page: A seal patrols the rocks of West Anvers Island waiting for penguin chicks to head to sea. Facing page, top: After several threat displays, this four-meter-long female relaxed with the photographer and began to bring him offerings of penguins. Below: A juvenile gentoo penguin takes a look under water before going into the sea. Penguins are a favored element of the leopard seal diet. (story continues)

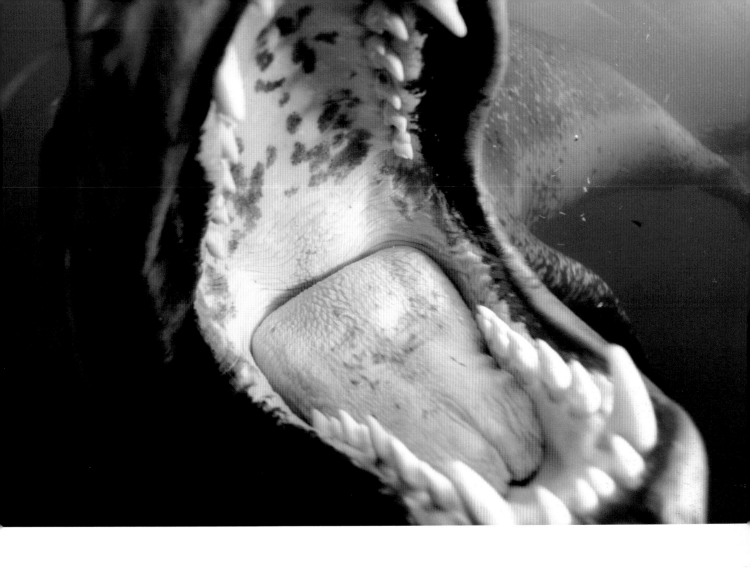

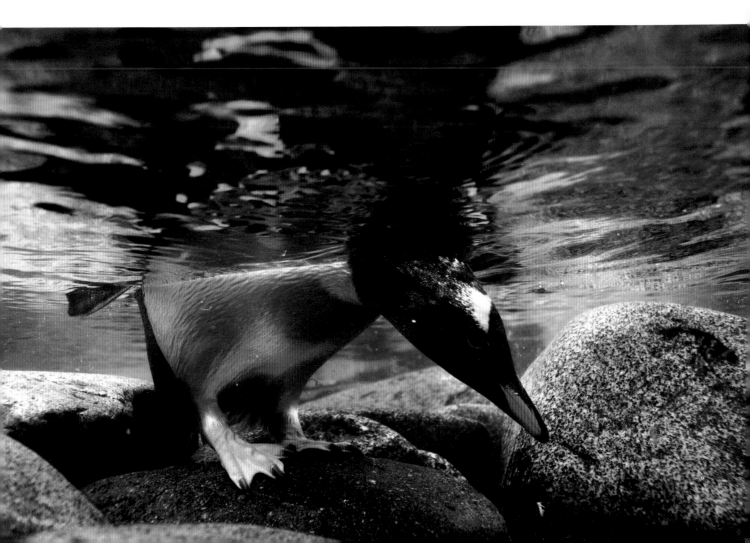

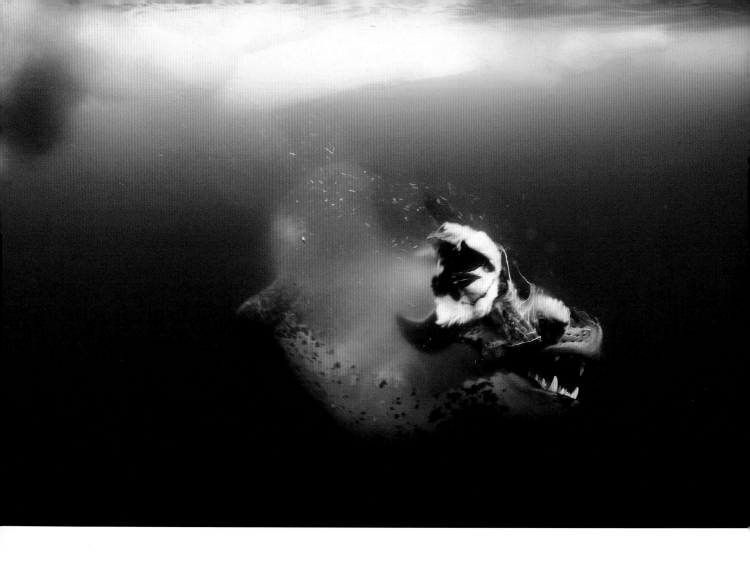

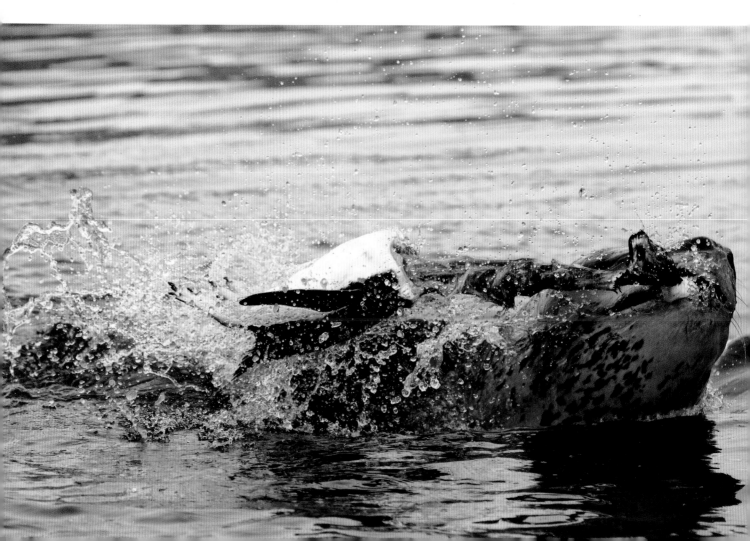

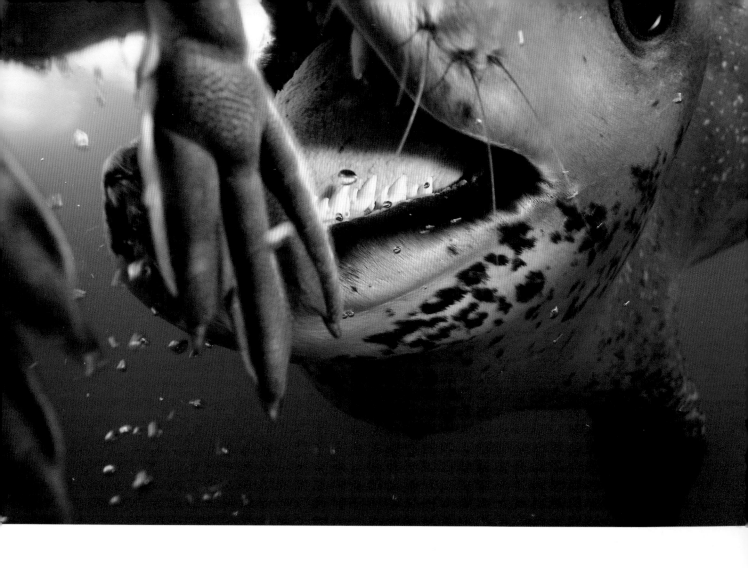

(continued) Penguins will sometimes make long detours on foot if they are aware of leopard seals in the water. Once one penguin heads for the sea, others follow en masse, as a seal will generally take one chick at a time. Facing page, top: A leopard seal uses its sharp molars to cut through penguin flesh. Below: A seal attempts to rip off a bite-sized piece of meat by whipping the penguin from side to side. This page: The female leopard seal places a penguin on top of the photographer's camera. Over several days she grew agitated as he could not accept her offerings.

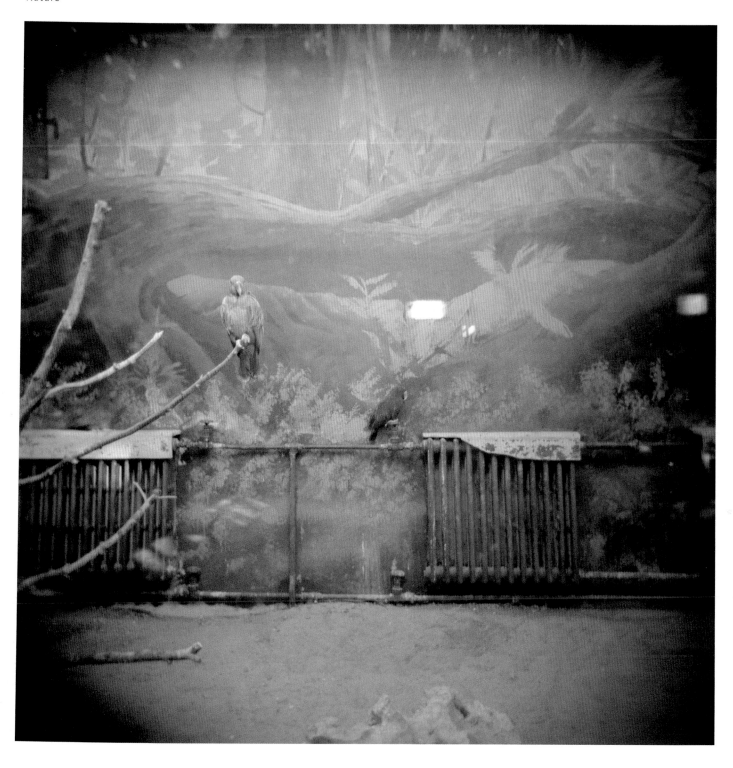

Chang He
People's Republic of China,
Oriental Morning Post
2nd Prize Stories

In the years following the foundation
of the People's Republic of China in
1949, a number of zoos were built as
part of a move to improve quality of
life for people living in cities. Today,
many zoos suffer from worn-out
infrastructure and lack of funds. In a
booming economy costs have been

going up. Many zoos are overstaffed,
and rising salaries eat up a large
portion of the budget. This page:
Heating and a tropical backdrop
created an environment for parrots.
Facing page: A skunk gets its head
stuck in a can that has been thrown
into its cage. (continues)

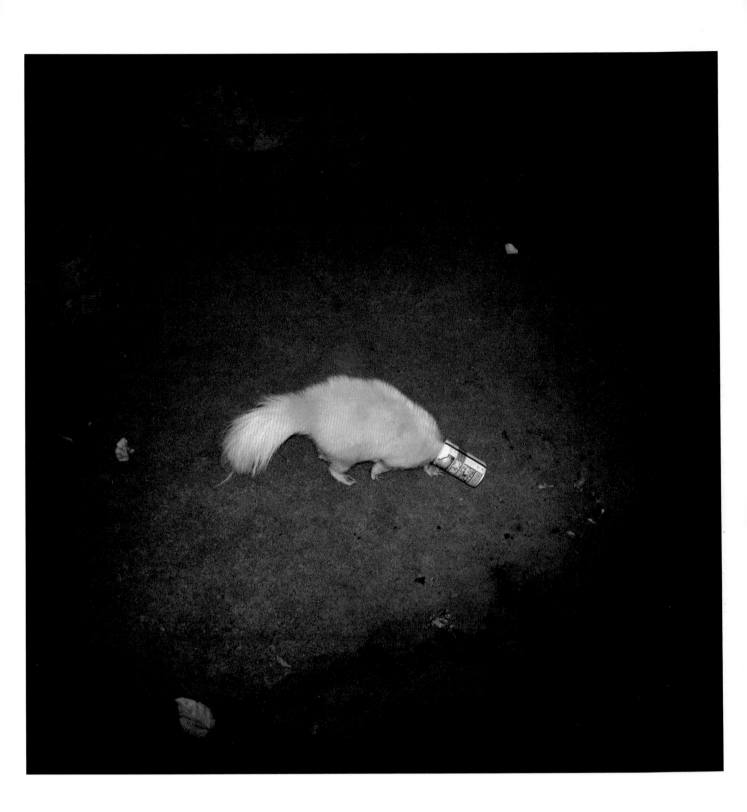

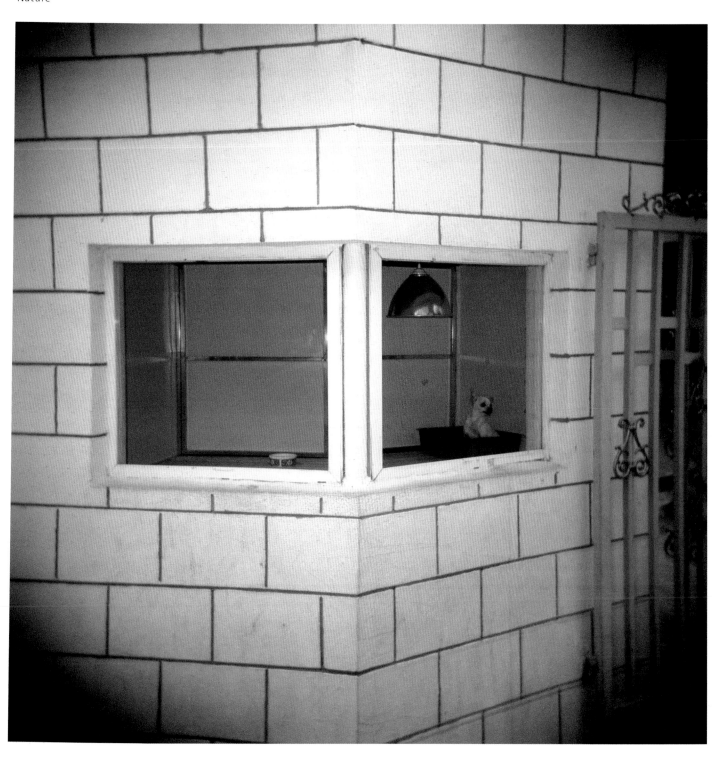

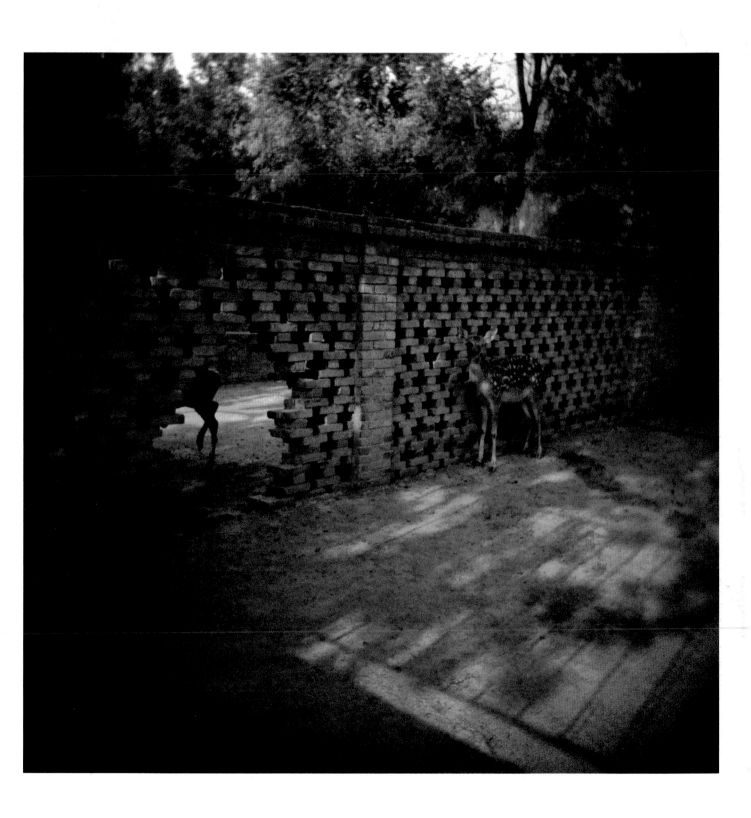

(continued) Zoos have also been badly hit by a drop in income from ticket sales. They are no longer popular with children who are growing used to computer games and more interactive forms of entertainment. As zoos often occupy highly desirable real estate in city centers, there is pressure on many to close, or to move to country districts.

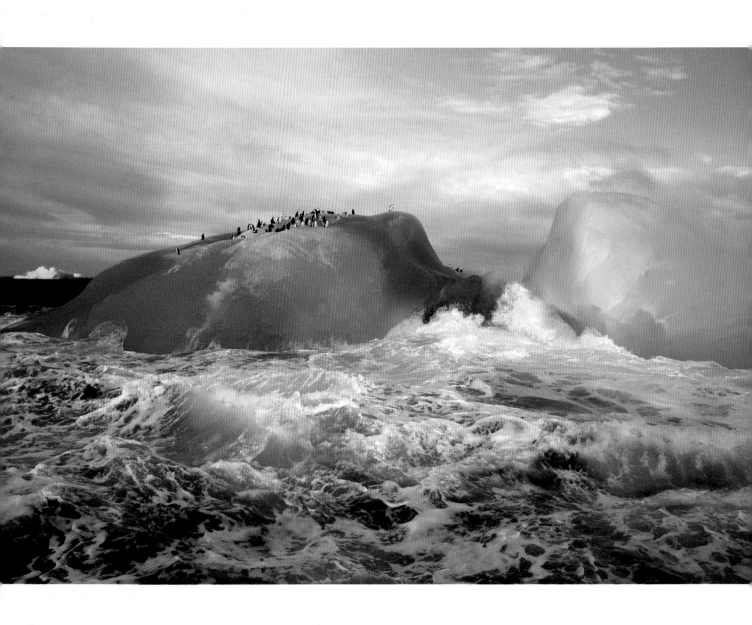

Maria Stenzel
USA, for National Geographic
Magazine
3rd Prize Stories

Every summer, millions of chinstrap penguins, having spent seven months at sea, arrive on the remote South Sandwich Islands in the southern Atlantic Ocean to breed. Protected by rough seas and severe storms, the islands are uninhabited by humans, but are home to the largest penguin colony in the world.

The penguins, which get their name from a distinctive black band under their heads, lay around two eggs that are incubated by both male and female. Chicks hatch after 35 days, and gain their adult plumage after around two months. This page: Chinstrap penguins on an iceberg near Candlemas Island. Blue icebergs

are older and more compressed than white ones, with little air left between the ice crystals. Facing page, top: Penguins catch shrimp-like krill, their main diet, off Zavodovski Island. Middle: Birds jump from a cliff to catch krill. Below: A march across a glacier on Thule, one of the southernmost islands in the chain.

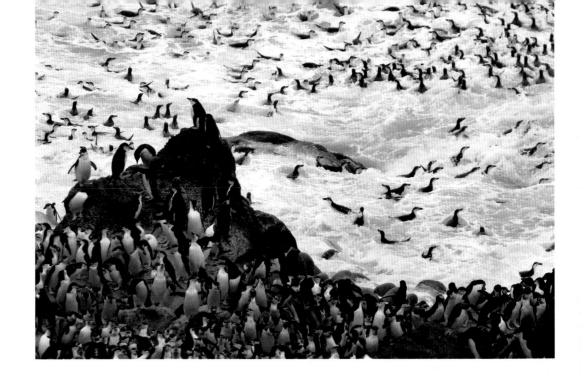

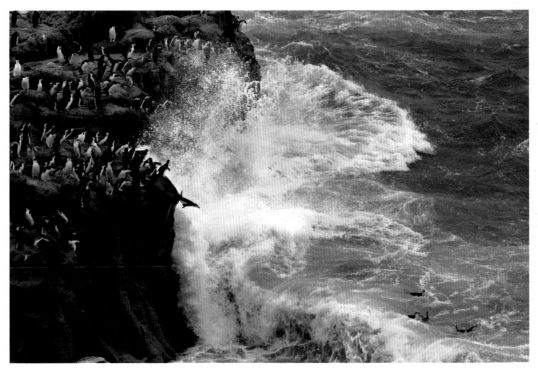

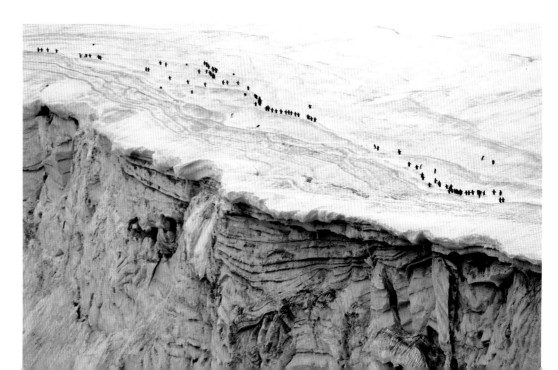

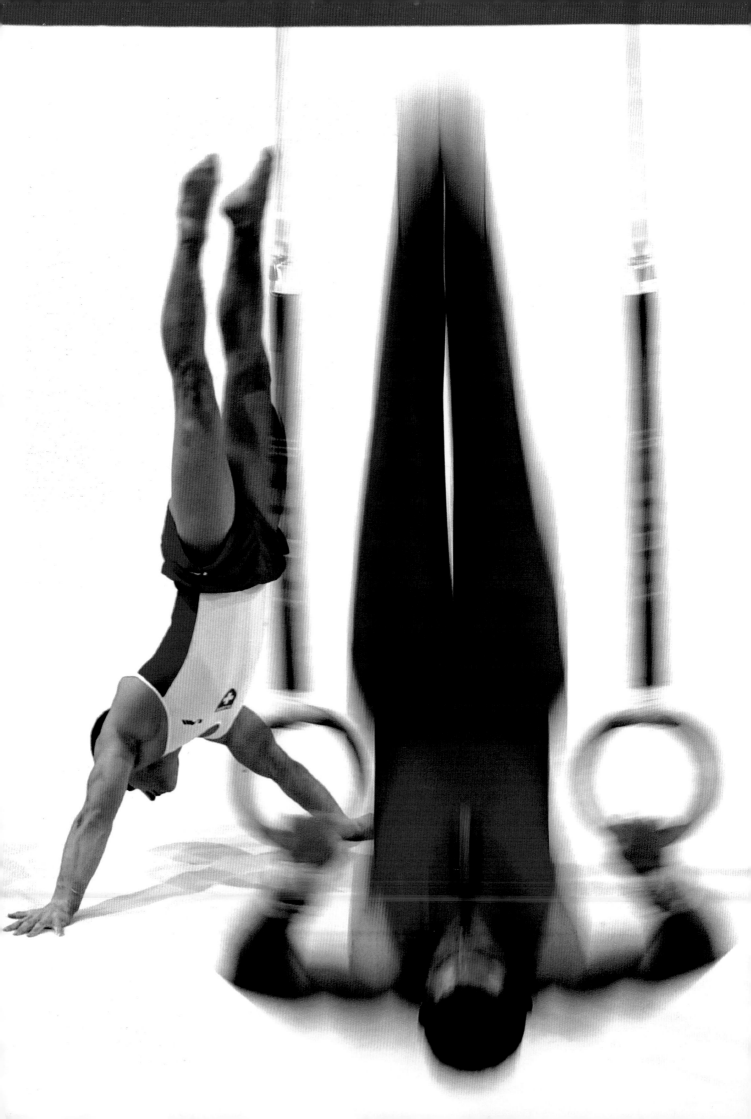

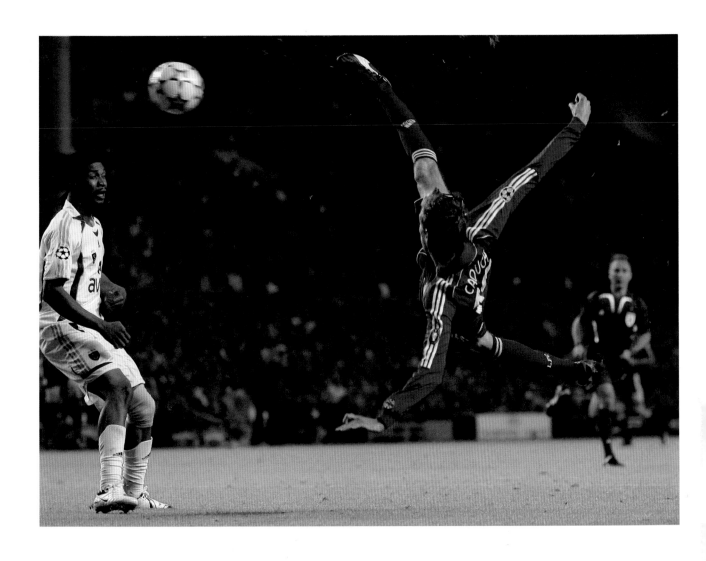

Alex Livesey
United Kingdom, Getty Images for
Sports Illustrated
2nd Prize Singles

Max Rossi
Italy, Reuters
1st Prize Singles

Romania's Dorin Razvan Selariu
competes on the rings, as Niki
Boeschenstein of Switzerland
participates in the floor event, on the
first men's qualification day of the
Artistic Gymnastics World
Championships in Aarhus, Denmark
in October. Romania came second in
the tournament overall, but the
championship was dominated by
China, which took eight out of a
possible fourteen gold medals.

Liverpool striker Peter Crouch
performs an acrobatic kick to score
against Galatasaray, in a match
during the group stage of the UEFA
Champions League at Liverpool's
Anfield Stadium, in September. It
was Crouch's second goal in what
became a 3-2 victory against the
Istanbul team. Liverpool led their
group in the Champions League – a
tournament between the 32 top
football clubs in Europe – going on
to the first knockout round of the
championship.

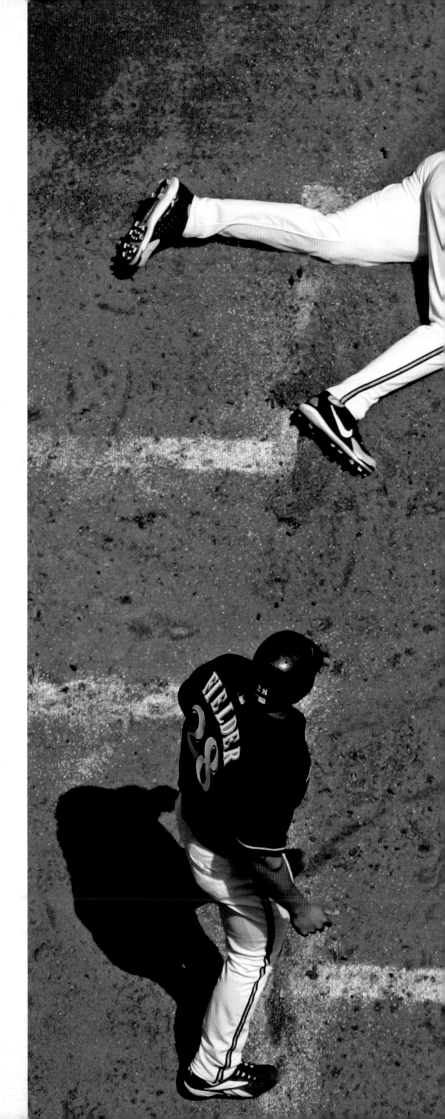

Jeffrey Phelps
USA, The Associated Press
3rd Prize Singles

Milwaukee Brewers runner Prince
Fielder (bottom left) is safe at home
base after barreling into San
Francisco Giants catcher Todd
Greene (bottom center) in the first
inning of the US National League
baseball game in Milwaukee. Greene
was injured and left the game.
Moments after the smashup Corey
Koskie also tried to score for the
Brewers, but pitcher Brad Hennessey
(top) tagged him at the last second.
The Giants lost 4-7 to the Brewers.

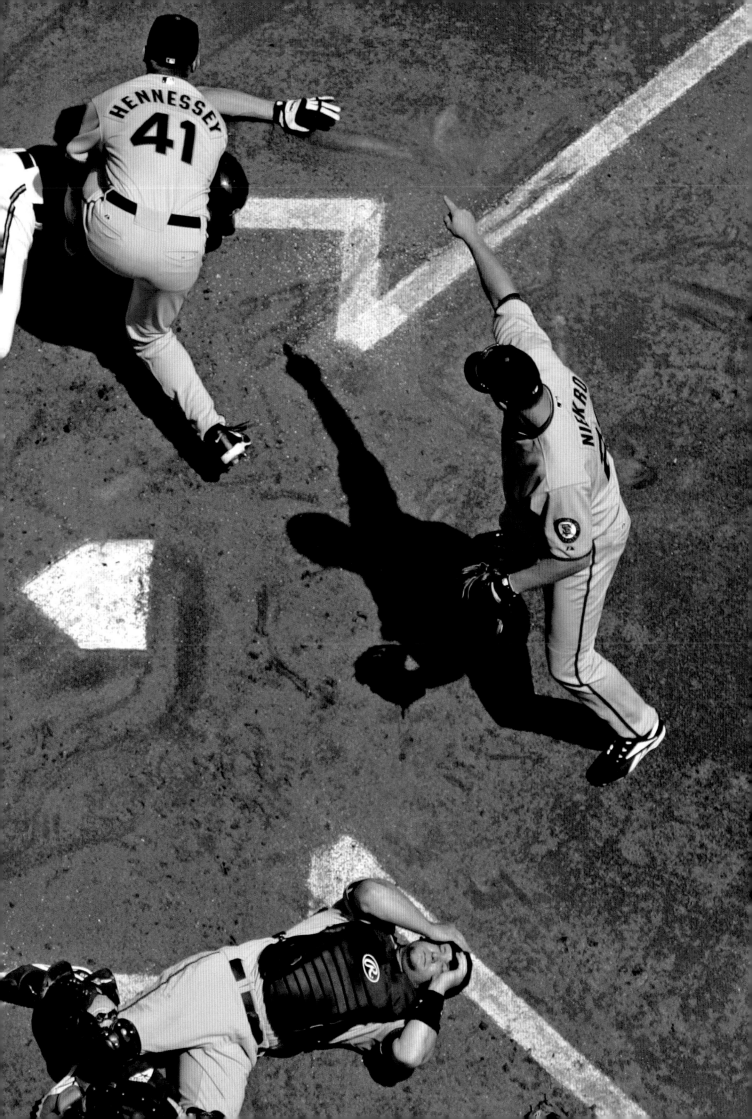

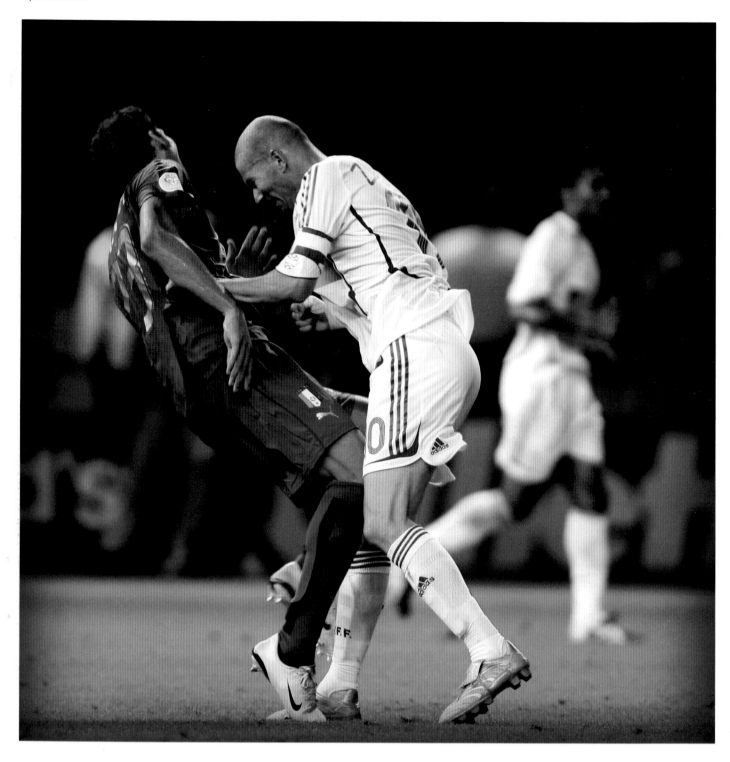

Peter Schols
The Netherlands, Dagblad
De Limburger/GPD/Reuters
1st Prize Stories

Top French football player Zinédine Zidane was sent off the field for butting Italian Marco Materazzi in the chest towards the end of extra time of the World Cup final between France and Italy, in Berlin on July 9. As a result Zidane, one of the top goal-scorers ever, could not participate in a penalty shootout which saw Italy win 5-3. Zidane had previously announced that this was to be his final match before retirement from football. Materazzi was said to have provoked Zidane with personal insults. Despite the incident, Zidane received the Golden Ball for the most outstanding player of the tournament. Facing page, top left: Italian goalkeeper Gianluigi Buffon expresses incomprehension while Zidane spits. Right: Referee Horacio Elizondo, who did not appear to have seen the off-ball confrontation, consults with Zidane and his teammates. Below, left: The referee shows Zidane the red card. Right: Zidane leaves the field.

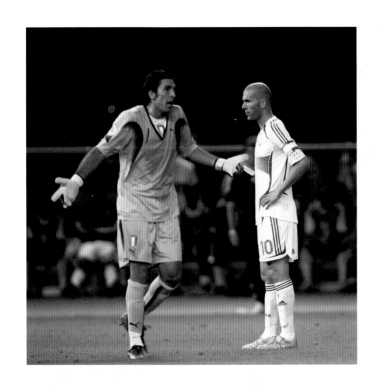 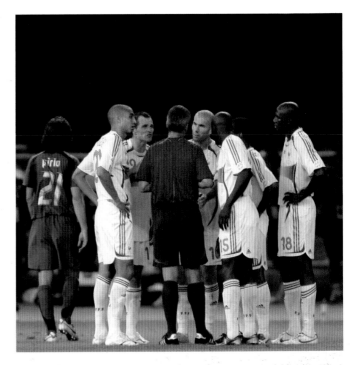

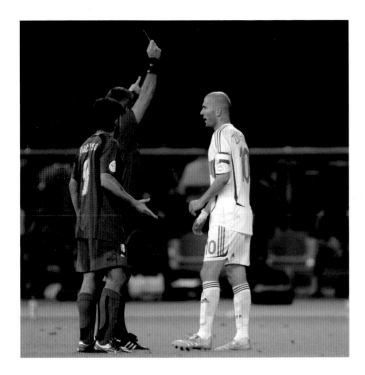 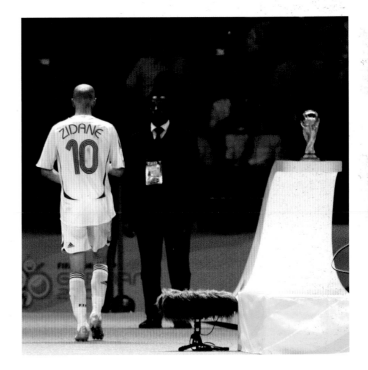

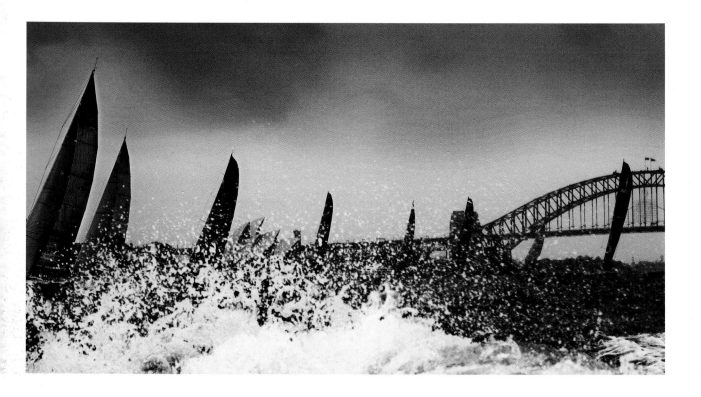

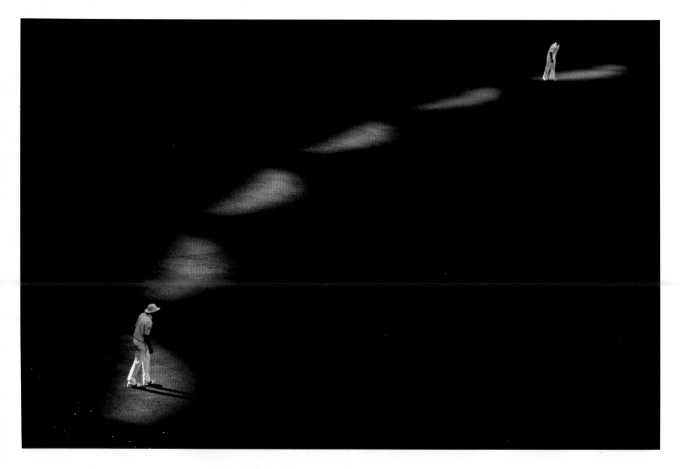

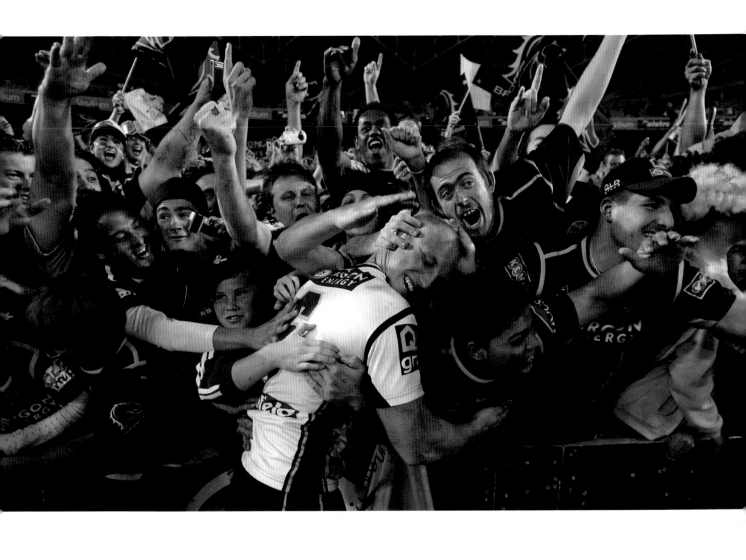

Craig Golding
Australia, Sydney Morning Herald
2nd Prize Stories

Sports portfolio. Facing page, top: Yachts participate in the Big Boat Challenge in Sydney harbor, one of a series of events leading up to the Sydney Hobart Yacht Race on Boxing Day. Below: England's Paul Collingwood and James Anderson field out on the boundary in the late afternoon of the initial day's play of the first Ashes match between Australia and England, at the Gabba Cricket Ground in Brisbane. Australia trounced England 5-0 in the series, winning back the trophy they had lost eighteen months earlier. The Ashes contest between England and Australia is the most celebrated rivalry in international cricket, dating back to 1882. This page: Darren Lockyer, captain of the Brisbane Broncos, is mobbed by fans after the Broncos won the rugby league grand final against Melbourne Storm at the Telstra Stadium in Homebush.

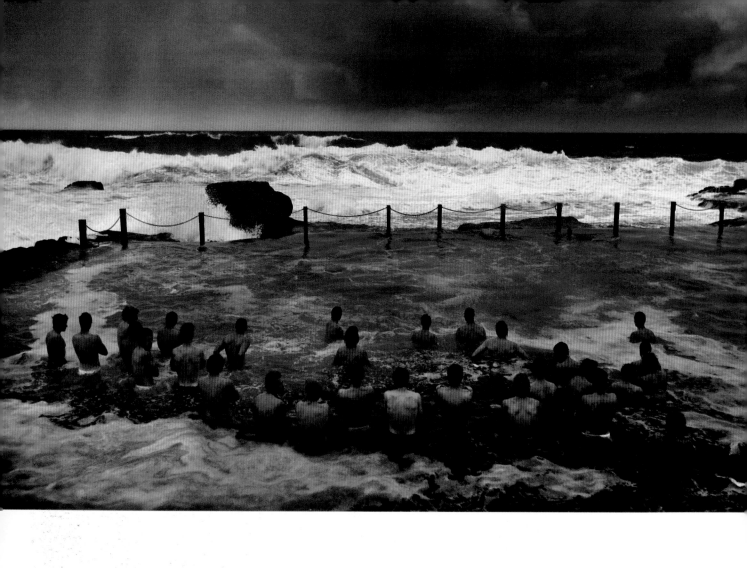

Steve Christo
Australia, Sydney Morning Herald
3rd Prize Stories

Sports portfolio. This page: The Sydney Swans Australian football team swim at Maroubra beach, one of their favorite haunts, during a recovery session. Facing page, top: Ben Kennedy, captain of the Manly-Warringah Sea Eagles rugby league team, after a game against the Wests Tigers. His inspirational impact on the team was such that his retirement at the end of the season raised questions about its future success. Middle: Women watching the Synchronized Swimming at the 2006 Commonwealth Games, in Melbourne in March. Below: Spectators at the Birdsville Races, one of Australia's most famous horse racing events. The races, which have been held annually for the past 125 years in the remote Australian Outback town of Birdsville, swell the local population from around 100 to 6,000 for two days.

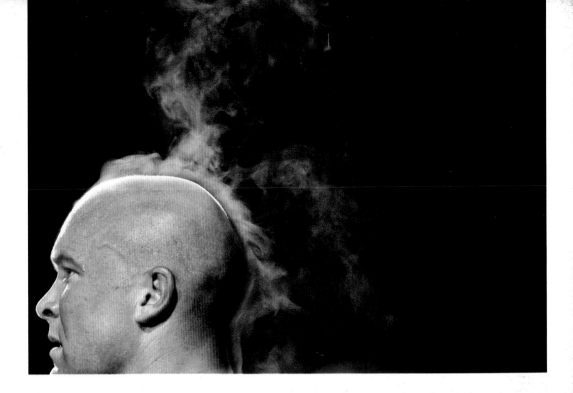

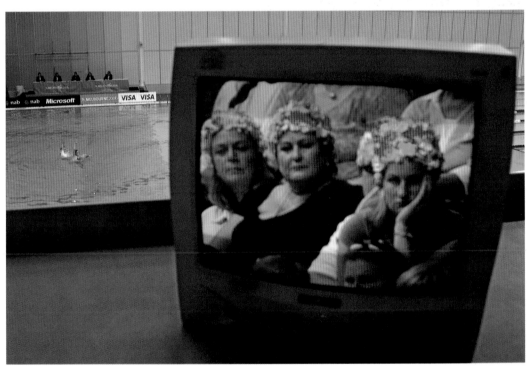

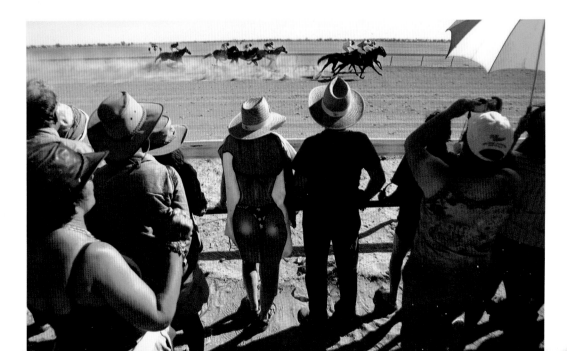

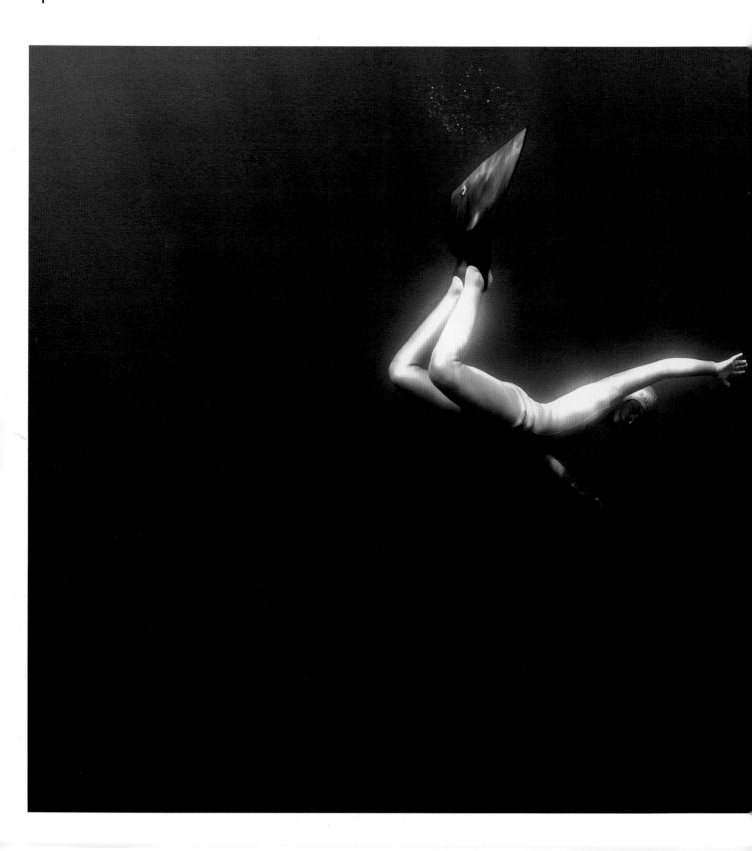

Franck Seguin
France, Deadline Photo Press
1st Prize Singles

Guillaume Néry, 24, of France, trains for his attempt to break the world freediving record, off the coast of Nice in July. Freediving is carried out without oxygen tanks, and participants try to reach as great a depth as possible. Néry succeeded in his record-breaking quest with a 109-meter-deep dive on September 6. The record held only until December, when it was beaten by a 111-meter dive by Austrian Herbert Nitsch. Néry has been freediving since he was 14 years old, and participates in the Constant Weight category, in which divers descend and ascend using fins and/or arms, without changing ballast. They are allowed just one pull on an underwater rope to turn descent into ascent.

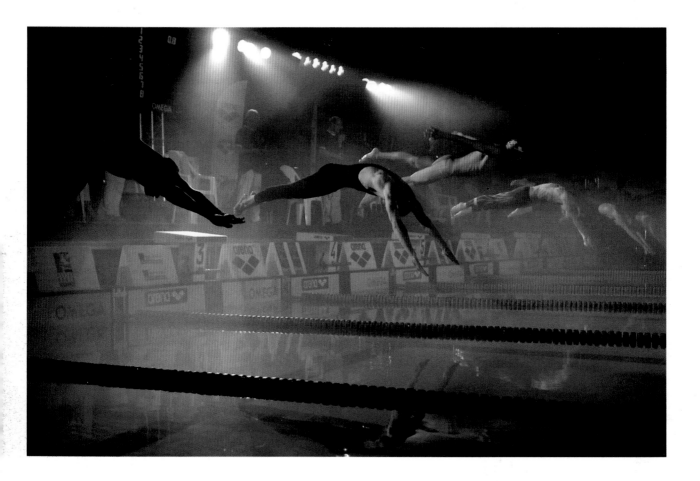

Nicolas Gouhier
France, Abaca Press for
Sports Illustrated
2nd Prize Singles

Contestants take a dive during the
Arena Sprint swimming competition
at the Centre Sportif Guy Boissière in
Rouen, France, in November. The
annual contest attracts top swimmers
from around the country, who
participate in 25-meter sprints. The
event involves considerable spectacle,
with music and a festival atmosphere.

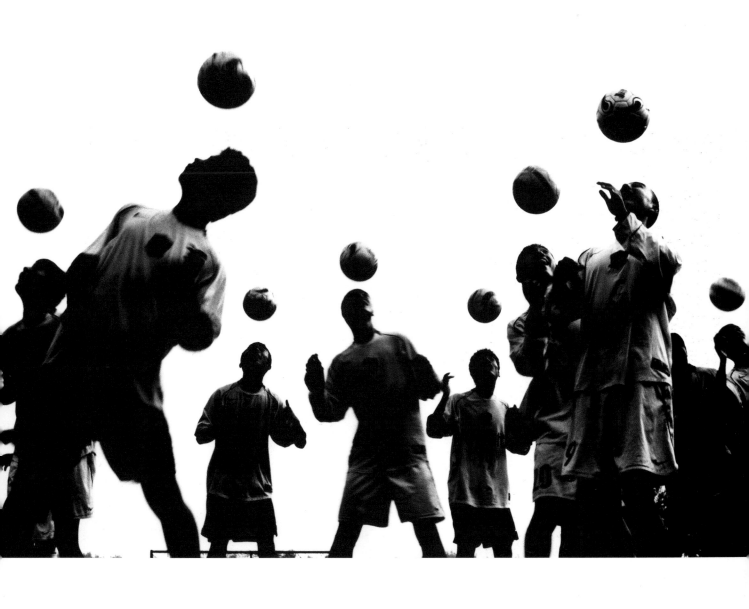

Lorenzo Cicconi Massi
Italy, Contrasto
3rd Prize Singles

Students at the Beijing Guoan Football Club school practice heading techniques. The school is in an isolated spot about 70 kilometers from Beijing, and has some 200 pupils between the ages of 15 and 18. They are selected from all over China, and have to go through rigorous tests before being accepted. The boys all board at the school, and the curriculum focuses entirely on physical training and soccer techniques. On weekends the young students play matches against other Chinese youth teams.

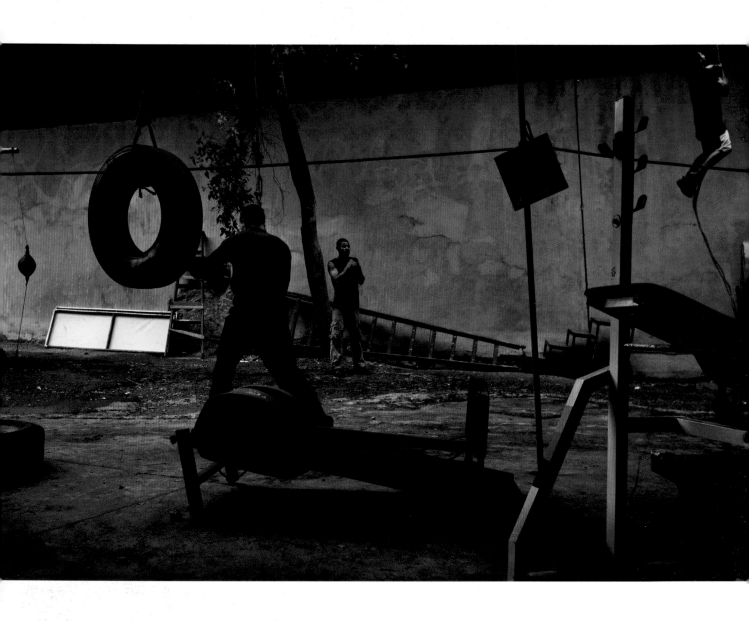

João Kehl
Brazil, Cia de Foto
1st Prize Stories

Garrido's boxing gym is located under a viaduct in the central area of the Brazilian city of São Paulo, a quarter with one of the highest rates of homelessness in the city. The fighters are people who survive in difficult conditions, often without having a place to live, but believing that boxing is a way towards a more dignified life. This page: Training methods are not always conventional. Jaílton, 19, pummels an improvised punch-bag,

while a friend scales a rope tied to the viaduct. Facing page, top: Security guard Jack Welson, 26, a Brazilian champion aiming at a South American title, is a role model to the young boxers at the gym. Middle: Garrido, 50, lives alone beneath the viaduct beside his gym. Below: Jaílton gives an interview before the second professional fight of his career, 250 kilometers from São Paulo. Following pages: Garrido's gym.

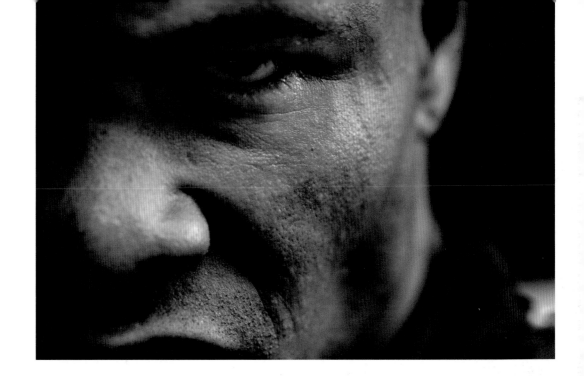

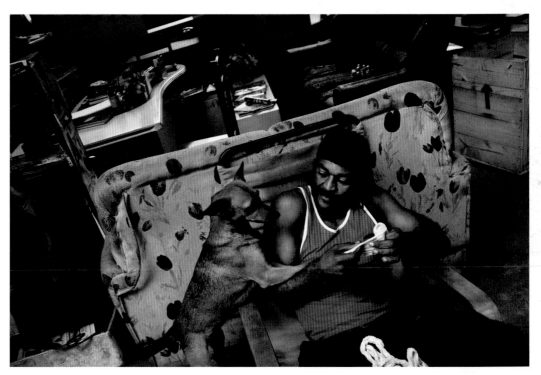

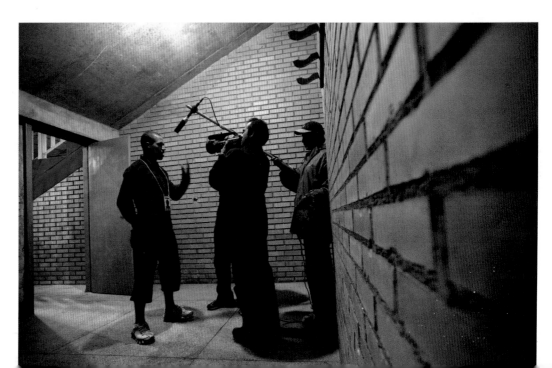

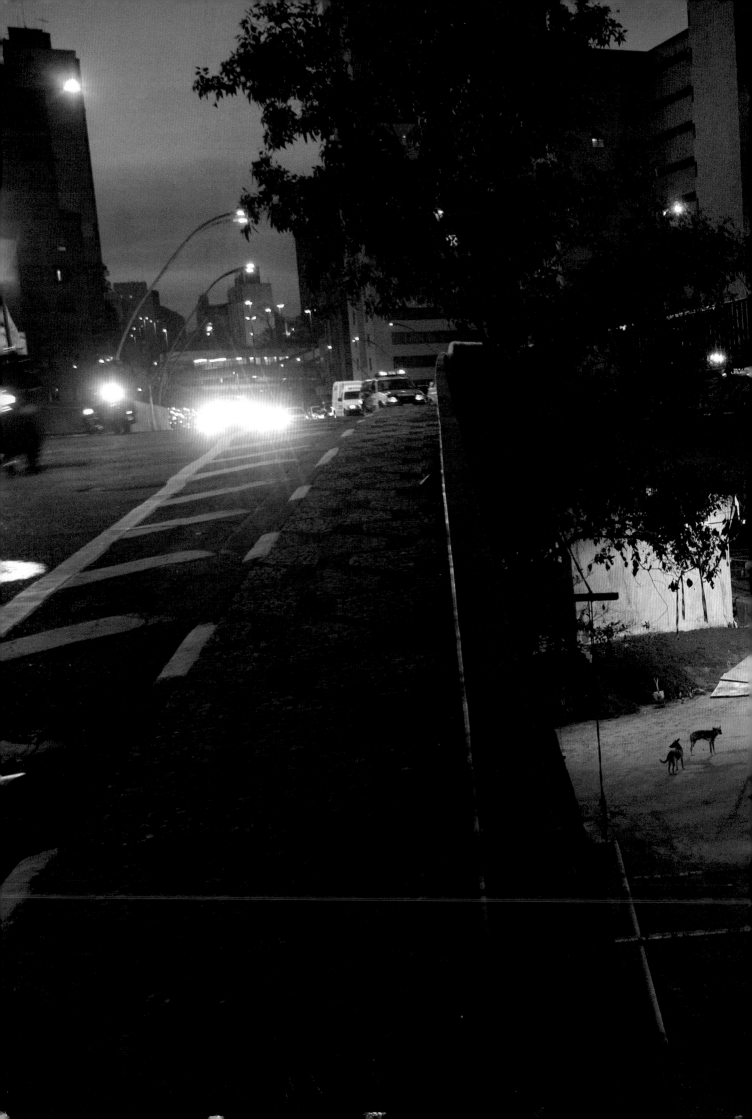

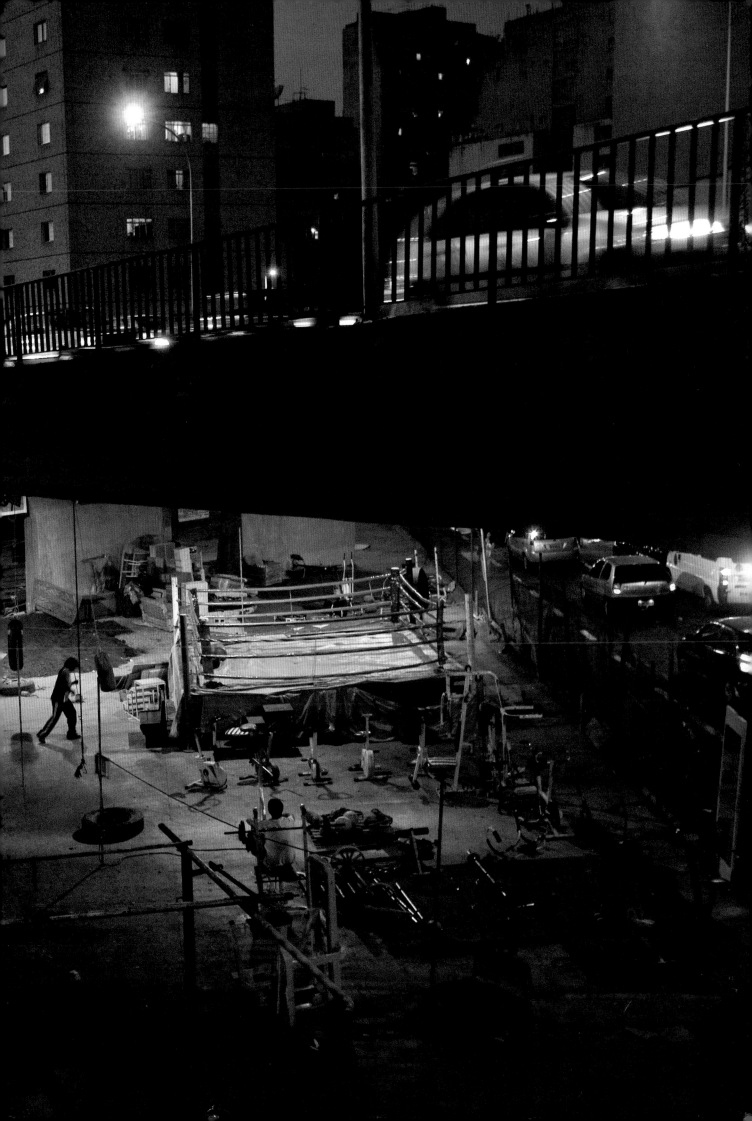

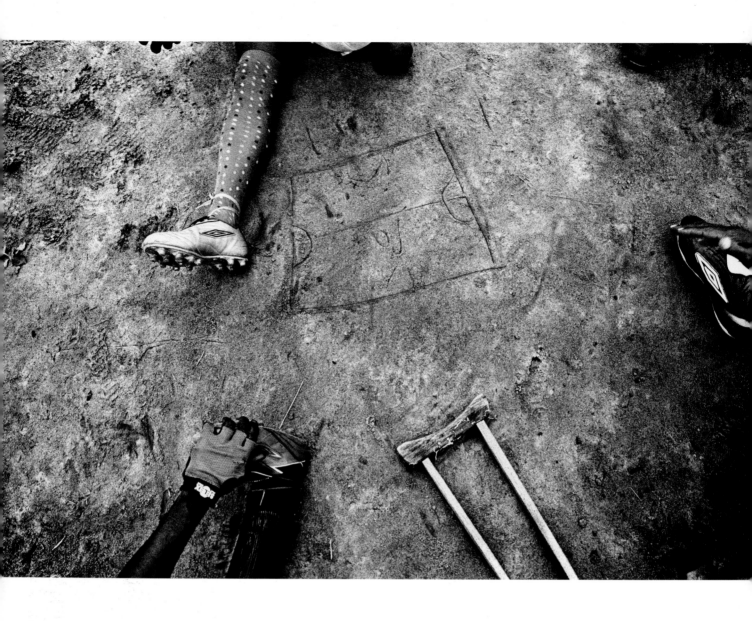

Pep Bonet
Spain, Panos Pictures
2nd Prize Stories

As Sierra Leone rebuilds itself following a ten-year-long civil war, members of the Single Leg Amputee Sports Club aim to play against other international teams, and make a living from their sport. Most of the 22 members of the club live in the Murray Town Camp for Amputees in Freetown, having had limbs cut off by rebel forces during the war. In

February 2007 the club – which had already competed in matches in Britain, Russia, and Brazil – hosted the first ever All-African Amputee Football Tournament. This page: Players discuss tactics before a game. Facing page, top: The team prays before a match. Middle: The game is underway. Below: A player shoots a penalty in a match between the club's two teams.

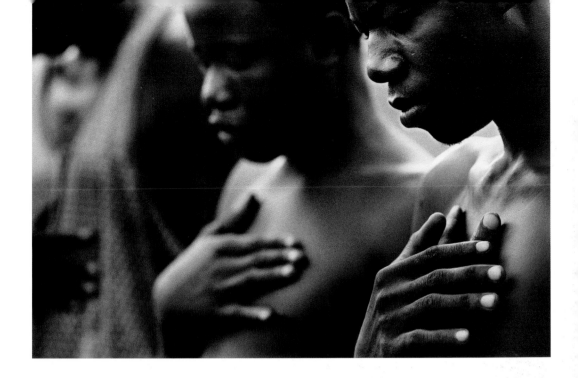

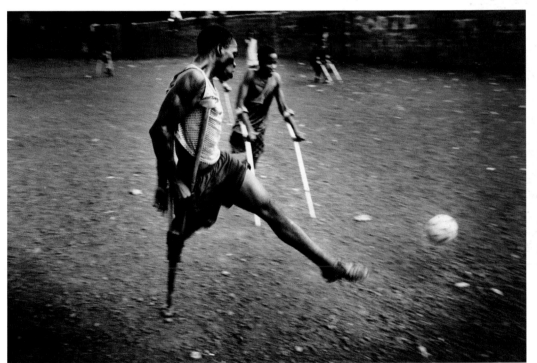

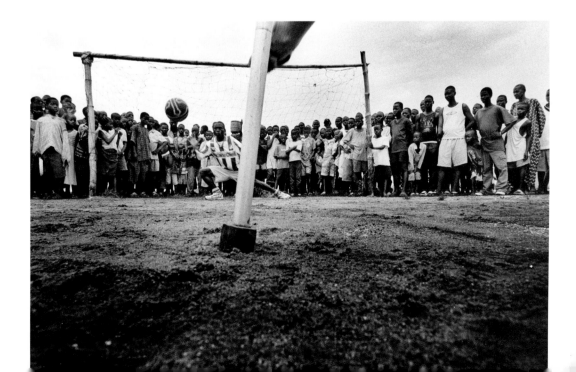

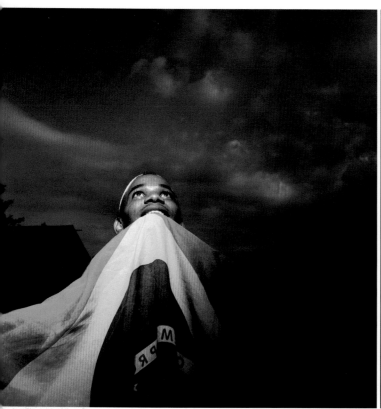
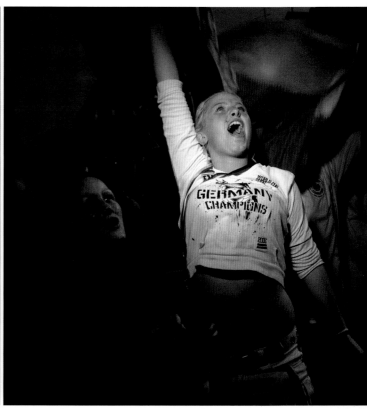

David Klammer
Germany, Visum
3rd Prize Stories

The 2006 World Cup was held in
Germany in June and July. The
football championship, which after
the Olympics is the world's biggest
and most watched sporting event,
involved 32 different national teams
playing in twelve cities across the
country. This page, left: A Brazilian fan
stares at an outdoor screen during
the match between Brazil and
Croatia on June 13. Right: A German
fan cheers a goal as her team plays
Costa Rica in the opening match of
the tournament on June 9. Facing
page, left: Mexican fans comfort each
other after Argentina eliminated
Mexico in a Round of 16 match. Right:
A British girl crouches in an outdoor
public viewing area in Gelsenkirchen,
during the quarter-final on July 1, in
which Portugal knocked England out
of the competition.

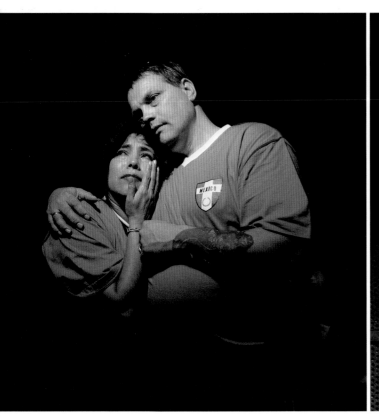
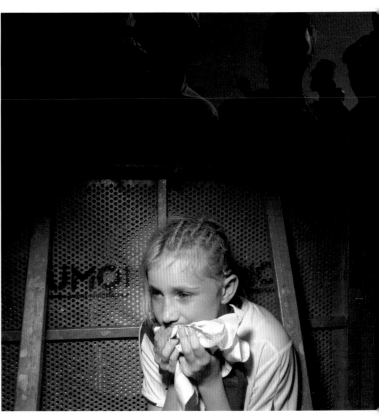

Prizewinners 2007

World Press Photo of the Year 2006
Spencer Platt, USA, Getty Images
Lebanese drive through devastated Beirut neighborhood, 15 August

Page 4

The World Press Photo of the Year 2006 Award honors the photographer whose photograph, selected from all entries, represents an event, situation or issue of great journalistic importance in that year, and demonstrates an outstanding level of visual perception and creativity.

Spot News Singles
1 Akintunde Akinleye, Nigeria, Reuters
Man after pipeline explosion, Lagos, Nigeria, 26 December

Page 10

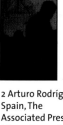

2 Arturo Rodríguez, Spain, The Associated Press
Migrants await transfer, Tenerife, Spain, 7 September

Page 11

3 Mohammed Ballas, Palestinian Territories, The Associated Press
Execution of suspected collaborator, Jenin, West Bank, 13 August

Page 12

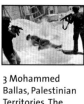

Honorable Mention Jeroen Oerlemans, The Netherlands, Panos Pictures
Paramedics show body of child to press, Lebanon, 30 July

Page 13

 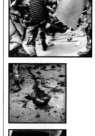

Spot News Stories
1 Davide Monteleone, Italy, Contrasto
Israeli bombings of Lebanon, July

Page 14

 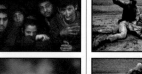

2 Agnes Dherbeys, France, Cosmos/Eve
Protests against monarchy, Nepal, April

Page 18

  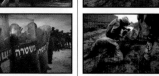 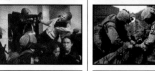 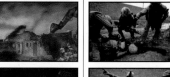 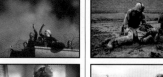

3 Yonathan Weitzman, Israel, Reuters
Forced evacuation of Amona outpost, West Bank, 1 February

Page 22

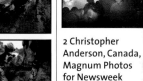

Honorable Mention Joao Silva, South Africa, The New York Times
Sniper attack, Karmah, Iraq, 31 October

Page 24

People in the News Singles
1 Oded Balilty, Israel, The Associated Press
Settler struggles with Israeli security officer, Amona outpost, West Bank, 1 February

Page 26

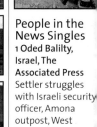

2 Christopher Anderson, Canada, Magnum Photos for Newsweek
President Chávez of Venezuela, 27 November

Page 28

3 Stephanie Sinclair, USA, NPR
Family flee Israeli bombings, Lebanon, 27 July

Page 29

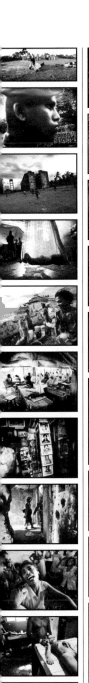

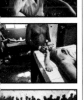

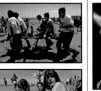

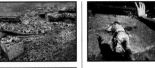

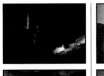
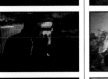
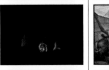

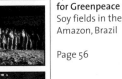
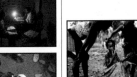

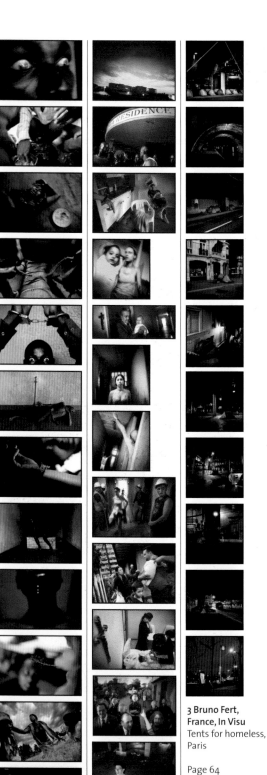

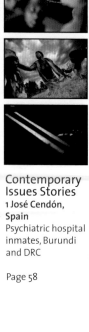

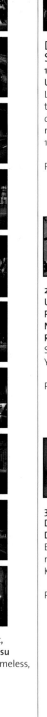

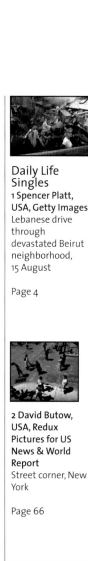

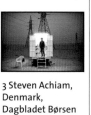

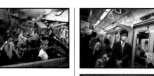

Daily Life Singles

1 Spencer Platt, USA, Getty Images
Lebanese drive through devastated Beirut neighborhood, 15 August

Page 4

2 David Butow, USA, Redux Pictures for US News & World Report
Street corner, New York

Page 66

3 Steven Achiam, Denmark, Dagbladet Børsen
Bangladeshi migrant worker, Kuwait

Page 67

3 Bruno Fert, France, In Visu
Tents for homeless, Paris

Page 64

2 Massimo Berruti, Italy, Grazia Neri
Condemned residence, Rome

Page 62

Contemporary Issues Stories

1 José Cendón, Spain
Psychiatric hospital inmates, Burundi and DRC

Page 58

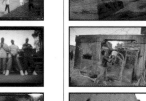

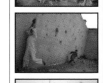

Daily Life Stories

1 David Guttenfelder, USA, The Associated Press
The lonely man, Tokyo

Page 68

2 Jon Lowenstein, USA, Aurora Photos
Chicago South Side

Page 72

3 Moises Saman, Spain, Newsday
Afghanistan

Page 76

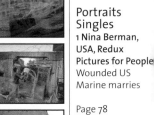

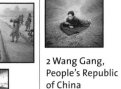

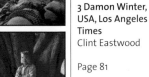

Portraits Singles

1 Nina Berman, USA, Redux Pictures for People
Wounded US Marine marries

Page 78

2 Wang Gang, People's Republic of China
Yi shepherd, Sichuan province, China

Page 80

3 Damon Winter, USA, Los Angeles Times
Clint Eastwood

Page 81

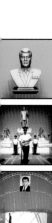

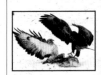

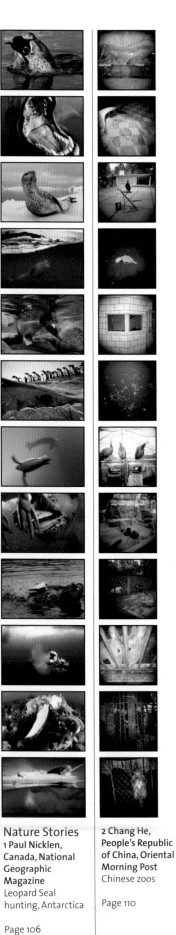

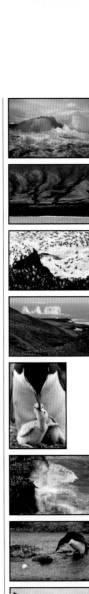
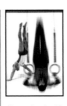

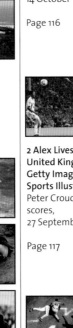

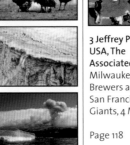

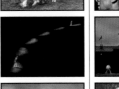

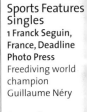

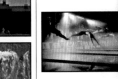

Nature Stories
1 Paul Nicklen,
Canada, National
Geographic
Magazine
Leopard Seal
hunting, Antarctica

Page 106

2 Chang He,
People's Republic
of China, Oriental
Morning Post
Chinese zoos

Page 110

3 Maria Stenzel,
USA, for National
Geographic
Magazine
Chinstrap penguins,
South Sandwich
Islands

Page 114

Sports Action
Singles
1 Max Rossi, Italy,
Reuters
World
Championship
Gymnastics,
Denmark,
14 October

Page 116

2 Alex Livesey,
United Kingdom,
Getty Images for
Sports Illustrated
Peter Crouch
scores,
27 September

Page 117

3 Jeffrey Phelps,
USA, The
Associated Press
Milwaukee
Brewers against
San Francisco
Giants, 4 May

Page 118

Sports Action
Stories
1 Peter Schols,
The Netherlands,
Dagblad De
Limburger/GPD/
Reuters
Zidane's exit from
World Cup final,
Berlin, 9 July

Page 120

2 Craig Golding,
Australia, Sydney
Morning Herald
Sports portfolio

Page 122

3 Steve Christo,
Australia, Sydney
Morning Herald
Sports portfolio

Page 124

Sports Features
Singles
1 Franck Seguin,
France, Deadline
Photo Press
Freediving world
champion
Guillaume Néry

Page 126

2 Nicolas Gouhier,
France, Abaca Press
for Sports
Illustrated
Arena Sprint
swimming
competition,
Rouen, France,
3 November

Page 128

3 Lorenzo Cicconi
Massi, Italy,
Contrasto
Students of Beijing
Guoan Football
Club school
exercise

Page 129

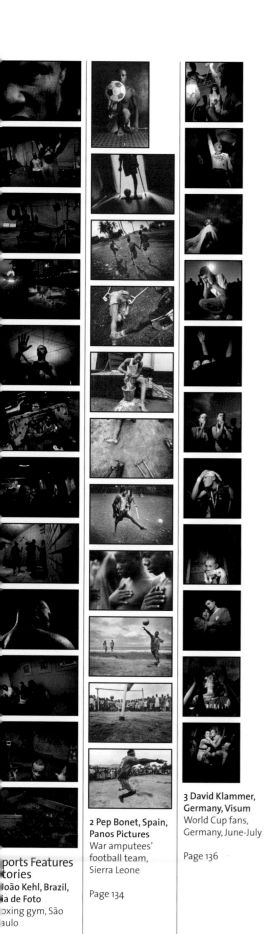

Participants 2007 Contest

In 2007, 4,460 photographers from 124 countries submitted 78,083 entries. The participants are listed here according to nationality as stated on the contest entry form. In unclear cases the photographers are listed under the country of postal address.

AFGHANISTAN
Ahmad Masood
Musadeq Sadeq

ALBANIA
Bevis Fusha
Zhani Terpini

ALGERIA
Idjeraoui Atmane
Zohra Bensemra
Mohamed Messara

ARGENTINA
Marcelo F. Aballay
Rodrigo Abd
Luis Carlos Abregú
Martin Acosta
Humberto Lucas Alascio
Fer Arias
Walter Astrada
Diego Azubel
Carlos Barria
Blas Martinez
Eduardo Blidner
Sandra Mariel Cartasso
Maria Eugenia Cerutti
Daniel Cima
Pablo Cuarterolo
Jorge Duro
Walter Echazu
Benito Francisco Espindola
Oriana Eliçabe
Fernando Gutierrez
Javier Heinzmann
Gustavo Jononovich
Emiliano Lasalvia
Pablo De Luca
Guillermo Luna
Sebastian Marjanov
Blas Martinez
Jose Angel Mateos
Juan Medina
Ali Burafi
Luis Micou
Hernan Gustavo Ortiz
Natacha Pisarenko
Ricardo Ramirez
Tomás Rawski
Héctor Rio
Delfo Rodriguez
Hernán Rojas
Miru Trigo
Enrique Rosito
Juan Sandoval
Carlos Sarraf
Ezequiel Scagnetti
Sebastian Scheiner
Jose Enrique Sternberg
Gustavo Marcelo Suarez
Patricia Tetzlaff
Omar Torres
Juan José Traverso
Nestor Troncoso
Tony Valdez
Leonardo Vincenti
Henry von Wartenberg
Hernan Zenteno

ARMENIA
Gayane Harutyunyan
Anahit Hayrapetyan
Piruza Khalapyan
Ruben Mangasaryan
Karen "Emka" Mirzoyan
Nelli Shishmanyan

AUSTRALIA
Jack Atley
Ben Baker
Daniel Berehulak
Paul Blackmore
Vasil Boglev
Polly Borland
James Brickwood
Angela Brkic
Patrick Brown
Will Burgess
Vince Caligiuri

David Callow
Glenn Campbell
Robert Carew
Steve Christo
Robert Cianflone
Warren Clarke
Tim Clayton
Nuno da Costa
Michael Coyne
Tamara Dean
John Donegan
Stephen Dupont
Brendan Esposito
Jenny Evans
Ashley Gilbertson
Kirk Gilmour
Craig Golding
David Gray
Lee Griffith
Natalie Grono
Duane Hart
Mathias Heng
Ian Hitchcock
Sean Hobbs
Adam Hourigan
Jessica Hromas
Martin Jacka
Anthony Johnson
Quentin Jones
David L. Kelly
Nicholas Laham
Paul Lakatos
Tanya Lake
Wade Laube
Andrew Lee
Dean Lewins
Guy Little
Vince Loveccio
Jesse Marlow
Régis Martin
Brendan McCarthy
Marc McCormack
Fiona McDougall
Chris McGrath
Andrew Meares
Andrew Merry
Georgia Metaxas
Palani Mohan
Nick Moir
Lindsay Moller
Peter Morris
Dean Mouhtaropoulos
Debrah Novak
Renee Nowytarger
Jason O'Brien
Warrick Page
David Dare Parker
Thomas Pickard
Ryan Pierse
Adam Pretty
Andrew Quilty
Mark Ralston
Tony Reddrop
Jon Reid
Brad Rimmer
Joanne Saad
Dean Sewell
Russell Shakespeare
Robert Shakespeare
Steven Siewert
Barry Slade
Ellen Smith
Troy Snook
Cameron Spencer
Hamish Ta-mé
Dave Tacon
Jay Town
Therese Tran
Terry Trewin
Angelo Velardo
Astrid Volzke
Tamara Voninski
Ian Waldie
Barbara Walton
Clifford White
Thomas Wielecki
Annette Willis
Craig Wilson
Tim Wimborne
Krystle Wright
Megan Young

AUSTRIA
Heimo Aga
Michael Appelt
Harald Arnold
David Bacher
Heinz-Peter Bader
Marcus E. Deák
Dominic Ebenbichler

Robert Fleischanderl
Philipp Horak
Christopher Klettermayer
Miro Kuzmanovic
Helmut Ploberger
Reiner Riedler
Gregor Sailer
Norbert Schiller
Dagmar Schwelle
Aram Voves

AZERBAIJAN
Ancelika Babayera
Agdes Baghirzade
Ilgar Djafarov
Rafiq Gambarov
Samira Gdsimova
Nonna de Gubek
Osman Karim
Emil Khalilov
Yelena Patsina
Denis Safronov

BAHRAIN
Hamad Mohammed

BANGLADESH
Abir Abdullah
Maruf Hasan
G.M.B. Akash
J.A. Akash
Shahidul Alam
Monirul Alam
K.M. Jahangir Alam
Shafiqul Alam Kiron
Amin
Sheikh Wahid Adnan Bashar
Hassan Bipul
M.N.I. Chowdhury
Emdadul Islam Bitu
Farjana Godhuly
Ashanul Haque
M. Shafiqul Islam
Momena Jalil
Juthika Howlader
Naymuzzaman Prince
Tanvir Murad Topu
Abu Taher Khokon
Munem Wasif
Rashid Un Nabi
Shahadat Parvez
Kazi Md. Golam Quddus
Jewel Samad
Khaled Sattar
Partha Talukdar
Mohamed Main Uddin
MD. Akhlas Uddin
Shehab Uddin
Jashim Uddin

BARBADOS
Michael D. Cadogan

BELARUS
Vladimir Bazan
Kliashchuk Anatoli
Sasha Veledzimovich

BELGIUM
Malek Azoug
Nicolas Bouvy
Alain Breyer
Jean-Michel Clajot
Frederic Courbet
Thomas Dashuber
Joost De Raeymaeker
Tim Dirven
Cédric Gerbehay
Harry Goossens
Brigitte Grignet
Tomas van Houtryve
Gert Jochems
Carl De Keyzer
Firmin de Maitre
Wendy Marijnissen
Frederic Materne
Bart van der Moeren
Samer Mohdad
Dario Pignatelli
Philip Reynaers
Thierry Roge
Sébastien Smets
Lieve Snellings
Bruno Stevens
Dieter Telemans
Gaël Turine
Sarah Van den Elsken
Stephan Vanfleteren
Davy Vanham
Alex Vanhee

John Vink
Warnand Julien

BOLIVIA
Patricio Crooker
Pedro Laguna
Fernando Ovellar Otero
Carlos Hugo Vaca
Wara Vargas

BOSNIA-HERZEGOVINA
Amel Emric
Ziyah Gafic
Damir Sagolj
Darko Zeljkovic

BRAZIL
Elexandre Aparecido da Silva
Kardec Epifânio Marques
Euler Paixão Alves Peixoto
Paulo Amorim
Keiny Andrade
Alberto César Araújo
Alexandro Auler
Leonardo Aversa
Joao Bacellar
Sonia Bacha
Beto Barata
Nário Barbosa
Caetano Barreira
Jorge Bechara
Alexandre Belém
Jefferson Bernardes
Gustavo Bettini
Jamil Bittar
Julio Bittencourt
Oiram Bourges
Tiago Brandão
Alexandre Brum
André Camara
Rubens Cardia
Marcelo Carnaval
Weimer Carvalho
João Castilho
Francilins Castilho Leal
Sergio Castro
Vidal Cavalcante
André Coelho
Jose Luis da Conceição
Julio Cordeiro
Antonio Costa
Marizilda Cruppe
Fernando Dantas
Pedro David
José Francisco Diorio
Bruno Domingos
Leo Drumond
Armando Favaro
Marcos Fernandes
Alcione Ferreira
Pio Figueiroa
Orlando Filho
Márcia Foletto
Marco Antonio Fontes de Sá
Priscila Forone
André François
Leticia Freire
Evelson de Freitas
Nilton Fukuda
Dado Galdieri
Antônio Gaudério
Apu Gomes
Miriam Gomes
Rivaldo Gomes
Valéria Gonçalvez
Ivo Gonzalez
Yone Guedes
André Henriques
Rafael Jacinto
Isabela Kassow
João Kehl
Andrea König Graiz
Juliana Leitão
Odair Leal
Antônio Lima
Mauricio Lima
Rodrigo Lôbo
Helvio Romero Lopes
Jean Lopes
Moacyr Lopes Junior
Tiago Queiroz Luciano
Gustavo Magnusson
Teresa Maia
Bruno Magalhaes
Eduardo Martino
Luiz Maximiano
Márcia Mendes
Alexandre Meneghini
Antônio Menezes
Gleice Mere

Carlos Mesquita
Sergio Moraes
Ricardo Moraes Castellar
Divaldo Moreira
Sebastião Moreira
Fabio Motta
Pedro Motta
Marta Nascimento
Eduardo Nicolau
Diego de Campos Padgurschi
Joao Padua
Paulo Pampolin
Marcos D'Paula
Marcos Piffer
Jean Pimentel
Paulo Pinto
André Porto
Sergio Quissak
Marcos Ramos
Mastrangelo Reino
Davi Ribeiro
Levy Ribeiro
Ernesto Rodrigues
Jonne Roriz
Joao Marcos Rosa
Anderson Schneider
Roberto Scola
Rogério Alonso Senaha
Francisco De Souza
Rogério Stella
Marco Antonio Flores Teixeira
Andrea Testoni
José Varella
Luiz Vasconcelos
André Vieira
Tadeu Vilani
Roberto Vinicius
Leonardo Wen
Ricardo Yamamoto
Mônica Zarattini

BULGARIA
Mladen Antonov
Svetlana Bahchevanova
Dimitar Dilkoff
Nikolay Doychinov
Hristo Hristov
Dimitar Kyosemarliev
Aziz Mehmed
Stoyan Nenov
Petar Petrov
Ivaylo Velev
Georgy Velichkov
Yellowman
Boris Voynarovitch

BURKINA FASO
Ramata Soré

CAMBODIA
Tang Chhin Sothy

CAMEROON
Eustache Djitouo Ngouagna

CANADA
Patrick Alleyn
Christopher Anderson
Tyler Anderson
Benoit Aquin
Terry Asma
Olivier Asselin
Brian G. Atkinson
Anthony Shiu Hung Au
Jill Beshiri
Shaun Best
Mike Blake
Laëtitia Boudaud
Bernard Brault
Joe Bryksa
Shaughn Butts
Kitra Cahana
Glenn Campbell
Phil Carpenter
Ryan Carter
Frédéric Chartrand Jr.
Andy Clark
Paul Couvrette
Barbara Davidson
Mike Dean
Ivanoh Demers
Don Denton
Daniel Desmarais
Andrew Eccles
Bruce Edwards
Rick E. Eglinton
Heather Faulkner
Elliot Ferguson
Brent Foster
Kevin Frayer

Ricky Friedlander
Brian J.Gavriloff
Guang Niu
Jane Eaton Hamilton
Olivier Hanigan
John Hasyn
Simon Hayter
James Helmer
Jim Henderson
Veronica Henri
Gary Hershorn
Harry How
J. Adam Huggins
Les Jones
Kari Medig
Todd Korol
Robert Laberge
Richard Lautens
Aislinn Leggett
John Lehmann
Rita Leistner
Brent Lewin
David Clifford
Lorne Carl Liesenfeld
Karen Longwell
John Lucas
Fred Lum
Rod C. MacIvor
Doug MacLellan
Rick Madonik
John Mahoney
Liam Maloney
Peter McCabe
Jeff McIntosh
Mandel Ngan
Sandy Nicholson
Paul Nicklen
Farah Nosh
Gary Nylander
Brennan O'Connor
Finbarr O'Reilly
Marcus Oleniuk
Lucas Oleniuk
George Omorean
Ed Ou
Louie Palu
Jean-Sébastien Perron
Wendell Phillips
Vincenzo Pietropaolo
Christopher Pike
Robert Polidori
Peter Power
Duane Gregory Prentice
Ryan Pyle
Andrew Querner
Alain Roberge
Jim Ross
Steve Russell
Derek Ruttan
Rick Rycroft
Sarah Hoibak
Robert Semeniuk
Dave Sidaway
Steve Simon
Jack Simpson
Sami Siva
Lana K. Slezic
David W. Smith
Timothy Smith
Randi Sokoloff
Lyle Stafford
Robert Tinker
Martin Tremblay
Stephen Uhraney
Kevin Unger
Jeff Vinnick
Julian Abram Wainwright
George Webber
Donald Weber
Dana Wilson
Larry Wong
Adrian Wyld
Tory Zimmerman
Iva Zimova

CHILE
Ivan Alvarado
Alejandro Balart
Roberto Candia
Gustavo Corvalán
Edgard Garrido
Rodrigo Garrido Fernández
Luis Hidalgo
Hugo Infante
Julio David Lillo Gallardo
Santiago E. Llanquín Caceras
Max Montecinos
Waldo Nilo
Pedro Rodriguez
Victor Rojas

Victor Daniel Salas Araneda
Sebastian Sepulveda
Pedro Ugarte
Marco Ugarte
Jorge Uzon
Carlos Vera Mancilla
Eduardo Verdugo
Aníbal Vivaceta de la Fuente

COLOMBIA
Luis Cristobal Acosta Castro
Roberto Africano
Henry Agudelo
Gabriel Aponte Salcedo
Eliana Aponte
Juan Manuel Barrero
Felipe Caicedo Chacón
Juan Fernando Cano
Gerardo Chaves
Milton Diaz
Edgar Domínguez Cataño
César Flórez
Javier Galeano Naranjo
Jose Miguel Gomez
Juan Pablo Gomez
Mario Hernandez Jr
Albeiro Lopera Hoyos
William Fernando Martinez
Daniel Munoz
Eduardo Munoz
Jorge E. Orozco Galvis
Jaime Pérez
Luis Ramirez
Patricia Rincon-Mautner
Henry Romero
Camilo Rozo
Robinson Vargas
Jaime Saldarriaga
Manuel Saldarriaga
Juan A. Sanchez Ocampo
Juan Carlos Sierra
Joana Toro
Guillermo Torres
Hernan Vanegas
John W. Vizcaino
Donaldo Zuluaga Velilla

COSTA RICA
Jeffrey Arguedas
Mayela López
Alexander Otarola
Rafael Pacheco Granados
Mónica Quesada C.
Tomas Stargardter
Juan Carlos Ulate Moya
Kattia Vargas Araya

COTE D'IVOIRE
Issouf Sanogo

CROATIA
Darko Bandic
Antonio Bat
Filip Horvat
Tino Juric
Miroslav Kis
Vanda Kljajo
Vlado Kos
Sandra Krunic
Zeljko Lukunic
Dragan Matic
Damir Rajle
Alen Sajina
Sanjin Strukic
Ivo Vucetic
Sasha Zinaja

CUBA
Ginle Cubillas
Gonzo González
Ramsés H. Batista
Cristóbal Herrera Ulashkevich
Giorgio Viera
José Martí
Alejandro Ernesto
Luis Quintanal
Randy Rodriguez Pagés
Adalberto Roque

CYPRUS
Nicolas Iordanou
Petros Karadjias
George Rahmatoulin

CZECH REPUBLIC
Jaroslav Bocek
Vladimir David
Jiri Dolezel
Alena Dvorakova
Viktor Fischer

Michael Fokt
Hynek Glos
Martin Hurda
René Jakl
Kaman Juraj
Antonin Kratochvil
Standa Krupar
Veronika Lukasova
Dan Materna
David Neff
Michal Novotny
Jir Rezc
Hana Schäfer
Jan Schejbal
Robert Sedmik
Filip Singer
Barbora Slapetova
Vladimír Slobodzian
Frantisek Staud
Jan Symon
Jiri Turek
Jiri Urban
Ales Vasicek
Vaclav Vasku
Ivan Vetvicka
Jan Zatorsky

DENMARK
Steven Achiam
Joachim Adrian
Christian Als
Nicolas Asfouri
Casper Balslev
Soren Bidstrup
Anders Birch
Jonathan Bjerg Møller
Michael Barrett Boesen
Thomas Borberg
Sisse Brimberg
Martin Bubandt Jensen
Jeppe Carlsen
Klavs Bo Christensen
Cotton Coulson
Jan Dago
Casper Dalhoff
Jakob Dall
Miriam Dalsgaard
Jens Dresling
Jacob Ehrbahn
Mik Eskestad
Lene Esthave
Jørgen Flemming
Thomas Fredberg
Jan Grarup
Mads Greve
Peter Grosen
Bjorn Stig Hansen
Martin Stampe
Tine Harden
Rudy Hemmingsen
David Høgsholt
Niels Hougaard
Simon Jeppesen
Martin N. Johansen
Nils Jorgensen
Reimar Juul
Anna Kari
Lars Krabbe
Joachim Ladefoged
Jesper Langhoff
Claus Bjørn Larsen
Thomas Larsen
Martin Lehmann
Bax Lindhardt
Jesper Mauritzen
Rikke Milling
Lars Moeller
Morsi
Esben Nielsen
Thomas Nielsen
Mads Nielsen
Miklas Njor
Sigrid Nygaard
Charlotte Oestervang
Peter Hove Olesen
Soren Pagter
Ulrik Pedersen
Betina Skovbro
Carsten Snejbjerg
Martin Søby
Camilla Stephan
Jorn Stjerneklar
Sisse Stoyer
Michael Svenningsen
Bo Tornvig
Jan Unger
Ditte Valente
Thomas Wilmann

DOMINICAN REPUBLIC
Miguel Gomez

EAST TIMOR
Ze'sopol C. Caminha

ECUADOR
Amelia Andrade
Richard Castro Rodriguez
Stalin Agustin Diaz Suarez
Karla Gachet
Carlos Granja Medranda
Ana Belen Jarrin
Alfredo Ernesto Lagla Lagla
Alex Lima
Jonathan Miranda Vanegas
Gerardo Mora
César Morejón
Jimmy J. Negrete Vera
Galo Paguay
Bolivar A. Parra
Alejandro Reinoso
Edison Riofrío Barros
Santiago Serrano
Eduardo Valenzuela
Christian Vasconez
Angel Estuardo Vera
Jorge Vinueza G.

EGYPT
Khaled El Fiqi
Omar Khodeir

EL SALVADOR
Francisco Alemán
Mario Amaya
Félix Amaya
Mercedes Arias
Mauro Arias
José Cabezas
Francisco Campos
Omar Carbonero
Nelson Dueñas
Milton Flores
Angel Gómez
Rony González Guadrón
Oscar Leiva Marinero
Lissette Lemus
Borman Marmol
Roberto Escobar
Rene Rodriguez
Salomón Vásquez
Claudia Zaldaña de Mármol

ERITREA
Girmay Abrha
Kidane Teklemariam

ESTONIA
Annika Haas
Tairo Lutter
Raimond Raadik
Tiit Räis

FINLAND
Tommi Anttonen
Mikaela Berg
Joonas Brandt
Rami Hanafi
Hannes Heikura
Esko Jämsä
Markus Jokela
Sami Kero
Kari Kuukka
Timo Marttila
Elina Moriya
Juhani Niiranen
Heidi Piiroinen
Timo Pyykkö
Erkki Raskinen
Jukka Ritola
Eetu Sillanpää

FRANCE
Pierre Adenis
Christophe Agou
Antoine Agoudjian
Patrice Aguilar
Christian Alminana
Bruno Amsellem
JB Autissier
Patrick Aventurier
Alain Le Bacquer
Capucine Bailly
Patrick Bard
Joan Bardeletti
Pascal Bastien
Patrick Baz
Arnaud Beinat
Christian Bellavia

Christophe Bertolin
Cyril Bitton
Patrick Blanche
Romain Blanquart
Olivier Boëls
Samuel Bollendorff
Régis Bonnerot
Youssef Boudlal
Denis Boulanger
Alexandra Boulat
Pierre Boutier
Gabriel Bouys
Philippe Brault
Patrick Bruchet
Hervé Bruhat
Jerome Brunet
Catherine Cabrol
Christophe Calais
Serge Cantó
Sarah Caron
Jérôme Cartillier
Amandine Cau
Cyril Cavalié
Julien Chatelin
Aurelien Chauvaud
Olivier Chouchana
Pierre Ciot
Sebastien le Clezio
Thomas Coex
Jerome Eagland-Conquy
Cyrus Cornut
Olivier Corsan
Olivier Coulange
Gilles Coulon
Pierre Crom
Olivier Culmann
Francois Daburon
Denis Dailleux
Viviane Dalles
Julien Daniel
William Daniels
Denis Darzacq
Georges Dayan
Jean Noël de Soye
Gautier Deblonde
Manoocher Deghati
Luc Delahaye
Jerome Delay
Francis Demange
Michel Denis-Huot
Jean-François Deroubaix
Philippe Desmazes
Bertrand Desprez
Patrick Dewarez
Agnes Dherbeys
Oliver Douliery
Claire Doutremepuich
Frédéric Dufour
Emmanuel Dunand
Rachida El Ghazali
Alain Elorza
Christophe Ena
Isabelle Eshraghi
Patricio Estay
Eric Estrade
Hubert Fanthomme
Gilles Favier
Jerome Favre
Pascal Fayolle
Eric Feferberg
Olivier Fermariello
Bruno Fert
Franck Fife
Olivier Fitoussi
Sylvie Francoise
Mélanie Frey
Simon Gade
Eric Gaillard
Sebastien Galea
Eric Garault
Baptiste Giroudon
Pierre Gleizes
Georges Gobet
Julien Goldstein
Nicolas Gouhier
Mathieu Grandjean
Elodie Grégoire
Diane Grimonet
Olivier Grunewald
Bertrand Guay
François Guillot
Jean-Paul Guilloteau
Valery Hache
Eric Hadj
Azim Haidaryan
Philippe Haÿs
Philippe Henry
Guillaume Herbaut
Patrick Hertzog
Kristina Hruska

Arja Hyytiainen
Olivier Jobard
Gérard Julien
Guilad Kahn
Sylvette Kandel
France Keyser
Stephane Klein
Gregoire Korganow
Patrick Kovarik
Jean Philippe Ksiazek
Benedicte Kurzen
Olivier Laban Mattei
Fréderic Lafargue
Jean Pierre Lagarde
Francis Latreille
Didier Lefevre
Rene Limbourg
Thierry Lopez
Philippe Lopparelli
Jean-Marc Lubrano
John MacDougall
Gregoire Maisonneuve
Etienne de Malglaive
Alexandre Marchi
Jean Marmeisse
Pierre Mérimée
Isabelle Merminod
Bertrand Meunier
Meyer
Marcel Mochet
Olivier Morin
Jean Claude Moschetti
Vincent Mouchel
Frédéric Mouchet
Jean-Pierre Muller
Freddy Muller
Jacky Naegelen
Roberto Neumiller
Alain Noguès
Anaïs Pachabezian
Jef Pachoud
Jean-Philippe Pariente
Claude Pauquet
Celia Pernot
Bruno Perousse
Renaud Philippe
Jean-Marc Pochat
Kevin Poirier
Philippe de Poulpiquet
Olivier Puccia
Julie Pudlowski
Noël Quidu
Hubert Raguet
Raveendran Pradeepan
Pascal Rossignol
Marc Roussel
Denis Rouvre
Cyril Ruoso
Lizzie Sadin
Joël Saget
Stephane De Sakutin
Frédéric Sautereau
David Sauveur
Sylvain Savolainen
Pascal Le Segretain
Franck Seguin
Philippe Servent
Jérôme Sessini
Will Sterns
Susset-Lacroix
Patrick Swirc
Taamallah Mehdi
Myriam Tangi
Benoit Tessier
Patrick Tourneboeuf
Eric Travers
Jean-Michel Turpin
Eric Vandeville
Pierre Verdy
Jean-Christophe Verhaegen
Maya Vidon
Veronique de Viguerie
Laurent Weyl
Nadia Wicker
Philippe Wojazer
Stephan Zaubitzer

GEORGIA
Mariam Amurvelashvili
Levan Kherkheulidze
Yuri Lobodin
Ketevan Mgebrishvili
Dato Rostomashvili
Merabishvili Shorena
Niko Tarielashvili
Beso Uznadze

GERMANY
Valeska Achenbach
Ingo Arndt

Bernd Arnold
Nils Bahnsen
Julia Baier
David Baltzer
Christoph Bangert
Lars Baron
Theodor Barth
Christian Bauer
Max Becherer
Siegfried Becker
Sandra Behne
Fabrizio Bensch
J. Berger
Guido Bergmann
Birgit Betzelt
Fabian Bimmer
Olaf Blecker
Christoph Boeckheler
Joerg Boethling
Sebastian Bolesch
Stefan Boness
Kai Bornhöft
Marcus Brandt
Hermann Bredehorst
Carsten Bredhauer
Gero Breloer
Hansjürgen Britsch
Till Budde
Sven Buschmeier
Dirk Claus
Sven Creutzmann
Peter Dammann
Uli Deck
Andrea Diefenbach
Günter Distler
Sven Doering
Volker Döring
Alfred Drossel
Jens Dünhölter
Thomas Dworzak
Philipp Ebeling
Winfried Eberhardt
Thomas Ebert
Thorsten Eckert
Tameer Gunnar Eden
Bastian Ehl
Thekla Ehling
Eckhard Elmer
Johannes Eisele
Florian Eisele
Andreas Endermann
Stefan Enders
Diether Endlicher
Philipp Engelhorn
Frank Eppler
Thomas Ernsting
Volker Essler
Daniel Etter
Stefan Falke
Bernd Feil
Sibylle Fendt
Peter Franke
Juergen Freund
Amira Fritz
Sascha Fromm
Kurt Fuchs
Maurizio Gambarini
Dirk Gebhardt
Uwe Gerig
Markus Gilliar
José Giribás
Bodo Goeke
Lukas Gold
Nina N. Greipel
Jens Grossmann
Philipp Guelland
Patrick Haar
Kirsten Haarmann
Michael R. Hagedorn
Matthias Hangst
Alfred Harder
Markus Hass
Alexander Hassenstein
Laura Hegewald
Gerhard Heidorn
Kay-Christian Heine
Katja Heinemann
Oliver Heisch
Klaus Helbig
Katharina Hesse
Markus C. Hildebrand
Annegret Hilse
Antje Hoefer
Thomas Holtrup
Helge Holz
Milan Horacek
Eva Horstick-Schmitt
Andreas Hub
Lara Huck
Wolfgang Huppertz

145

Christian Irrgang
Claudia Janke
Karlheinz Jardner
Carmen Jaspersen
Judith Jockel
Bernd Jonkmanns
Matthias Jung
Hagen Kaelberer
Enno Kapitza
Anja Kessler
Claus Kiefer
Thomas Kienzle
Ulla Kimmig
Silke Kirchhoff
David Klammer
Christian Klein
Wolfgang B. Kleiner
Brigitta Klotz
Jens Knappe
Herbert Knosowski
Kai-Uwe Knoth
Carsten Koall
Hans-Jürgen Koch
Heidi Koch
Thomas Köhler
Ralph Köhler
Bernd König
Christof Köpsel
Reinhard Krause
Gert Krautbauer
Jens Küsters
Peter Lammerer
Karl Lang
Martin Langer
Paul Langrock
Ralph Larmann
Joerg Letz
Ralf Lienert
Maximilian Ludwig
Uwe H. Martin
Noel Tovia Matoff
Fabian Matzerath
Daniel Maurer
Andreas Meichsner
Günther Menn
Dieter Menne
Uwe S. Meschede
Jens Meyer
Denis Meyer
Belaid le Mharchi
Markus Milde
Thorsten Milse
Benjamin Antony Monn
Cathrin Mueller
Christian Muhrbeck
Hardy Müller
Anja Niedringhaus
Kay Nietfeld
Ernesto Oehler
Jan Oelker
Ingo Otto
Jens Palme
Isabela Pacini
Laci Perenyi
Carsten Peter
Kai Pfaffenbach
Thomas Pflaum
Fritz Pölking
Cornelius Popovici
Wolfgang Quednau
Emanuel Raab
Britta Radike
Andreas Reeg
Wolfgang Reiher
Renate Reimann
Pascal Amos Rest
Sascha Rheker
Astrid Riecken
Julian Röder
Frederik Roeh
Daniel Roland
Jens Rötzsch
Martin Sasse
Sabine Sauer-Hetzer
Henning Schacht
Peter Schatz
Christiane J.B. Scheidt
Günter Schiffmann
Peter Schilde
Benjamin Schilling
Roberto Schmidt
Axel Schmidt
Harald Schmitt
Martin Schoeller
Markus Schreiber
Annette Schreyer
Michel Schüler
Bernd Schuller
Frank Schultze
Eckehard Schulz

Jochen Schulze
Stephan Schütze
Tobias Schwarz
Hartmut Schwarzbach
Oliver Sehorsch
Yvonne Seidel
Patricia Sigerist
Roland Sigwart
Hans Silvester
Stefan Sobotta
Martin Specht
Günter Standl
Matthias Steinbach
Berthold Steinhilber
Marc Steinmetz
Björn Steinz
Peter Steudtner
Carsten Stormer
Julian Stratenschulte
Kai Stuht von Neupauer
Jens Sundheim
Stefan Syrowatka
Andreas Teichmann
Andreas Thelen
Isabella Thiel
Christian Thum
Murat Türemis
Markus Ulmer
Heinrich Voelkel
Friedemann Vogel
Vanja Vukovic
Paul Wagner
Richard Walch
Tim Wegner
Mario Weigt
Maurice Weiss
Sönke C. Weiss
Udo Weitz
Gordon Welters
Philipp Wente
Sabine Wenzel
Kai Wiedenhöfer
Arnd Wiegmann
Claudia Yvonne Wiens
Michael Wolf
Xiaoling Wu
Monique Yazdani
Solvin Zankl
Fabian Zapatka
Jan Zappner
Frank Zauritz
Sven Zellner
Christian Ziegler
Gregor Zielke
Harf Zimmermann

GREECE
Konstantinos Antonopoulos
Kostas Argyris
Yannis Behrakis
Evangelos Bougiotis
John Cazolis
Greg Chrisohoidis
Nikos Chrisikakis
Vassilis Constantineas
Vasilis Germanis
Louisa Gouliamaki
Yiorgos Karahalis
Yannis Kontos
Eleftherios Kostans
Evangelos Kousiora
Alexandros Lamprovasilis
Kostas Mantziaris
Aris Messinis
Stefania Mizara
Orestis Panagiotou
Nikos Pilos
Lefteris Pitarakis
Vladimir Rys
Aris Vafeiadakis
Vagelis
Alexis Michael Vassilopoulos

GUATEMALA
Jesús Alfonso
Moisés Castillo
Luis Echeverria
Enrique Hernandez Avila
Antonio Rodriguez
Sandra Sebastian

GUYANA
Nikki Kahn

HAITI
Carl Juste

HONDURAS
Orlando Sierra

HUNGARY
Laszlo Antalfay
Éva Arnold
Karoly Arvai
Bácsi Róbert László
László Balogh
Szabolcs Barakonyi
Zsolt Batar
Laszlo Beliczay
Imre Benkö
Gyula Czimbal
Katalin Darnay
Tamas Dezso
Bela Doka
Tivadar Domaniczky
Szabolcs Dudás
Imre Földi
Balazs Gardi
György Gáti
Norbert Hartyanyi
Kálmánfi Gábor
Gabor Kapolka
Szilárd Koszticsák
Nanoq Nakokrii
Daniel Kovalovszky
Marczi
Simon Móricz
Andras Peter Nemeth
Reviczky
Gergely Rónai
Csaba Segesvari
Mark Simon
Gyula Sopronyi
Zsuzsanna Spilak
Sandor H. Szabo
Peter Szalmas
Bela Szandelszky
József L. Szentpéteri
Zsolt Szigetváry
Kovacs Tamas
Paczai Tamas
Gabor F. Toth
Zoltán Tuba
Bala'zs Turay
Imre Varga
Zoltán Varga
Daniel Vegel
Péter Zádor

ICELAND
Hrönn Axelsdóttir
Ragnar Axelsson
Vilhelm Gunnarsson
Kristinn Ingvarsson
Thorvaldur Kristmundsson
Arni Torfason

INDIA
Ajay Aggarwal
Sanjay Ahlawat
Srinivas Akella
Daniel Alexander
Aditya Anupkumar
Binsar Bakkara
Anand Bakshi
Utpal Baruah
Vikram S. Barwal
Shyamal Basu
Salil Bera
Achinto Bhadra
Amit Bhargava
Ch.Vijaya Bhaskar
Mahesh Bhat
Piyal Bhattacharjee
Pradeep Bhavsar
Sawan Bohra
S. Burmaula
Rana Chakraborty
Bharat Chanda
Rahul Chandawarkar
Sajal Chatterjee
Sandipan Chatterjee
Anindya Chattopadhyay
Yeshe Choesang
Deshakalyan Chowdhury
Bikas Das
Sanjit Das
Saurabh Das
Shantanu Das
Sucheta Das
Sudipto Das
Amit Dave
Rajib De
Praveen Dixit
Sima Dubey
Santosh Dutta
Nilayan Dutta
Subir Kumar Dutta
Diptendu Dutta
Subham Dutta

Dudhalkar Gajanan
Sanjib Ghosh
Manob Ghosh
Krishnendu Halder
Adeel Halim
Abu Hashim
Prakash Hatvalne
Shah Hemendra
Sohrab Hura
Fawzan Husain
Sumeet Inder Singh
Anand Ishwarappa Murgod
Danish Ismail
Rijo Joseph
Fayaz Kabli
Sankha Kar
Soumik Kar
Harikrishna Katragadda
Ruhani Kaur
Pawan Kumar
Naleen Kumar
Bijoy Kumar Jain
Varun Kumar Jaiswal
Brijesh Kumar Singh
Rajesh Kumar Singh
Pradeep Kumar Surya
Vino Kutt
Atul Loke
Shalini Maheshwari
Swaroop Majumder
Rafiq Maqbool
Max Martin
Kailash Mittal
Muherjee
Paroma Mukherjee
Omprakash Munisamy
Prashant Nadkar
Pankaj Nangia
Ch. Narayana Rao
Dev Nayak
Yawar Nazir Kabli
Gurinder Osan
Nick Oza
Prashant Panjiar
Punit Paranjpe
Swapan Parekh
Ganesh Parida
Shriya Patil
G. Pattabiraman
Indranil Paul
Ravi Posavanike
Vasant Prabhu
Jitendra Prakash
Singh Prakash
Neeraj Priyadarshi
Altaf Qadri
Abdul Qayoom Wani
Aijaz Rahi
Ritesh Ramchand
Uttamchandant
K. Ramesh Babu
R. Raveendran
Prashant Ravi
Nilanjan Ray
Manpreet Romana
Tamal Roy
K.K. Santhosh
Parth Sanyal
Ruby Sarkar
Debajyoti Sarkar
Pankaj Sekhsaria
Arijit Sen
Samik Sen
Bijoy Sengupta
R. Senthil Kumaran
Javeed Shah
Ashish Shankar
Sondeep Shankar
S.Shanmugasundaram
Thevar
Subhash Sharma
Money Sharma
Jayanta Shaw
Anand Shinde
Selvan Shiv Kumar
Qamar Sibtain
Bandeep Singh
Prakash Singh
Gautam Singh
Dijeshwar Singh
Rajib Singha
Manish Sinha
Ajit Solanki
Nitin Sonawane
Shekhar Soni
T. Srinivasa Reddy
P.V. Sujith
S.Sundaram
Adesara Sunil
Manish Swarup

Mustafa Taussef
Harish Tyagi
Regi Varghese
Manan Vatsyayana
Prashanth Vishwanathan
Himanshu Vyas
Dar Yasin
Altaf Zargar

INDONESIA
Yuyung Abdi
Adiat
Yuniadhi Agung
Nogo Agusto Alimin
M. Anshar
Arif Ariadi
Oka Barta
Beawiharta
Andry Bey
Ali Budiman Lo
Chalid MN
Andi Cristop
Sugeng Deas
Adam Dwi Putra
Riza Fathoni
Junaidi Gandy
Guslan Gumilang
Afriadi Hikmal
Hadiyanto
Wawan Hadi Prabowo
Jongki Handianto
Said Harahap
Hariyanto
Raditya Helabumi
Pang Hway Sheng
Bagus Indahono
Sandhi Irawan
Mast Irham
Jakop Iskandar
Kemal Jufri
Mak Pak Kim
Pradeep Kocharekar
Andi Lubis
Ali Lutfi
Molamarbun
Made Nagi
Eka Nickmatulhuda
Dwi Oblo
Bayu Pamungkas
Ivan N. Patmadiwiria
Lucky Pransiska
Hermanus Prihatna
Priyombodo
Edy Purnomo
Didi Rahardjo
Agung Rahmadiansyah
Arif Ramdan
Ahmad "Deny" Salman
Toto Santiko Budi
Agung Sastro
Ferdy Siregar
Poriaman Sitanggang
Denny Sitohang
Boy Slamet
Arief Suhardiman
Toni Suhartono
Jurnasyanto Sukarno
Arief Sunarya
Agus Susanto
Ng Swan Ti
Maha Eka Swasta
Andika Wahyu
Sophan Wahyudi
Adi Weda
Wasis Wibowo
Taufan Wijaya
Veronica Wijaya
Totok Wijayanto
Yan Rafsanjani
Yayus Yuswoprihanto

IRAQ
Ghaith Abdul-Ahad
Mohammed Adnan
Ahmed Hamza Al-Fadhil
Ahmad Al-Rubaye
Ali Al-Saadi
Sabah Arar
Ceerwan Aziz
Muhannad Fala'ah
Ali Haider
Karim Kadim
Hadi Mizban
Khalid Mohammed
Ibrahim Sulaiman Nadir
Ali Youssef

IRELAND
Alan Betson
Marcus Bleasdale

Noel Bowler
Deirdre Brennan
Aidan Crawley
Colman Doyle
Denis Doyle
Nic Dunlop
Arthur Ellis
Kieran Galvin
Don McNeill Healy
Andrew Hetherington
James Horan
Steve Humphreys
John C Kelly
Dan Linehan
Dara Mac Dónaill
David Maher
John McDermott
Ross McDonnell
John D. McHugh
Cathal McNaughton
Frank Miller
Denis Minihane
Brendan Moran
Seamus Murphy
Jeremy Nicholl
Bryan O'Brien
Joe O'Shaughnessy
Niall O'Shea
Alan Place
Ivor Prickett
Dave Ruffles
David Sleator
Paul Stewart
Dermot Tatlow
Morgan Treacy
Ian Walton
Eamon Ward

ISLAMIC REPUBLIC OF IRAN
Aalimanesh
Ali Agharabie
Arash
Mohammad Babaei
Kaveh Baghdadchi
Ali Bagheri
Alireza Emtiaz
Vahid Faraji
Farnood
Hossein Fatemi
Caren Firouz
Ali Ghalamsiah
Hasan Ghareeb
Mehdi Ghasemi
Siavash Habibollahi
Dariyoosh Hariri
Kamran Jebreili
Farzaneh Khademian
Mohammad Kheirkhah
Mohammedreza Kowsari
Siavash Laghai
Katayoun Massoudi
Behrouz Mehri
Javad Moghimi
Mina Momeni
Mohammad Namazi
Mansour Nasiri
Baqer Nassir
Ahad Nazarzadeh
Morteza Nikoobazl-e
Motlagh
Morteza Noormohammadi
Ebrahim Noroozi
Labkhand Olfatmanesh
Amir Masoud Oskouilar
Roohilius
Payam Rouhani
Saba
Taher Sadati
Vahdat Sadr Mohammadi
Hosein Saki
Vahid Salemi
Nousha Salimi
Mohsen Sanei Yarandi
Hasan Sarbakhshian
Shahrouz Sharifynasab
Mahmoudi Soleyman
Alireza Sotakbar
Pooyan Tabatabaei
Alfred Yaghobzadeh
Azin Zanjani

ISRAEL
Liron Almog
Tomer Appelbaum
Lihee Avidan
Oded Balilty
Mohammed Ballas
Rafael Ben-Ari
Yaron Brener
Rina Castelnuovo

Raanen Choen
Gil Cohen Magen
Yori Costa
Eli Dassa
Natan Dvir
Nir Eilon
Nir Elias
Michal Fattal
Yoav Galai
Eddie Gerald
Elad Gershgoren
Amnon Gutman
Nir Kafri
Menahem Kahana
Kaprov Edward
Julia Komissaroff
Ziv Koren
Eyal Landesman
Yoav Lemmer
Yoray Liberman
Amit Magal
Shay Mehalel
Ilan Mizrahi
Nadav Neuhaus
Eldad Rafaeli
Alex Rozkovsky
Ariel Schalit
Ahikam Seri
Amit Shabi
Avihu Shapira
Nati Shohat
Uriel Sinai
Yuval Tebol
Pierre Terdjman
Gali Tibbon
Miriam Tsachi
Eyal Warshavsky
Yonathan Weitzman
Noam Wind
Pavel Wolberg
Kobi Wolf
Danny Yanai
Ilia Yefimovich
Max Yelinson
Yossi Zamir
Ronen Zvulun

ITALY
Francesco Acerbis
Edoardo Agresti
Vito Amodio
Mario Anzuoni
Roberto Arcari
Giampiero Assumma
Giovanni Attalmi
Fabiano Avancini
Antonietta Baldassarre
Danilo Balducci
Isabella Balena
Marco Baroncini
Massimo Bassano
Cristiano Bendinelli
Massimo Berruti
Guia Besana
Alfredo Bini
Valerio Bispuri
Paolo Bona
Tommaso Bonaventura
Fabrizio Borella
Alberto Bortoluzzi
Michele Borzoni
Mauro Bottaro
Giovanni Del Brenna
Luca Bruno
Talos Buccellati
Alberto Buzzola
Roberto Caccuri
Jean Marc Caimi
Guy Calaf
Simona Caleo
Alberto Cambone
Alberto Cambone
Maristella Campolunghi
Federico Caponi
Giuseppe Carotenuto
Marco Casale
Davide Casella
Sergio Cecchini
Giancarlo Ceraudo
Francesco Chiorazzi
Donato Chirulli
Lorenzo Cicconi Massi
Alex M. Cipollini
Giordano Cipriani
Francesco Cito
Pier Paolo Cito
Noris Cocci
Ignacio Maria Coccia
Francesco Cocco
Giovanni Cocco

Elio Colavolpe
Gianluca Colla
Massimo Colombo
Antonino Condorelli
Daniele Coricciati
Matt Corner
Marilisa Cosello
Marzia Cosenza
Alessandro Cosmelli
Claudio Cricca
Pietro Cuccia
Pierfranco Cuccuru
Fabio Cuttica
Alfredo D'Amato
Maria Silvia D'Ambrosio
Enrico Dagnino
Daniele Dainelli
Daniel Dal Zennaro
Andrea Dapueto
Rocco De Benedictus
luca desienna
Marco Di Lauro
Armando Di Loreto
Giovanni Diffidenti
Alessandro Digaetano
Dario de Dominicis
Simone Donati
Sara Elter
Salvatore Esposito
Luca Eugeni
Gughi Fassino
Luca Ferrari
Peef Fiorillo
Nanni Fontana
Adolfo Franzò
Andrea Frazzetta
Lorenzo Galassi
Alessandro Gandolfi
Riccardo Gangale
Marco Garofalo
Tony Gentile
Carlo Gianferro
Francesco Gioia
Carola Giordano
Alberto Giuliani
Maria Elena Giuliani
Alessandro Grassani
Paola de Grenet
Gianluigi Guercia
Daniele Gussago
Luca Lo Iacono
Marina Imperi
Mattia Insolera
Roberto Isotti
Stefano Jesi Ferrari
Giuseppe
Franco Lannino
Laudanna Saba
Gino Lazzarin
Alessandro Lazzarin
Marco Longari
Peppino Longobardo
Stefano de Luigi
Alessandro Majoli
Livio Mancini
Emiliano Mancuso
Milko Marchetti
Claudio Marcozzi
Giovanni Marrozzini
Andrea di Martino
Enrico Mascheroni
Masi Roberto
Massimo Mastrorillo
Andrew Medichini
Giovanni Mereghetti
Mimi Mollica
Livia Monami
Riccardo Montanari
Laura Montanari
Luana Monte
F. Filippo Monteforte
Davide Monteleone
Silvia Morara
Morelli Stefano
Alberto Moretti
Lorenzo Moscia
Emanuele Mozzetti
Sara Munari
Gianni Muratore
Filippo Mutani
Giulio Napolitano
Francesco Nencini
Michele Nucci
Antonello Nusca
Oliviero Olivieri
Bruna Orlandi
Diego Orlando
Agostino Pacciani
Isabela Pacini
Franco Pagetti

Andrea Pagliarulo
Fabio Palli
Stefano Paltera
Partesi
Mila Pavan
Stefano G. Pavesi
Alice Pedroletti
Samuele Pellecchia
Paolo Pellegrin
Paolo Pellizzari
Viviana Peretti Legramante
Giorgio Perottino
Carlo Pettinelli
Marco Pighin
Vincenzo Pinto
Pamela Pioli
Fabio Polenghi
Duilio Polidori
Paolo Porto
Roberto Radimir
Raffaello Raimondi
Sergio Ramazzotti
Alberto Ramella
Pino Rampolla
Stefano Rellandini
Chris Ricco
Simone Romeo
Rorandelli Rocco
Max Rossi
Andrea Sabbadini
Ivo Saglietti
Francesco Sammicheli
Giorgio Sandrone
Marco Saroldi
Loris Savino
Giuseppe Sboarina
Claudio Scaccini
Andrea Scaringella
Stefano Schirato
Massimo Sciacca
Manuel Scrima
Livio Senigalliesi
Tonino Sgrò
Giuliani Silvio
Christian Sinibaldi
Massimo Siragusa
Andreas Solaro
Mauro Spanu
Andrea Staccioli
Alessandro Stellari
Francesco Survara
Alessandro Tarantino
Vincenzo Tessarin
Kash G Torsello
Alessandro Tosatto
Ivano Trabalza
Lorenzo Tugnoli
Cristian Umili
Giuseppe Ungari
Albertina d' Urso
Antonio Vacirca
Giuseppe Valente
Paolo Vanda
Cristina Vatielli
Riccardo Venturi
Paolo Verzone
Fabrizio Villa
Massimo Vitali
Lorenzo Vitturi
Theo Volpatti
Paolo Volponi
Marta Zaccaron
Fabrizio Zani
Francesco Zizola
Dana de Luca
Vittorio Zunino Celotto

JAMAICA
Norman Grindley
Bebeto Matthews
Kazuyoshi Ehara

JAPAN
Chieko Hara
Shiro Harada
Takumi Harada
Yasunari Itayama
Taichi Kaizuka
Chiaki Kawajiri
Tetsuya Kikumasa
Takao Kitamura
Thoshifumi Kitamura
Yoshiki Kitaoka
Junji Kurokawa
Naoki Maeda
Yuzo Uda
Fumiko Matsuyama
Shigeki Miyajima
Toru Morimoto

Takuma Nakamura
Motoya Nakamura
Masahiro Nakamuta
Takuya Okabe
Kosuke Okahara
Jiro Ose
Takashi Ozaki
Q Sakamaki
Kiriko Shirobayashi
Akira Suemori
Dai Sugano
Ryuzo Suzuki
Kuni Takahashi
Ari Takahashi
Kimitaka Takeichi
Atsushi Taketatzu
Daisuke Wada
Yoichi Watanabe
Haruyoshi Yamaguchi
Tsuyoshi Yoshioka

JORDAN
Kholoud Majed Abu Shakra
Osama Abughanim
Omar Al-Daher
Najd Al-Hamdan
Amerah Al-Hemsi
Wael Al-Hijazeen
Hanady Issa Al-Ramahi
Khaleel Issa Al-Ramahi
Ali Mousa Al-Sahouri
Ammar Awad
Da'ad Rafiq Dallal
Tanya Habjouqa
Rula Halawani
Salman Madanat
Nasser Nasser

KAZAKHSTAN
Aziz Mamirov

KENYA
Kuria J.Burugu
Antony Kaminju
Boniface Mwangi
Ogutu M. Elvis
Thomas Omondi

KYRGYZSTAN
Vyacheslav Oseledko

LATVIA
Aigars Eglite
Ruta Kalmuka
Andris Kozlovskis
Wilhelm Mikhailovsky
Janis Pipars

LEBANON
Nicolas Abi Haidar
Anwar Amro
Mohamed Azakir
Dina Debbas
Mustafa Elakhal
Wael Hamzeh
Hamzi Haydar
Nabil Hassan Mounzer
Haitan Mussawi
Marwan Naamani

LITHUANIA
Aleksandravicius Algimantas
Giedrius Baranauskas
Ramunas Danisevicius
Zenonas Gricius
Valdas Kopustas
Kazimieras Linkevicius
Petras Malukas
Renaldas Malychas
Egle Melinauskiene
Rolandas Parafinavicius
Alfredas Pliadis
Andrius Repsys
Sigitas Stasaitis
Jonas Staselis
Romualdas Vaitkus

LUXEMBOURG
Claude Diderich
Jean-Claude Ernst
Georges Schneider
Alain Schroeder
Wagner Tom
Wagner Christian

MACEDONIA
Ivan Blazhev
Dimitrov Petar
Ognen Teofilovski

MALAWI
Bonex Julius

MALAYSIA
Jaafar Abdullah
Sawlihim Bakar
Esther Cheach
Art Chen
Glenn Guan
Bob Lee Keng Siang
Lai Seng Sin
Lee Chee Keong
Chin Hwan Lei
Leong Chun Keong
Jeffry Lim Chee Yong
Azhar Mahfof
Bazuki Muhammad
Pan Kah Vee
Abd Rahman Saleh
Kamal Sellehuddin
Shum Fook Weng
Tan Chik Sang
Kevin Tan
Tan Ee Long
Tan Woei Hwa
Teh Eng Koon
Vincent Thian
Tim Chong
Andy Wong Sung Jeng
Aswad Yahya
Yang Zixiong

MALTA
Matthew Mirabelli
Darrin Zammit Lupi

MAURITIUS
Georges Michel

MEXICO
Carlos Abraham Slim
Daniel Aguilar
Javier Aguilar
Marcela Alonso López
Enrique Alvarez del Castillo
Guillermo Arias
Armando Arorizo
Hebert Camacho
Luis Castillo
Carlos Cazalis
Julieta Cervantes
Luis Cortes
José Luis Cuevas
Alfredo Dominguez Noriega
Oscar Estevez
Alfredo Estrella Ayala
Gonzalo Fuentes Moreno
Javier Garcia
Héctor García
Alejandro G. Bedoya
José Carlo González
Susana Gonzalez Torres
Claudia Guadarrama
Hector Guerrero Skinfill
Fernando Gutiérrez-Juárez
Edgar Hernández Barrera
Elizabeth Dalziel
Miguel Juarez
Leopoldo Kram
Pericles Lavat Guinea
Gilberto Marquina
Alejandro Meléndez
David de la Paz
Gilberto Meza
Alberto Millares
Octavio Nava Hernandez
Antonio Nava
Bernardo De Niz
Mauricio Palos
Rosauro Pozos Villanueva
Alberto Puente
Luis Quiroz
Arturo Ramos Guerrero
Rafael del Rio
Jose Rosales
Xolotl Salazar
Enrique Sifuentes Ramos
Jorge Silva
Marcela Taboada
Antonio Turok
Marco Aurelio Vargas Lopez
Federico Vargas Somoza

MONGOLIA
Erdenetuya Gurrinchin
Vandandorj Battulga

MALAWI
Bonex Julius

NAMIBIA
Karel Prinsloo

NEPAL
Mukunda Kumar Bogati
Bimal Gautam
Chandra Shekhar Karki
Sailendra Kharel
Bibi Funyal
Naresh Kumar Shrestha
Prasant Shrestha
Narendra Shrestha
Shruti Shrestha
Shaligram Tiwari

NEW ZEALAND
Mark Baker
Scott Barbour
Greg Bowker
Melanie Burford
Jonathan Cameron
Ben Campbell
Jocelyn Carlin
Marion van Dijk
Andrew Gorrie
David Hancock
Maarten Holl
Dave Hunt
Jimmy Joe
Robert Kitchin
Alan Knowles
Mark McKeown
Marty Melville
Mike Millett
Sandra Mu
Vivek Prakash
Dean Purcell
Peter James Quinn
Phil Reid
Richard Robinson
Kenny Rodger
Martin de Ruyter
Keith Andrew Scott
Dwayne Senior
Alex Shea
Craig Simcox
Mark Taylor
William West
Murray Wilson

NICARAGUA
Guillermo Flores
Alejandro Sánchez

NIGERIA
Sunday Olufemi Adedeji
Kunle Ajayi
Akintunde Akinleye
Pius Utomi Ekpei
Sunday Ohwo
Muyiwa Osifuye
George Osodi

NORWAY
Paul Sigve Amundsen
Odd Andersen
Jonas Bendiksen
Stein Jarle Bjorge
Pal Christensen
Tomm W. Christiansen
Ellen Lande Gossner
Pål Hermansen
Jan Johannessen
Daniel Sannum Lauten
Henning Lillegärd
Gunnar Mjaugedal
Mimsy Moller
Otto von Münchow
Eivind H. Natvig
Fredrik Naumann
Karin Beate Nøsterud
Kristine Nyborg
Christopher Olsson
Espen Rasmussen
Haavard Saeboe
Pia Solberg
Knut Egil Wang

PAKISTAN
Ameer Hamza
Zahid Hussein

PALESTINIAN TERRITORIES
Mohamed Abed
Jamal Aruri
Jaafar Ashtiyeh
Hazem Bader
Mahmud Hams
Said Khatib
Wissam Nassar

Fayez Nureldine
Suhaib Salem
Mohammed

PANAMA
Demóstenes Angel Quiroz
Eric Batista
Jorge Fernandez
Bernardino Freire
Tito Herrera
Anselmo Mantovani
Davis Mesa
Jihan Rodriguez
Maydée Romero

PARAGUAY
Luis Vera

PEOPLE'S REPUBLIC OF CHINA
Bai Jikai
Cai Jingrui
Cao Tong
Cao Zhi Zheng
Cao Zhi-gang
Chan Man Lung
Chan Wai Hing
Chang Gang
Chang He
Chennan
Chen Zhou
Chen Hui
Chen Da Yao
Chen Qinggang
Chen Yi Huai
Cheng Bing Hong
Cheng Jiang
Cheng Ning
Cheng Gang
Cheng Heping
Cheng Qiling
Chu Cancan
Cui Wenbin
Cui Zhishuang
Cunyun Zhou
Deng Xiaowei
Deng Bo
Du Hai
Du Jianxiong
Fan Jinyu
Fang Qianhua
Fei Maohua
Fu Guangxin
Fu Keqiang
Fuyongjun
Gan Nan
Gao Wei
Gao Baoyan
Gao Hetao
Gao Jian Ping
Gao Teng
Guo Lei
Haibo Yu
Han Yan Betsy
Han Wei
Han Yi Ming
Handan
Hao Jiang
Hong'en Yu
Hou Shu-Wang
Hu Lingyun
Hu Qing Ming
Hu Tiexiang
Hu Weiming
Huang Jingda
Huang Yue-Hou
Ji Dong
Jia Guorong
Jiang ShengLian
Jiang Bo
Jiang Hongjing
Jiang Jianhua
Jiangang Li
Jason Lee
Jin Cheng
Jin Siliu
Jing Yan
Li Jinhe
Edward Ju
Ju Yang
Ma Jun
Kang Jing
Lang Shuchen
Lee Thomas
Li Zhen Yu
Li Yue
Li Yalong
Li Yonggang
Li Feng
Li Guang Cheng
Li Wei

Li Wending
Li Xiaogang
Li Yong
Lian Xiang Ru
Liangmeng
Liang Chao
Liang Wang
Liao Yujie
Lim Stan
Linxi
Liu Liqun
Liu Hong Qun
Liu Qiang
Liu Hongyang
Liu Hang
Liu Dajia
Liu Jin
Liu Ke
Liu Tao
Liu Yingyi
Lu Haitao
Lu Guang
Lu Xu Yang
Lu Zhong Bin
Mai Qixuan
Miao Bo
Mo Wei Nong
Mu Jiwu
Ng Robert
Ni Huachu
Ning Feng
Ning Zhouhao
Pan Haiqi
Paul Hu
Paul
Pu Feng
Qi Xiaolong
Qi JieShuang
Qi Hong
Qian Dong Sheng
Qiang Zeng
Qin Bin
Qiu Yan
Qiu Mim
Qiu Weirong
Qui Min
Shan Zeng Hui
Shen Zhong
Sheng Kun Yang
Shi Chen ren
Shi Lifei
Shi Xunfeng
Shiri Su
Song Simon
Song Aly
Tao Sun
Tan Wei Shan
Tan Qingju
Tang Huiji
Tian Yuzhuang
Tianyue
Tian Fei
Tian Li
Tian Xi
Tong Ryan
Tong Jiang
Tsang Chun Nam
Wang Chun
Wang Huisheng
Wang Jianying
Wang Jing
Wang Hui
Wang Yishu
Wang Xiaoming
Wangyi
WangHongda
Wang Xiao
Wang Fei
Wang Gang
Wang Guijiang
Wang Haixin
Wang Jie
Wang Juliang
Wang Xinke
Wangyan
Wang Yao
Wang Zhao-hang
Wang Zhen
Wang Zhou
Wen Xiang Liang
Wu Zhonglin
Wu Lei
Wu Fang
Wu Jun Song
Wu Niao
Wu Po-Yuan
Wu Zhangjie
Wung Tiewei
Xi Haibo
Xiao Huaiyuan

Xiao Langping
Xie Fucheng
Xie MingGang
Xin Zhou
Xinan Wei
Xing Guangli
Xu Jiajun
Xu Haifeng
Yan Bailiang
Yan Yuhong
Yan Ming
Yan Liang
Yang Bo
Yang Xi
Yang Huan
Yang Kejia
Yip Bobby
You Jie
Yu Vincent
Yuan K. Zhen
Yu Liang
Yu Wenguo
Yuchuan Jia
Zhang Feng
Zhang Deng Wei
Zhang Yanhui
Zhang Paul
Zhang Mohan
Zhang Lijie
Zhang Jian
Zhang Nicky
Zhang Jianhua
Zhang Wanshan
Zhang Hongjiang
Zhang Jun
Zhang Weiqing
Zhang Yan
Zhang Yi
Zhao Hang
Zhao Gang
Zhao Jing
Zhao Qing
Zhao Bin
Zhao Kang
Zhen Hongge
Zhong Min
Zhou Guoqiang
Zhou Chao
Zhou Wei
Zhou Yan Ming
Zhuang Xiaolong
Zhuang Yingchang
Zong Lu Fan
Zu Yuan Bin

PERU
Eitan Abramovich
Mariana Bazo
Ernesto Benavides del Solar
Martin Bernetti
Manuel Berrios
Roberto Cáceres
Ana M. Castaneda
Juan Sebastian Castaneda
Enrique Castro Mendivil
José Chuquiure
Romina Cupen
Hector Emanuel
Leon Esteban Felix Alfaro
Carlos Garcia Granthon
Cesar Garcia
Manuel Garcia-Miro
Marco Garro
Richard Hirano Moreno
Gary Manrique
Hector Mata
Maria Ines V. Menacho Ortega
Karel Navarro Pando
Lenin Nolly
Alberto Orbegoso
Susana Raab
Daniel Silva Yoshisato
Gihan Tubbeh
Gonzalo Villena Villar
Sulsba Yépez Schwartz

PHILIPPINES
Jes Aznar
Joseph J. Capellan
Erasmo "Sonny" Espiritu
Aaron Favila
Pepito D. Frias
Romeo Gacad
Joe Galvez
Renato Gandia
Marvi Sagun Lacar
Dennis Borja Mallari
Bullit Marquez
Romeo Ranoco
Cheryl Ravelo

Joaquin Ruste
Dennis M. Sabangan
Jake Verzosa
Rem Zamora

POLAND
Mariusz Adamski
Judit Berekai
Krystian Bielatowicz
Robert Boguslawski
Ms Monika Bulaj
Kuba Dabrowski
Jacenty Dedek
Dembinski Grzegorz
Irek Dorozanski
Arkadiusz Dziczek
Ania Freindorf
Grzegorz Galezia
Tomasz Gawalkewicz
Andrzej Georgiew
Lukasz Glowala
Anna Gluszko
Wojciech Grzedzinski
Tomasz Gudzowaty
Heyda
Marzena Hmielewicz
Marcin Jamkowski
Piotr Jasiczek
Maciej Jeziorek
Jacub Kaminski
Mariusz Kapala
Pawel Kleineder
Roman Konzal
Pawel Kopczynski
Kacper Kowalski
Andrzej Kramarz
Witold Krassowski
Bogdan Krezel
Przemyslaw Krzakiewicz
Robert Krzanowski
Bartlomiej Kudowicz
Piotr Lelek
Wojciech Lembryk
Andrei Liankevich
Marcin Lobaczewski
Weronika Lodzinska
Agnieszka Luczakowska
Katarzyna Mala
Piotr Malecki
Krzysztof Miekus
Justyna Mielnikiewicz
Rafal Milach
Karolina Misztal
Maciej Nabrdalik
Adam Nocon
Wojciech Nowicki
Wojciech Oksztol
Krystyna Okulewicz
Adam Panczuk
Mieczyslaw Pawlowicz
Wojciech Prazmowski
Zorka Project
Konrad Pustola
Aleksander Rabij
Agnieszka Rayss
Szymon Roginski
Olgierd Rudak
Bartek Solik
Waldemar Sosnowski
Pawel Stauffer
Tomasz Stepien
Mikolaj Suchan
Przemek Swiderski
Team Imago Mundi
Team Visavis
Tomasz Tomaszewski
Piotr Trybalski
Lukasz Trzcinski
Tomasz Wiech
Luke Wolagiewicz
Bartek Wrzesniowski

PORTUGAL
Jose Antunes
Sérgio Azenha
Gustavo Bom
Alfredo Cunha
Vitor Costa
Rodrigo Cabrita
Antonio Carrapato
José Carlos Carvalho
Susana Maria Cerdeira Paiva
Armindo Cerqueira
Carlos Costa
Hugo Delgado
Paulo Duarte
Paulo Escoto F
Nuno Ferreira Santos
Jorge Firmino
Paulo Freitas

Vitor Gordo
Pedro Guimarães
Nuno Guimaraes
Francisco Leong
Rui M. Leal
Gonçalo Lobo Pinheiro
Artur Machado
João Mariano
Pedro Jorge Melo
Bruno Rascão
Armando Ribeiro
Miguel Ribeiro Fernandes
Odette Rodrigues
Pedro de Sampayo Ribeiro
Jose Sousa Coutinho R. Coelho
Miguel De Sousa Dias
Nuno Veiga
Marta Vitorino

PUERTO RICO
Xavier J. Araujo
Carlos J. Ortiz
Ramón Tonito Zayas

ROMANIA
Daniel Baltat
Mihai-Alexandru Barbu
Cosmin Bumbut
Mihai Burlacu
Horia Calaceanu
Petrut Calinescu
Bogdan Cristel
Bogdan Croitoru
Egyed Ufó Zoltán
Zsolt Fekete
Vadim Ghirda
Florin Iorganda
Stefan Jora
Liviu Maftei
Bogdan Maran
Matei Silviu
Daniel Mihailescu
Marius Nemes
Calin Piescu
Dana Popa
Mircea Restea
Gicu Serban
Radu Sigheti
Andreea Tanase
Tudor Vintiloiu

RUSSIA
Lana Abramova
Andrey Arkhipov
Armen Asratyan
Alexandre Astafiev
Maxim Babkin
Kirill Ciaplinskiy
Dmitry Beliakov
Elena Blednykh
Sergey Bondarev
Alexey Bushov
Dmitry Chebotaev
Andrey Chepakin
Alexandra Demenkova
Nikolay Dementiev
Vladimir Fedorenko
Sergey Gagauzov
Mikhail Galustov
Alexey Golubtsov
Grigory Golyshev
Valeriy Gorokhov
Pavel Gorshkov
Alexander Gronsky
Vasily Gulin
Olga Gumenyuk
Solmaz Guseynova
Dmitry Gushchin
Sergei Isakov
Misha Japaridze
Yuri Kadobnov
Pavel Kashaev
Sergey A. Kompaniychenko
Tanya Kotova
Yuri Kozyrev
Evgeny Kozyrev
Vladimir Larionov
Oleg Lastochkin
Sergei L. Loiko
Dmitry Lovetsky
Lukmanov Philipp
Said
Tatjana Makeyeva
Nekto V
Andrey Malashkevich
Maxim Marmur
Sergey Maximishin

Arseniy Neskhodimov
Valeri Nistratov
Valentinas Pecininas
Alexander Petrov
Vladimir Pirogov
Anna Piunova
Kirill Pochivalov
Vitaliy Podgurchenko
Alexandr Polyakov
Alexei Sazonov
Ivan Sekretarev
Shapran Andrei
Sergei Shchekotov
Shihin Dmitry
Vladimir Shootofedov
Vladimir Sichov
Alexander Sidorov
Denis Sinyakov
Andrey Sladkov
Pavel Smertin
Igor Starkov
Igor Tabakov
Alexander Taran
Alexey Tikhonov
Nikolay Titov
Vrindan Lila Dasi
Alexey Tsarev
Viktor Vasenin
Serezha Vasilyev
Vladimir Velengurin
Sergei Vinogradov
Vladimir Voronin
V. Vyatkin
Alex Zamorkin
Konstantin Zavrazhin
Alexander Zemlyanichenko

SAUDI ARABIA
Musleh Jameel
Baker Sindi

SERBIA
Zoran Anastasijevic
Nenad Bojic
Josip Buljovic
Aleksandar Dimitrijevic
Marko Djokovic
Djordje
Novak Djurovic
Marko Drobnjakovic
Andrej Isakovic
Djordje Jovanovic
Nemanja Jovanovic
Dejan Kostic
Ferdi Limani
Mihály Moldvay
Igor Pavicevic
Branislav Puljevic
Nikola Solaja
Goran Tomasevic
Tanja Valic

SIERRA LEONE
Allieu Jalloh
Bockarie Koroma

SINGAPORE
Aziz Hussin
Bryan van der Beek
Caroline Chia Su-Min
Chin Fook Chew
Chua Chin Hon
Desmond Wee Teck Yew
Edwin Koo
Ernest Goh
How Hwee Young
Jeff Chouw
Joyce Fang Hui-Lin
Kwong Kai Chung
Lim Wui Liang
Mike Lee CS
Nicky Loh
Norman Ng
Ng Sor Luan
Ooi Boon Keong
Ray Tan
Seah Kwang Peng
Sim Chi Yin
Stephanie Yeow
Terence Tan
Trevor Tan
Wang Hui Fen
Wee Teck Hian
Woo Fook Leong
Yeap Chin Tiong
Yen Meng Jiin
Zann Huizhen Huang
Zhuang Wubin

SLOVAKIA
Martin Bandzak
Jozef Barinka
Peter Brenkus
Jana Cavojska
Dusan Guzi
Maros Herc
Vladimir Kampf
Joe Klamar
Martin Kollar
Pavel Maria Smejkal

SLOVENIA
Jaka Adamic
Luka Cjuha
Jure Erzen
Jaka Gasar
Arne Hodalic
Manca Juvan
Matjaz Kacicnik
Borut Peterlin
Matej Povse
Klemen Razinger
Igor Skafar

SOMALIA
Abdu Kadir Ahmed Olad
Mohamed Sheikh Adow

SOUTH AFRICA
Nick Aldridge
Werner Beukes
Jodi Bieber
M.C. Botha
Nic Bothma
Jennifer Bruce
Denis Farrell
Brenton Geach
Ilan Godfrey
Julian Goldswain
Phyllis Green
Themba Hadebe
Brian Hendler
Nadine Hutton
Andrew Ingram
Fanie Jason
Jeremy Jowell
Chris Kirchhoff
Adrian de Kock
Halden Krog
Henk Kruger
David Larsen
Steve Lawrence
Tebogo Letsie
Liza
Kim Ludbrook
Liam Lynch
Lebohang Mashiloane
Padi Matlala
Bathini Mbatha
Simphiwe Mbokazi
Bongiwe
Gideon Mendel
Eric Miller
Moeketsi Moticoe
Thobeka Zazi Ndabula
Wally Nell
Nqobizwe Elkarrah Ngwenya
Nonhlanhla Kambule Makbati
Neo Ntsoma
James Oatway
Johnny Onverwacht
Raymond Preston
Antoine de Ras
Samantha Reinders
John Robinson
Shayne Robinson
Karen Lee Sandison
Sydney Seshibedi
Siphiwe Sibeko
Dumisani Sibeko
Joao Silva
David Silverman
Alon Skuy
Brent Stirton
Giordano Stolley
Mikhael Subotzky
Caroline Suzman
Guy Tillim
Muntu Vilakazi
Rogan Ward
Natasja Weitsz
Mark Wessels
Gary van Wyk
Schalk Van Zuydam

SOUTH KOREA
Changwoo Ryu
Jean Chung
Joo Woo Chan

Han Sungpil
Haseon Park
Hyunsoo Leo Kim
Kim Kyung Sang
Kim Tae Hyeong
Lee Jin-Man
Young-Joon Ahn

SPAIN
Tomàs Abella
Miki Alcalde
Carmenchu Aleman
Delmi Alvarez
Eva Álvarez
Jesus Antoñanzas
Samuel Aranda
Javier Arcenillas
Manuel Asensio Garcia
Pablo Balbontin Arenas
Joan Manuel Baliellas
Alvaro Barrientos
Daniel Beltrá
Pep Bonet
Fernando Bustamante
Alfredo Caliz
Nacho Calonge
Enrique Calvo
Luis Camacho
Sergi Camara
Dani Cardona
Sergio Caro
José Manuel Carratalá
Daniel Casares Román
Juan Manuel Castro Prieto
José Manuel Cendón
Ignacio Cerezo Ortega
Xavier Cervera Vallve
Eduard Compte Verdaguer
Matias Costa
Joan Costa
Miguel Cuenca
Claudia Daut
Carlos de Andrés
Marcelo Del Pozo
Eduardo D. de San Bernardo
Miguel Diez Perez
Daniel Duart
Javier Echezarreta
Sergio Enríquez - Nistal
Eduardo Escudero
Joaquim Fabregas Elias
Alvaro Felgueroso Lobo
Mónica Ferreirós
Andres Fraga
Victor Fraile
Isaac Freijo
Raul Gallego Abellan
Jesús Vallinas
Alvaro Garcia Coronado
Xoan Garcia Huguet
Ricardo Garcia
Albert Gea
Luis Gene
Moncho Gil
Rafael Gil
Joaquin Gomez Sastre
Elena de la Vega
Pedro Armestre
Pasqual Gorriz
Jose Haro
Francisco de las Heras
Isaac Hernández
X. M. Laburu
Xavier Landa
Fernando Lazaro Quintela
Alvaro Leiva
Laura Leon
Manuel Lerida Ortega
Daniel Loewe
Antonio Lopez Diaz
J. M. Lopez
Angel Lopez Soto
Jose Lores
Carlos Luján
Hermes Luppi
César Manso
Fernando Marcos Ibanez
Xurde Margaride
Robert Marquardt
Désirée Martin
Antonio M. Xoubanova
Ángel Colina
Antonio Arabesco
Pere Masramon
Héctor Mediavilla
Fernando Moleres
Alfonso Moral
Marc Morte
Isabel Muñoz
José Manuel Navia

Maria Nieto
Felix Ordoñez
Ricardo Ordoñez
Alberto Paredes
Gemma Parellada
Antonio Pérez
Rafa Perez
José Maria Pueche
Papu Garcia
Joan Pujol-Creus
Ferran Quevedo Bergillos
David Ramos Vidal
Eli Regueira
Miguel Riopa
Eva Ripoll
Nando Rivero
José Luis Roca
Luis Cobelo
Arturo Rodríguez
Paulino Rodriguez Villar
Amaya Roman
Víctor Romero
Alejandro Ruesga
Jesus F. Salvadores
Moises Saman
Cesar Sanchez
Luís Davilla
José Antonio De Lamadrid
Chico Sanchez
Lourdes Segade
Patricia Sevilla Ciordia
Miguel Sierra
Faustino Soriano
Nelson Souto
Carlos Spottorno
Javier Sulé
Luis Tejido
Javier Teniente
Gabriel Tizón
Juan Tomás
Rafael Trobat
Txomin Txueka
Raúl Urbina
Guillem Valle Ruiz
Lucas Vallecillos
Rosa Isabel Vázquez
Luis De Vega
Susana Vera Pascual
Jaime Villanueva
Pere Virgili
Enric Vives-Rubio
Alvaro Ybarra Zavala

SRI LANKA
Alefiya Akbarally
Karunarathna C. Somipath
Asanka Gunarathna
Isuru Perera
Premalal Ranawila

SURINAM
Roy Ritfeld

SWEDEN
Torbjörn Andersson
Sören Andersson
Peppe Arninge
Christian Åslund
Jens Assur
Elin Berge
Jocke Berglund
Julian Birbrajer
Henrik Björnsson
Nicklas Blom
Sophie Brandstrom
Lars Brundin
Henrik Brunnsgard
Swen Connrad
Lars Dareberg
Nils Patrick Degerman
Åke Ericson
Malin Fezehai
Linda Forsell
Niklas Hallen
Magnus Hallgren
Paul Hansen
Krister Hansson
Anders Hansson
Fredrik Härenstam
Frida Hedberg
Adam Ihse
Torbjörn Jakobsson
Ann Johansson
Jörgen Johansson
Thor Jonsson
Moa Karlberg
Tomas Karlsson
Magnus Liam
Peter Kjelleras
Martin Von Krogh

Peter Krüger
Björn Larsson Rosvall
Magnus Laupa
Jonas Lemberg
Jonas Lindkvist
Johan Lundahl
Joachim Lundgren
Chris Maluszynski
Markus Marcetic
Tommy Mardell
Karl Melander
Linus Meyer
Jack Mikrut
Thomas Nilsson
Nils Petter Nilsson
Brita Nordholm
Mikkel Örstedholm
Pekka Pääkkö
Per-Anders Pettersson
Lennart Rehnman
Kristofer Sandberg
Torbjörn Selander
Linnea Sellersjö
Anna Simonsson
Hakan Sjostrom
Åsa Sjöström
Sanna Sjösward
Johan Solum
Maria Steén
Pontus Tideman
Ola Torkelsson
Roger Turesson
Joachim Wall
Magnus Wennman
Karl-Göran Z. Fougstedt

SWITZERLAND
Zalmaï
Pius Amrein
Franco Banfi
Mathias Braschler
Markus Bühler-Rasom
Marcel Chassot
Fabrice Coffrini
Raphael Delaloye
Ladislav Drezdowicz
Philippe Dudouit
Monika Fischer
Peter Gerber
Michael von Graffenried
Michael Greub
Tobias Hitsch
Steeve Iuncter
Alexander Keppler
Patrick B. Kraemer
Yves Leresche
Cédric Marsens
Yann Mingard
Pascal Mora
Marco Paoluzzo
Nicolas Righetti
Didier Ruef
Roland Schmid
Andreas Schwaiger
Andreas Seibert
Daniel Tischler
Fabian Unternährer
Luca Zanetti
Marco Zanoni
Michael Zumstein

SYRIA
Khaled Al-Hariri
Thanaa Arnaout
Shadi Batal
Mouhamed Haj Kaab
Nouh Ammar Hammami
Hisham Zaweet

TAIWAN
Amos Chiang
Boheng Chen
Chang Tien Hsiung
Chiang Yung-Nien
Chih-Wei Yu
Fang Chun-Che
Keye Chang
Ma Li-Chun
Shen Chao-Liang
Simon Kwong
Tsung-Sheng Lin
Wang Fei Hwa
Wei-Sheng Huang
Wu Yi-Ping

TANZANIA
Mohamed A. Mambo

THAILAND
Vinai Dithajohn
Jetjaras
Pornchai Kittiwongsakul
Sarot Meksophawannagul
Korbphuk Phromrekha
Rungroj Yongrit

THE NETHERLANDS
Marc van der Aa
Laurens Aaij
Sabine Albers
Jan Banning
Amit Bar
Amber Beckers
Peter van Beek
Peter den Bekker
Bram Belloni
Victor Bergen-Henegouwen
Marcel van den Bergh
Leendert Jan Bergwerff
Hugo Bes
Peter Blok
Chris de Bode
Marco Borggreve
Jan van Breda
Joost van den Broek
Jasper Buninga
Erik Christenhusz
René Clement
Rachel Corner
Roger Cremers
Anoek de Groot
Martijn De Vries
Peter Dejong
Marc Deurloo
Jorge Dirkx
Taco van der Eb
Tara Fallaux
Flip Franssen
Philippe van Gelooven
Annie van Gemert
Brian George
Augustinus Joh. Mara Geurts
Martijn van de Griendt
Remon Haazen
Olaf Hammelburg
Roderik Henderson
Piet Hermans
Thijs Heslenfeld
Chrisje van den Heuvel
W.S. Hiralal
Pieter ten Hoopen
Hans Hordijk
Kaspar Jansen
Martijn de Jonge
Jasper Juinen
A.M.A. Kaag
Geert van Kesteren
Chris Keulen
Harry Kikstra
John Klijnen
Cor de Kock
Ton Koene
Niels Kooyman
Marc van der Kort
Olaf Kraak
Jeroen Kramer
Inez van Lamsweerde
Frans Lanting
Gé-Jan van Leeuwen
Florian Lems
Jaco van Lith
Kadir van Lohuizen
Elmer van der Marel
Vinoodh Matadin
Robert Meij
Vincent Mentzel
Kees Metselaar
Eric de Mildt
Adrie Mouthaan
Robert Mulder
Benno Neeleman
Jeroen Oerlemans
Marco Okhuizen
Erik-Jan Ouwerkerk
Isabelle Pateer
Willem Poelstra
Patrick Post
Pauline Prior
Judith Quax
Pim Ras
Martin Roemers
Michiel de Ruiter
Raymond Rutting
Diana Schetters-Scheilen
Peter Schols
Levon Schuller
Ruud Sies
Geert Snoeijer

Corné Sparidaens
Friso Spoelstra
Anoek Steketee
Jan-Joseph Stok
Ruud Taal
Roy Tee
Sven Torfinn
Robin Utrecht
Jeroen van Herk
Catrinus van der Veen
Kees van de Veen
Sjaak Verboom
Peter Verdurmen
Jan Vermeer
Dirk-Jan Visser
Karen Vlieger
Robert Vos
Dick Vos
Rob Voss
Paul Vreeker
Marc Vreuls
Koen van Weel
Klaas Jan van der Weij
Eddy van Wessel
Emily Wiessner
Herbert Wiggerman
Petterik Wiggers
Alex Wolf
Paolo Woods
Herman Wouters
Daimon Xanthopoulos

TRINIDAD AND TOBAGO
Andrea de Silva

TUNISIA
Karim Ben Khelifa
Sarah Mabrouk

TURKEY
Mustafa Abadan
Tolga Adanali
Ibrahim Arslan
Husamettin Bahge
Kursad Bayhan
Umit Bektas
Ali Borovali
Hatice Ezgi Özçelik
Kenan Gürbüz
Burak Kara
Ali Riza Kutlu
Baran Ozdemir
Cevdet Özdemir
Riza Ozel
Mustafa Ozer
Ziya Sandikcioglu
Murad Sezer
Tolga Sezgin
Gökhan Tan
Tarik Tinazay
T. Kerem Uzel
Firat Yurdakul

UGANDA
Bruno Birakwate
John Omoding
Joseph W. Ouma

UKRAINE
Volodymyr Baleha
Konstantin Donin
Alexander A. Drozdov
Gleb Garanich
Dima Gavrysh
Vitaly Hrabar
Stanislav Ivasyuk
Kagan
Alexander Kharvat
Gennadiy Minchenko
Sergiy Pasyuk
Anatoliy Stepanov
Eduard Stranadko
Igor Strembitskyy
Sergei Supinsky
Viktor Suvorov
Olexander Techynskyy
Alexander Toker
Volodymyr Tverdokhlib
Vitaliy Zaporozhets

UNITED ARAB EMIRATES
Hussain Al-Numairy

UNITED KINGDOM
Lilly Lamia
Amos Aikman
Roger Allen
Timothy Allen
Brian Anderson
Kirsty Anderson

Cedric Arnold
Matthew Ashton
Helen Atkinson
Bob Aylott
Roger Bamber
Graham Barclay
Jane Barlow
Guy Bell
Suzy Bernstein
Chris Booth
Harry Borden
Shaun Botterill
Simon Bowcock
Anna Branthwaite
Clive Brunskill
Dillon Bryden
Henrietta Butler
Holly Cant
Matt Cardy
Brian Cassey
Angela Catlin
Peter Caton
Gareth Cattermole
Stephen Champion
Grenville Charles
Dave Charnley
Jake Chessum
Wattie Cheung
Mark Chilvers
Dave Clark
CJ Clarke
Jim Clarke
Rose Clive
Nick Cobbing
Rogan Coles
Chris Collingridge
Phil Coomes
Caroline Cortizo
Michael Crabtree
Tom Craig
Michael Craig
Georgina Cranston
Alan Crowhurst
Nicholas Cunard
Shaun Curry
Ben Curtis
Simon Dack
Nick Danziger
Prodeepta Das
Kate Davison
Jason Dawson
Adam Dean
Peter Dench
Adrian Dennis
Nigel Dickinson
Kieran Dodds
Luke Duggleby
Matt Dunham
Lucy Duval
Paul Ellis
Stuart Emmerson
Sophia Evans
Mark Evans
Sam Faulkner
Andrew Ferrato
Tristan Fewings
Liz Finlayson
Julian Finney
Adrian Fisk
Steve Forrest
Stu Forster
Lauren Forster
Andrew Forsyth
Ian Forsyth
Tim Foster
Stuart Freedman
Sam Frost
Andreas Fuhrmann
James Robert Fuller
Christopher Furlong
Robert Gallagher
Yishay Garbasz
Andrew Garbutt
Drew Gardner
George Georgiou
John Giles
Paul Gilham
David Gillanders
Paula Glassman
Henning Gloystein
Jonathan Goldberg
Mike Goldwater
Kyna Gourley
David Graham
David Graves
Charlie Gray
Stuart Griffiths
Malcolm Griffiths
Robert Hallam
Liza Hamlyn

Alex Handley
Rebecca Harley
Graham Harrison
Sahlan Hayes
Lionel Healing
Richard Heathcote
Mark Henley
Tim Hetherington
Mike Hewitt
Andrew Higgins
James Hill
Jack Hill
Paul Hilton
Adam Hinton
Alex Hofford
Dave Hogan
Jim Holden
Rip Hopkins
Mike Hughes
Richard Human
Richard Humphries
Jeremy Hunter
Mike Hutchings
Philip Ide
Darrell Ingham
Caroline Irby
Chris Ison
Chris Jackson
Justin Jin
Davy Jones
Shahrzad Kamel
Reseph Keiderling
Clare Kendall
Ross Kinnaird
Dan Kitwood
Gary Knight
Thomas Laird
Jed Leicester
Bryn Lennon
David Levenson
Nicky Lewin
Barry Lewis
Geraint Lewis
Karoki Lewis
Rob Leyland
Sacha Lilla
Paul Lindsay
Alex Livesey
Paul Lowe
Mikal Ludlow
Michael Lusmore
Emma Lynch
Peter Macdiarmid
Luke Macgregor
Alex MacNaughton
Toby Madden
Leo Maguire
Paul Marriott
Bob Martin
Guy Martin
Dylan Martinez
Leo Mason
Clive Mason
Jenny Matthews
Neil McCartney
Jamie McDonald
Mark McEvoy
Henry McInnes
Andrew McLeish
John McVitty
Toby Melville
Richard Mills
Jeff Mitchell
Steve Mitchell
Pramod Mondhe
James Muldowney
Eddie Mulholland
Omar Mullick
Rebecca Naden
Leon Neal
Peter Nicholls
Lucy Nicholson
Ian Nicholson
Phil Noble
Russ Nolan
Simon Norfolk
Jeremy O'Donnell
Charles Ommanney
Jeff Overs
Andy Palmer
Fabio De Paola
Peter Parks
Lindsey Parnaby
Nigel Parry
Andrew Parsons
Andrew Paton
David Pearson
Mark Pearson
Gerry Penny
Charles Pertwee

Gareth Phillips
Tom Pietrasik
Tom Pilston
Adam Pletts
Louis Porter
Mike Powell
Gary Prior
Léonie Purchas
Steve Pyke
Baz Ratner
Lucy Ray
Paul Read
Mark Read
Simon Renilson
Kiran Ridley
Simon Roberts
Graeme Robertson
Stuart Robinson
David Rose
Anita Ross Marshall
Mark David Runnacles
Honey Salvadori
David Sandison
Michael Sawyer
Oli Scarff
Mark Seager
David Shopland
John Sibley
Mike Simmonds
Dominic Simmons
Jamie Simpson
Tim Smith
Bill Smith
Ben Smith
Sean Smith
David Smithson
Claire Soares
Carl De Souza
Michael Steele
Tom Stockill
Tom Stoddart
Lee Karen Stow
Chris Stowers
Matt Stuart
Alex Sturrock
Justin Sutcliffe
Sean Sutton
Jeremy Sutton-Hibbert
Mark Parren Taylor
Aaron Taylor
Anastasia Taylor-Lind
Ian Teh
Edmond Terakopian
Andrew Testa
Mark Thompson
David Tipling
Mike Tipping
Kurt Tong
Dan Towers
Abbie Trayler-Smith
Simon de Trey-White
Felipe Trueba
Francis Tsang
Dominick Tyler
Fiona Hanson
James Veysey
Bruno Vincent
Howard Walker
Robert Wallis
James Warwick
Aubrey Washington
Geoff Waugh
Andy Weekes
Amiran White
Neil White
Lewis Whyld
Kirsty Wigglesworth
Greg Williams
James Williamson
Vanessa Winship
Jamie Wiseman
Philip Wolmuth
Alexander Yallop

URUGUAY
Leo Barizzoni
Gabriel Alejandro Cusmir Cneo
Quique Kierszenbaum

USA
Doug Abuelo
Daniel Acker
Gabriel Luis Acosta
Jeanie Adams-Smith
Michael Adaskaveg
Lynsey Addario
Noah Addis
Shakil Adil
Peter van Agtmael
Nabil Al-Jurani

Micah Albert
Jim Albright, Jr
Pablo Alcalá
William Albert Allard
Suzy Allman
Stephen L. Alvarez
Elise Amendola
Joe Amon
Jon Anderson
Kathy Anderson
Ryan Anson
Ron Antonelli
Antoine Antoniol
Samantha Appleton
Michael Appleton
Charlie Archambault
Ricardo Arduengo
Bernat Armague
Roger Arnold
Christopher T. Assaf
Lacy Atkins
Jocelyn Augustino
Alexandra Avakian
Paul Avallone
Tony Avelar
Brian Baer
Brian Bahr
Shawn Baldwin
Brendan Bannon
Leslie Barbaro
Jeffrey Barbee
Michael Barkin
Daniel Barry
Don Bartletti
David Bathgate
David Bauman
Will Baxter
Liz O. Baylen
Robyn Beck
Robert Beck
Keith Bedford
Natalie Behring
Al Bello
Doug Benc
Nicole Bengiveno
Brian Bennett
Bruce Bennett
Ruediger Bergmann
Nina Berman
Alan Berner
Adam Berry
Jeffrey F. Bill
Keith Birmingham
Matt Black
Teddy Blackburn
Victor James Blue
Caroline Blumberg
Lisa Blumenfeld
Willy Boeykens
Gary Bogdon
Peter Andrew Bosch
Mark Boster
Bie Bostrom
Gilbert R. Boucher II
Jim Bourg
Rick Bowmer
Jared Boyd
Tim Boyle
Heidi Bradner
Alex Brandon
William Bretzger
Paula Bronstein
Kate Brooks
Tiffany Brown
Joseph Brown
Milbert O. Brown, Jr.
Andrea Bruce
Stephanie Bruce
Simon Bruty
Michael Bryant
Vernon Bryant
Michael Bryant
Khue Bui
Gregory Bull
David Burnett
David Butow
Renée C. Byer
Dennis P. Callahan
Mary Calvert
Andrea Camuto
Carlos Chavez
Rob Carr
J. Carrier
Darren Carroll
J. Pat Carter
Antrim Caskey
Marco Castro
Nathan Caulford
Joe Cavaretta
Bryan Chan

Richard A. Chapman
Tia Chapman
Dominic Chavez
John Chiasson
Barry Chin
Paul Chinn
Ringo Chiu
Goh Seng Chong
Chien-Min Chung
Christopher Chung
Mary Circelli
Marshall Clarke
Thimothy A. Clary
Jay L. Clendenin
Victor José Cobo
Carolyn Cole
Fred R. Conrad
Greg Constantine
Kathryn Cook
Thomas R. Cordova
Molly Corfman
Gary Coronado
Ron Cortes
Carl Costas
Dean C.K. Cox
Andrew Craft
Bill Crandall
Ed Crisostomo
Stephen Crowley
Anna Curtis
Anne Cusack
Andrew Cutraro
Scott Dalton
Jim Damaske
Jonathan Daniel
Mike Darden
Darryl Bush
Meredith Davenport
Linda Davidson
Amy Davis
Ricardo De Luca
Sam Dean
Daron Dean
Suzanne Dechillo
Jason DeCrow
Rob Delorenzo
Danfung Dennis
DL Anderson
Chris Detrick
Charles Dharapak
Alan Diaz
Jessica Dimmock
Kevork Djansezian
Joginder Singh Dogra
Steven K. Doi
Bob Donnan
Jonathan Drake
Carolyn Drake
Jay Drowns
Michel DuCille
Stephen Dunn
David Durochik
Michael Eckels
Aristide Economopoulos
Ron Edmonds
Debbie Egan-Chin
Davin Ellicson
Bruce Ely
Douglas Harrison Engle
Peter Essick
Josh Estey
James Estrin
Jim Evans
Sarah Evans
Allen L. Eyestone
Rich-Joseph Facun
Timothy Fadek
Steven M. Falk
George Farah
Patrick Farrell
Chris Faytok
Michael Fein
Candace Feit
Gina Ferazzi
Jonathan Ferrey
Stephen Ferry
Melanie Fidler
Rob Finch
Brian Finke
Monika Fischer
Gail L. Fisher
Mikel Flamm
Kate Flock
Derek Henry Flood
Kathleen Flynn
Sasha G. Fornari
Tom Fox
Nikki Fox
Bill Frakes
Armando Franca

Jamie Francis
Danny Wilcox Frazier
Ruth Fremson
Lee Friedlander
Gary Friedman
Susanna Frohman
Nicole Frugé
Ana Elisa Fuentes
David Furst
Matt Gainer
Sean Gallup
Preston Gannaway
Alex Garcia
Marco Garcia
Chris Gardner
Mark Garfinkel
Elsa Garisson
Morry Gash
Robert Gauthier
Jim Gehrz
Sharon Gekoski-Kimmel
Hugh Gentry
Harraz N. Ghanbari
Mark Gilliland
C.M. Glover
Giovanna Godard
Matt Goins
David Goldman
Scott Goldsmith
Andres Gonzalez
Chet Gordon Jr.
Mark Gormus
Ronna Gradus
Michael Grecco
Kyle Green
Jill Greenberg
Bill Greene
Stanley Greene
Lauren Greenfield
John Gress
Morry Gash
Norbert von der Groeben
David I. Gross
Jeff Gross
David B. Grunfeld
Jorgen Gulliksen
Robert Gumpert
David Guralnick
David Guttenfelder
Carol Guzy
Marc Hall
Scott Halleran
Marsha Halper
Khalil Hamra
Mark M. Hancock
Andrew Harrer
Mark Edward Harris
Peter Harris
Richard Harrison
Rick Hartford
David Hartung
Mohammed Hato
Darren Hauck
Jeff Haynes
Steve Hebert
James Heil
Ann Heisenfelt
Todd Heisler
Kendra Helmer
Andrew Henderson
Mark Henle
Tyler Hicks
Stephen Hilger
Brian Hill
Ethan Hill
Edward Hille
Eros Hoagland
Evelyn Hockstein
Brendan Hoffman
Fritz Hoffmann
Jeremy Hogan
Jim Hollander
David S. Holloway
Matthew Holst
Derik Holtmann
Stan Honda
Chris Hondros
David Honl
Kevin Horan
Beverly Horne
Brad Horrigan
Eugene Hoshiko
Sarah Hoskins
Rose Howerter
Aaron Huey
Nam Y. Huh
Mark Humphrey
Brent Humphreys
Sarah Hunter
Thomas James Hurst

Jeffrey Daniel Hutchens
Andrew Innerarity
Walter Iooss, Jr.
Erik Ippel
Eddy Isango
Stuart H. Isett
Boza Ivanovic
Lance Iversen
Razak Jaber
Jed Jacobsohn
Julie Jacobson
Terrence Antonio James
Kenneth Jarecke
Janet Jarman
Ron Jenkins
Jennifer Brown
Crista Jeremiason
Cliff Jette
Joanna Jhanda
Ji Jianghong
Angela Jimenez
Lynn Johnson
Krisanne Johnson
Barbara L. Johnston
Joseph Johnston
Taylor Jones
Jonathan Jones
Renée Jones Schneider
Bonnie Josephson
Catherine J. Jun
Dan Jung
Greg S. Kahn
Mike Kamber
Mike Kane
Kang Hyungwon
Doug Kanter
Eli Kaplan
Sylwia Kapuscinski
Anthony Karen
Ivan Kashinsky
Carolyn Kaster
Reuven Kastro
Stephen M. Katz
Andrew Kaufman
Stephanie Keith
Caitlin M. Kelly
Brenda Ann Kenneally
David Hume Kennerly
Mike Kepka
Geof Kern
Laurence Kesterson
Carl Kiilsgaard
Yunghi Kim
John J. Kim
Kim Jae-Hwan
John Kimmich-Javier
Scott Kingsley
Kohjiro Kinno
Paul Kitagaki, Jr
Katherine Kiviat
Torsten Kjellstrand
Stephanie Klein-Davis
Heinz Kluetmeier
Kim Komenich
Jim Korpi
Brooks Kraft
Benjamin Krain
Lisa Krantz
Suzanne Kreiter
Amelia Kunhardt
Karna Kurata
Jack Kurtz
Branimir Kvartuc
Vincent Laforet
Christopher LaMarca
Ken Lambert
Rod Lamkey, Jr.
Nancy Lane
Jeremy Lange
Jerry Lara
Erika Larsen
Adrees Latif
B. Conrad Lau
Neal C. Lauron
Tony Law
Claudia B. Laws
Jared Lazarus
Michael J. LeBrecht II
Streeter Lecka
Chang W. Lee
Seokyong Lee
Sarah Leen
Brian Lehmann
Mark Lennihan
Paula Lerner
Will Lester
Andy Levin
Heidi Levine
Sivan Lewin
Shari Lewis

Jeff Lewis
William Wilson Lewis III
Brennan Linsley
Steve Liss
Jim Lo Scalzo
John Lok
David Longstreath
Rick Loomis
Dario Lopez Mills
Monica Lopossay
Jon Lowenstein
Benjamin Lowy
Pauline Lubens
Amanda Lucidon
Gerd Ludwig
Erik Lunsford
Lutton, Matt
Joshua Lutz
Patsy Lynch
Andy Lyons
Melissa Lyttle
Jeffrey MacMillan
Michael Macor
Chris Maddaloni
David Maialetti
Rick Maiman
Todd Maisel
Hussein Malla
Scott Manchester
Liz Mangelsdorf
Jeff Mankie
Yamina Manolova
Mary Ellen Mark
Pete Marovich
Dan Marschka
Joel Martinez
Ronald Martinez
Pablo Martinez Monsivais
Sean Masterson
Edgar Mata
Rania Matar
Rob Mattson
Robert Maxwell
Jimmy May
Robert Mayer
Larry Mayer
Mattew McClain
Karen McClean
Michele McDonald
David G. McIntyre
Jim McIsaac
Rick McKay
Joe McNally
Win McNamee
Chris McPherson
Eric Mencher
Peter J. Menzel
Thomas Meredith
Mike Mergen
Jim Merithew
Susan Merrell
Nhat V. Meyer
Peter Miller
Doug Mills
Lianne Milton
Donald Miralle, Jr.
Kevin Miyazaki
Logan Mock-Bunting
Bobby Model
Andrea Modica
Andrea Mohin
Genaro Molina
M. Scott Moon
John Moore
Viviane Moos
Zayra Morales
P. Kevin Morley
Christopher Morris
Toby Morris
Toby Morris
Gabrielle Motola
Hatem Moussa
Matthew Moyer
Ozier Muhammed
Muhammed Muheisen
Peter Muhly
Edward J. Murray
James Nachtwey
Adam Nadel
Donna E. Natale Planas
Anupam Nath
Sol Neelman
Michael Nelson
Scott Nelson
Greg Nelson
Gregg Newton
Ray Ng
NG Han Guan
Jehad Nga
Michael Nichols

Robert Nickelsberg
Steven Ralph Nickerson
Zia Nizami
Michael O'Neill
Stephanie Oberlander
Eyal Ofer
Katie Orlinsky
Edward A. Ornelas III
Francine E. Orr
Charles Osgood
José M. Osorio
Kevin Oules
Darcy Padilla
David B. Parker
Nancy Pastor
Bryan Patrick
Pete Pattisson
Peggy Peattie
John Pendygraft
Tom Pennington
Doug Pensinger
Hilda M. Perez
Michael Perez
William Alan Perlman
Richard Perry
Mark Peterson
Brian Peterson
Scott Peterson
Roberto Pfeil
Jeffrey Phelps
David J. Phillip
Mark D Phillips
Chad Pilster
Todd Pitman
Sylvia Plachy
Platon
Spencer Platt
Susan Fisher Plotner
William B. Plowman
Suzanne Plunkett
James Pomerantz
Wes Pope
Denis Poroy
Piotr Powietrzynski
Betty H. Press
Jake Price
Gene J. Puskar
Steve Pyke
Ethan Rafal
Asim Rafiqui
Ramin Rahimian
John Ranard
Danielle Rappaport
Laura Rauch
Patrick Raycraft
Lucian Read
Joe Readle
Anne Rearick
Jerry Redfern
Eric Reed
Jim Reed
Barry Reeger
Tom Reese
Tim Revell
Eugene Richards
Paul J. Richards
Joe Rimkus
Jessica Rinaldi
Steve Ringman
Carlos Antonio Rios
Frances Roberts
Katherine Robertson
Michael Robinson Chávez
Paul E. Rodriguez
Joseph Rodriguez
Mike Roemer
Chris Rogers
Dana Romanoff
Vivian Ronay
Pat Roque
Bob Rosato
Adam Rountree
Matt Rourke
Angela Rowlings
Norman Jean Roy
Raul Rubiera
Dina Rudick
Mario E. Ruiz
Benjamin Lee Rusnak
J.B. Russell
Tom Russo
Eva Russo
Orin Rutchick
David L. Ryan
Robert Sabo
Salvatore Sacco
Bob Sacha
Adrian Sanchez-Gonzalez
Paul Sancya
Wally Santana

Joel Sartore
Renée Sauer
April Saul
Steve Schaefer
F. Scott Schafer
Howard Schatz
Mindy Schauer
Michael Schennum
Emily Schiffer
Lucas Schifres
Beth Schlanker
Eric Schmadel
Chris Schneider
Jake Schoellkopf
Erika Schultz
Heidi Schumann
Shaul Schwarz
David Scull
Adam Seal
Eric Seals
Richard Sennott
Andres Serrano
Sam Sharpe
Sarah Shatz
Ezra Shaw
Callie Shell
Erin Siegal
Jacob Silberberg
Denny Simmons
Roger Simms
Taryn Simon
Stephanie Sinclair
Luis Sinco
Kevin Sites
Matthew B. Slaby
John Slavin
Tim Sloan
Bryan Smith
Brett K. Snow
Brian Snyder
Jared Thomas Soares
Brian Sokol
Lara Solt
Chip Somodevilla
Pete Souza
Scott Spangler
Alonzo Spann
Mike Spencer
Fred Squillante
Jamie Squire
Clayton Stalter
John Stanmeyer
Ms Sally Stapleton
R. Marsh Starks
John Starks
Tom Starkweather
Susan Stava
Sharon Steinmann
George Steinmetz
Maria Stenzel
Lezlie Sterling
Chris Stewart
Ruaridh Stewart
Sean Stipp
Mike Stocker
Matthew Stockman
Robert Stolarik
Wendy Stone
John W. Stoops
Scott Strazzante
David Strick
Bob Strong
Essdras Suarez
Anthony Suau
Justin Sullivan
Jon Super
Akira Suwa
Lea Suzuki
Chitose Suzuki
David Robert Swanson
Brad Swonetz
Joseph Sywenkyj
Sze Tsung Leong
Ramin Talaie
Mario Tama
Joe S. Tamborello
Allan Tannenbaum
Ross Taylor
David Teagle
Team Bloomberg 2007
Patrick Tehan
Sara Terry
Shmuel Thaler
Bob Thayer
Andrew Theodorakis
Irwin Thompson
Thu Hoang Ly
Al Tielemans
Lonnie Timmons III
Peter Tobia

Tara Todras-Whitehill
Amy Toensing
Billy Tompkins
Jonathan Torgovnik
Candice Towell
Erin Grace Trieb
Rob Tringali
Annie Tritt
Linda Troeller
Edna T. Simpson
Scout Tufankjian
David Turnley
Chris Tyree
Jane Tyska
Erik Monte Unger
Gregory Urquiaga
Chris Usher
John Valenzuela
Nuri Vallbona
John VanBeekum
Justin Vela
Fernando Vergara
Bethany Versoy
Lalo R. Villar
José Luis Villegas
Sarah Voisin
Libby Volgyes
Nicholas Von Staden
Stephen Voss
Dusan Vranic
Kat Wade
Diana Walker
Mark Wallheiser
Emile Wamsteker
Steve Warmowski
Paul Warner
Jennifer Warren
David M Warren
Lori Waselchuk
Lannis Waters
Guy Wathen
Jim Watson
Susan Watts
David H. Wells
Annie Wells
Brad Westphal
Kevin R. Wexler
Jeff Wheeler
Rodney White
Paul White
James Whitlow Delano
Max Whittaker
Jeff Widener
Erin Wigger
Jonathan L. Wiggs
Anne Chadwick Williams
Matthew Williams
Lisa Wiltse
Steve Winter
Damon Winter
Dan Winters
Michael Wirtz
Joshua Wolfe
Michael Woods
Steven Worthy
Ed Wray
Julia Xanthos
Mitsu Yasukawa
Dave Yoder
Craig A. Young
Reed Young
Mohammed Zaatari
Mark Zaleski
Mark V. Zalewski
Zoriah

VENEZUELA
Argenis Agudo
Jorge Aguirre
Pedro Antonuccio Sanó
Héctor Castillo
Nilo Rafael Jimenez Barrozzi
Ramon Lepage
Leo Liberman
Arnoldo Lopez
Carlos Ramirez
Pedro Ruiz
Carlos Sanchez
Juan Carlos Solorzano

VIETNAM
Anhtien Ho
Bui Dang Thanh
Hoang Quoc Tuan
Hoang Thach Van
Hoang Trung Thuy
Lai Khanh
Le Quang Nhat
Le Tung Khanh
Le Tung Nguyen

Mai Loc
Na Son
Nguyen Duc Bai
Nguyen Thi Thanh Son
Nguyen Viet Thanh
Pham Trac
Tuan Hai
Thai Son
Tran The Phong
Tran Van Minh
Tran Thanh Hai
Tran Duc Tai
Tran Ky
Tran Tam My
Tran The Long
Tran Tien Dung
Trang Dung
Vu Anh Tuan

YEMEN
Mustafa Al-Ezzi Naji
Mohamed Sanabani

ZAMBIA
Thomas Nsama

ZIMBABWE
Tsvangirayi Mukwazhi

151

Imagine a world without EOS

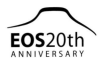

you can

Canon

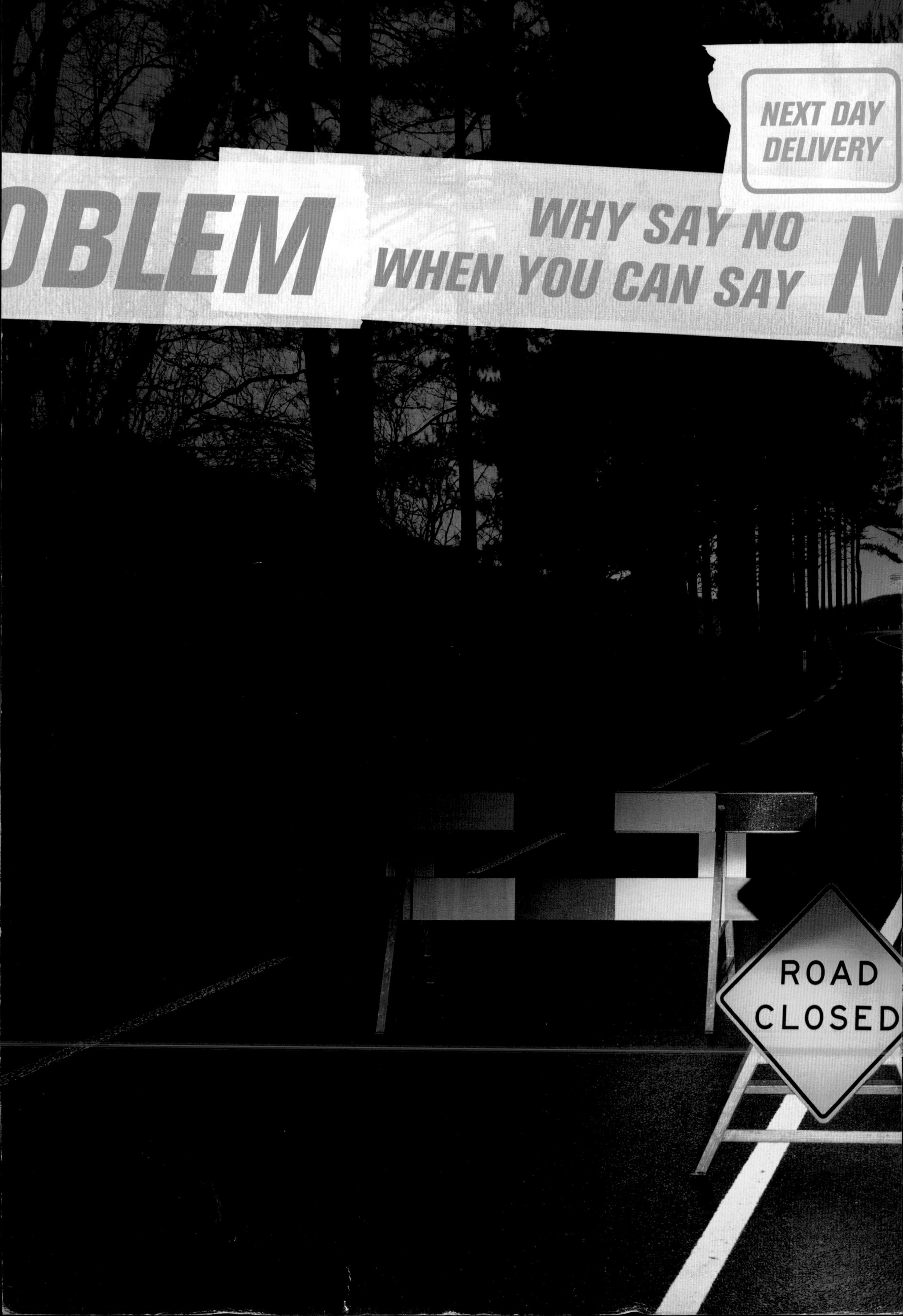
NEXT DAY
DELIVERY
OBLEM
WHY SAY NO
WHEN YOU CAN SAY
N
ROAD
CLOSED

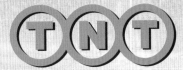

Copyright © 2007
Stichting World Press Photo, Amsterdam
Sdu Publishers, The Hague
All photography copyrights are held by the photographers

First published in Great Britain in 2007 by
Thames and Hudson Ltd,
181A High Holborn, London WC1V 7QX
www.thamesandhudson.com

First published in the United States of
America in 2007 by
Thames and Hudson Inc., 500 Fifth Avenue,
New York, New York 10110
thamesandhudsonusa.com

Art director
Teun van der Heijden
Advisors
Stephen Mayes
Bas Vroege
Design
Heijdens Karwei
Picture coordinators
Emily Kerckhoff
Madelijne Reijmerink
Nina Steinke
Captions & interview
Rodney Bolt
Editorial coordinators
Manja Kamman
Erik de Kruijf
Kari Lundelin
Editor
Elsbeth Schouten

Lithography
Maurice Tromp
Kleurgamma Photolab, Amsterdam
Paper
Hello Mat 135 g, quality Sappi
machine coated, groundwood-free paper
Cover
Hello Mat 300 g
Proost en Brandt, Diemen
Printing and binding
DeltaHage, The Hague
Production supervisor
Rob van Zweden
Sdu Publishers, The Hague

This book has been published under the
auspices of Stichting World Press Photo,
Amsterdam, The Netherlands.

British Library Cataloguing-in-Publication
Data: A catalogue record for this book is
available from the British Library

ISBN: 978-0-500-97667-8

Printed in The Netherlands

Cover picture
World Press Photo of the Year 2006
Spencer Platt, USA, Getty Images,
Young Lebanese drive through devastated
neighborhood of South Beirut, 15 August